JESUS

JeSuS

An Unconventional Biography

JACQUES DUQUESNE

Translated by Catherine Spencer

Triumph™ Books
LIGUORI, MISSOURI

Published by Triumph™ Books
Liguori, Missouri
An Imprint of Liguori Publications

© 1994 by Desclée de Brouwer/Flammarion
English translation © 1996 by Arthur James, Ltd.

Originally published as *Jésus* in 1994 by Desclée de Brouwer/Flammarion

This edition published 1997 by special arrangement with Arthur James, Ltd., Berkhamsted, United Kingdom

Library of Congress Cataloging-in-Publication Data

Duquesne, Jacques, 1930–.
    [Jésus, English]
    Jesus : an unconventional biography / Jacques Duquesne. — 1st U.S. ed.
        p. cm.
    Includes bibliographical references.
    ISBN 0-7648-0061-2
    1. Jesus Christ—Biography.   I. Title.
BT301.2.D8413   1997
232.9'01—dc20
[B]   96-30141

First U.S. Edition
01 00 99 98 97   5 4 3 2 1
Printed in the United Kingdom

Contents

Author's Thanks

Thanks are due to many friends and members of my family who helped, encouraged and supported me during the writing of this book (notably my wife Edith). But I am particularly indebted to Fr François Refoulé, a Dominican and New Testament specialist, former director of the Ecole Biblique of Jerusalem, who willingly undertook to read the manuscript, make comments and, when necessary, criticisms. That said, I alone should be held responsible for the contents of the book.   J.D.

Translator's Note

All the biblical quotations are from *The Jerusalem Bible* (popular edition), Darton, Longman and Todd, 1966, corresponding to the author's use of *La Bible de Jérusalem*; the English version was translated from the ancient texts but relied on the scholarship of the French version. Where a published translation of a quoted author exists, it has been used, with the exception of Ernest Renan's *Life of Jesus* (*Vie de Jésus*), of which there is no modern translation.

Acknowledgements

The publishers are grateful to the following for permission to quote copyright material:

1. Quotations taken from *The Jerusalem Bible*, published and copyright 1966, 1967 and 1968 by Darton Longman and Todd Ltd and Doubleday & Co. Inc. and used by permission of the publishers.

2. *The Interpretation of the 4th Gospel* by C. H. Dodd, 1953, given by Cambridge University Press.

3. *Jesus in His Time* by H. Daniel-Rops, 1950, given by Cambridge University Press.

4. *Jerusalem in the Time of Jesus* by Joachim Jeremias, SCM Press, 1969.

5. *Shadow of the Galilean* by Gerd Theissen, SCM Press, 1987.

6. *New Testament and Mythology* by Bultmann, SCM Press, 1985, ed. Schubert Ogden.

7. *Lecture de l'evangile selon Jean* by Xavier Léon-Dufour, © Editions du Seuil, 1990.

8. *Le Christ hébreu, la langue et l'age des Evangiles* by Claude Tresmontant, 1984, Guibert (Œil).

9. *La Vie quotidienne des hommes de la Bible* by André Chouraqui, © Hachette, 1978.

10. *Jésus* by Jean-Paul Roux, Fayard, 1989.

11. *Jesus and the 4 Gospels* by John Drane, Lion Publishing, 1979.

12. *Ce Que Je Crois* by Edmond Rostand, Editions Bernard Grasset, 1965.

13. *Jesus of Nazareth* by Bornkamm, Hodder and Stoughton, 1960.

14. *Jesus and the Zealots* by S. G. F. Brandon, Manchester University Press, 1967.

15. *Jésus Enfant* by France Quéré, Desclée (Fleurus Mame), 1992.

16. *La Parole qui Guerit* by Eugen Drewermann, Editions du Cerf, 1991.

17. *The Phenomenon of Man* by Pierre Teilhard de Chardin, © Editions du Seuil, 1970.

18. *Jesus Christ, Yesterday and Today* by Jacques Guillet, 1965, by permission of Geoffrey Chapman, an imprint of Cassell London.

19. *Jesus and the Word* by Rudolph Bultmann. Reprinted with the permission of Scribner, an imprint of Simon & Schuster, translated by Louise Pettibone Smith and Erminie Huntress. Copyright 1934 and renewed © 1962 Charles Scribner's Sons.

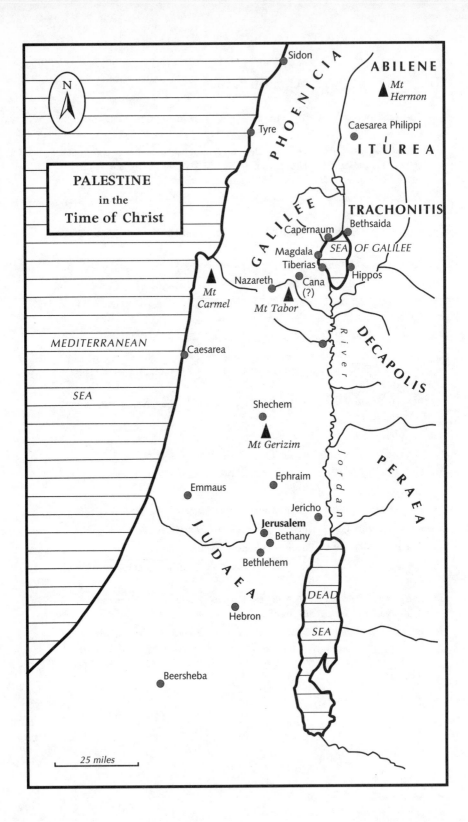

N

PALESTINE
in the
Time of Christ

MEDITERRANEAN

SEA

Sidon

PHOENICIA

Tyre

ABILENE

▲ Mt Hermon

Caesarea Philippi

ITUREA

GALILEE

TRACHONITIS

Capernaum

Bethsaida

Magdala

SEA OF GALILEE

Tiberias

Nazareth

Cana (?)

Hippos

Mt Carmel

Mt Tabor

DECAPOLIS

Jordan River

Caesarea

Shechem

▲ Mt Gerizim

PERAEA

Emmaus

Ephraim

Jericho

Jerusalem

JUDAEA

Bethany

Bethlehem

DEAD

SEA

Hebron

Beersheba

25 miles

I

The Boy and the Scribes

FROM time to time one of the scribes at the Temple breaks away from the little group, lifts a scroll of Scriptures down from a shelf, and cites a verse to illustrate the teaching he has just given. He replaces the scroll respectfully and, brushing aside a passing beggar, goes back to the youngsters to tell them again how great the God of Israel is – the One, the Only. Then he comments on a detail of the Law that the Eternal gave to Moses.

Another scribe takes over the teaching. The boys may be tired, their attention wandering; good teachers allow a little relaxation. So he reads a passage from the Haggadah, scriptural stories full of poetry and humour: Why, for example, did God use Adam's rib to create Eve? Because God said to Himself, 'I will not use Adam's head, or she will lift up her own too proudly; not his eye, or she will be too curious; not his ear, or she will eavesdrop; not his mouth, or she will talk too much; not his hand, or she will be too extravagant; not his foot, or she will be forever going outside the house. I shall make her from an invisible part of the body, so that she will be modest.' But another scribe countermands the quote with a second text from the Haggadah: 'God gave women more intelligence than men.'

The boys laugh at this debate. They are all thirteen – or soon will be – the age when they can go from the women's courtyard to the men's, closer to the altar on which sheep and doves are sacrificed, and closer to the Holy of Holies. Back in their villages, from now on they will don the prayer shawl, the *tallith*, before entering the synagogue; they will be able to give blessings and to carry the scrolls of the Law when these are displayed to the faithful for

9

their adoration. The boys have begun to matter in the adult world. They are, and from now on will be, important in religious terms. They are here in the synagogue of the Temple, the unique Temple at the heart of the world. They are listening to the scribes so as to complete their religious education before they reach the age of majority, and in order to demonstrate, in their replies to the scribes' questions, their knowledge of the Law.[1]

It is Passover, Pesah, which commemorates the end of the Jews' slavery in Egypt. This is one of the three festivals of pilgrimage that bring the crowds to Jerusalem. The scribes, unpaid scholars who also work in the 'honourable' professions (joiners, carpenters and silversmiths, as opposed to 'dishonourable' weavers and tanners), go into the Temple to speak to the pilgrims and to welcome the boys who are to be initiated. But, once inside, they do not know which way to turn. There is no time, now, to engage in their much loved and lengthy discussions over the interpretation of the Scriptures, no chance of deepening their religious scholarship or multiplying the precepts that will safeguard their fellow-countrymen against impurity and sin. The visitors overwhelm them.

Hundreds of thousands of these pilgrims have invaded Jerusalem, which normally consists of some 20,000 inhabitants (25,000 according to the highest estimates). The visitors clog up the alleys and the streets of the 'high town' around the Temple. They camp – on the ground, under a makeshift tent – outside its walls, mostly grouped together by village or by family. They pray; they listen to the rabbis explaining that Man is the being of Passover, of journeys, the link between Creator and created; they sing psalms:

> How I rejoiced when they said to me,
> 'Let us go to the house of Yahweh!'
> And now our feet are standing
> in your gateways, Jerusalem.'[2]

* * *

Considering this scene some two thousand years later, it is neither difficult nor inappropriate to imagine amongst them the boy named Jesus, who had travelled from Nazareth with Joseph and Mary. According to the evangelist Luke, they came down (in the geographical sense) or went up (in the religious sense) to Jerusalem every year. This would have been a clear sign of piety, since the annual pilgrimage to the Temple was compulsory only for men, and the journey of about seventy-five miles was tiring, sometimes dangerous – a far cry from our late-twentieth-century tourist pilgrimages.

Galilee, a rectangle about twenty-five by fifty miles, was a fruitful place. 'Everywhere is fertile and vegetated,' the Jewish historian Flavius Josephus enthused, 'and covered with every variety of tree. Even the least energetic men are inspired to cultivate; every piece of land is exploited, no field lies fallow. Cities and towns are numerous, for food is abundant in the region.'[3] Flowers, too: 'The red anemone reigns on the prairies, poppies and asters enliven the hills.' But to journey from one of these numerous towns to another, the traveller had little choice but to go by bad roads. This was partly because the Roman occupier, that indefatigable builder of roads, had barely penetrated the territory. What would be the point? It was the country of Herod Antipas, who had nothing but good will towards the Caesars and their underlings. The Romans' military presence was also limited in Palestine – 3,000 men at Caesarea, on the coast, and a cohort of 600 men at Jerusalem.

Judaea, in the south, was another matter; the roads improved somewhat as one approached Jerusalem. The Judaeans had nothing but contempt for the Galileans, with their country-bumpkin accents and their clumsy pronunciation – one Judaean expression was 'as stupid as a Galilean'. The Judaeans were also jealous of the Galileans' supposed wealth: 'To get riches, go north; to get wise, go south,' was the saying in Jerusalem. To reach the capital from Galilee, travellers had also to make their way across dry, rocky, tortured country, riddled with caves which served as hide-outs for the bandits who terrorised the roads.

And then – there it was, high up on its hills and enclosed by walls. The City, the unique City – Jerusalem!

> Jerusalem, if I forget you, may my right hand wither!
> May I never speak again if I forget you! [4]

sang the psalmist.

It is not difficult to imagine the feelings of the young boy on seeing the City rise up in the distance, like an island in the barren landscape. The Romans had moved their headquarters from Jerusalem to Caesarea, but that did not matter much to the pilgrims, who, like all Jews, greatly reviled the occupiers. For them, as for all Jews, Jerusalem was the religious heart of the world. The Temple had been built there, and in the Temple was the Holy of Holies, the empty sanctum where the one God was miraculously both present and absent. Only the High Priest could enter that holy place, once a year on Yom Kippur, the Day of Atonement, after having prayed, fasted and purified himself in every way. Once inside, he would pronounce the name of Yahweh in fear and trembling, and implore Him to forgive all the iniquities and transgressions committed by the people whom He had chosen.

The boy would have known all this. Parents as pious as Joseph and Mary would have explained to him how the other priests and the people would prostrate themselves the instant the High Priest entered the Holy of Holies, crying in unison, 'May the Lord be praised for ever!' As they journeyed down from the north they would have glimpsed the high colonnades of the Temple (partly obscured by the Antonia tower from which the Romans – may they be cursed! – kept watch). But, they would have told him, the Temple was nothing, absolutely nothing, however beautiful and grand it might seem, compared with the Other Temple in the sky. And as his parents put up the simple piece of cloth that would serve as their tent, and their Nazarene companions prepared the meal, the boy could have gazed at the city, hearing the hubbub emerging from the crowds and the distant cries of animals being brought for sacrifice, replaced, as the evening drew on, by the cries of the Roman guards at the Antonia tower and on the ramparts.

That influx of pilgrims would have come in a spectacular manifestation of piety not only from all over Palestine but also from every part of the Mediterranean to which the Jews had scattered. Together with the Greek, Syrian and Egyptian tourists and the traders, anxious to sell their trinkets and cloth, their arrival always brought the Romans close to panic. Generally loathed and considered 'impure' by a population obsessed with purity, the occupiers feared that civil riots and uprisings – common at the time – would break out. So they strengthened the usual garrison with troops from Caesarea, and restricted the pilgrims to designated routes so as to keep a closer eye on them.

The boy and his relatives would therefore probably have had to cross the valley of Josaphat and the Mount of Olives, where the traders would already be gathering. The money-changers would be there with their stalls; people could go into the Temple or pay the Temple tax demanded each year from every Israelite only with Temple, as against Roman, money. Sacrificial animals were also sold here, pigeons and doves for the poorest, cows for the richest, sheep for the rest. It is easy to picture the boy in that throng: the dusty, farmyard atmosphere, the smell of dung and of spices, the smoke from grilling meat, the babble and the surging of the crowd, the incantations of the most pious.

At the city gates, the pilgrims would have been stopped by the guardians, a kind of customs officer, whose function was to separate the pure from the impure. For it was written on the Temple scroll: 'The city that I have sanctified with the residence of my Name and with my sanctuary will be holy, pure from all impurity that would contaminate it; everything within it and everything brought into it must be pure.' This meant, in practice, that fruit and vegetables, dairy products, cereals and wood had to be purified by the payment of a tax. The import of skins, leather and fleeces was banned outright – with all the more reason if they had come from Samaria or from pagan cities (with which trade was nevertheless developing). The ban would naturally have delighted the tanners who lived in the lower part of the city, doubtless affording them some solace at being ranked among the base professions.

Then, once this curious customs post had been cleared, there would be the first cordons of Roman soldiers. Their helmets and coats of mail would have glinted in the sun. With an unsheathed sword at their sides and a baton in their hands, the soldiers would have filtered the long procession, scarcely bothering to hide their contempt for the Jews. (The historian Tacitus echoed the general Roman feeling when he described them some years later as 'an abominable race'.) The legionaries would have been blond or dark, swarthy or fresh-faced – recruited from every territory into which the Empire had stretched its hand. They would have exchanged mocking comments in a strange mixture of Latin, Greek, Aramaic and a whole range of other languages and dialects whilst the pilgrims, a dusty crowd in blue, white and grey, would have surged towards the Temple, pretending that the soldiers were invisible.

The Temple! At that time, it would have been still under construction, as it had been for years – perhaps thirty when the boy went to the scribes.[5] Herod intended it as a vast and magnificent monument to his own glory, but it was also his attempt at appeasing the Jews, to whom he was a collaborator and a turncoat. Not content with acting as a recruiting agent for the Roman armies throughout the East, had he not built a large temple of white marble at Caesarea, dedicated to Caesar and to Rome? After the destruction of Solomon's Temple, and on their return from exile, the Jews had built another temple – a modest, unpretentious affair, all that a conquered people could afford. Herod knew that for his people the Temple was both the place where God was absent – for He could not be captured, contained in a construction of stone – and present, the radiant manifestation of His Royalty. A text written by the rabbis explained:

Lord of the world, kings of nations have palaces with a table, chandeliers and other symbols of royalty so that their kingship can be recognised. And Thou, our king, liberator and saviour, wilt Thou not have symbols of royalty so that all the inhabitants of the earth may recognise that Thou art King of all?

The new Temple therefore had to be worthy both of the Eternal and of Herod. The priests must have leaped for joy, been overcome with emotion, when the project was announced. They would have been wary, however, about the details; this Herod was too steeped in Greek philosophy, slavishly following Greek fashions and adorning himself, like the Athenians, in rich silk tunics and jewellery. He had built himself a dozen or so Corinthian-style palaces in the desert, and if he had his way he would build them a *Greek* temple – a pagan monument.

The Jewish nation had been entrusted with a sacred message. Alone in the known world, that small group of people had made a covenant with the one God. It had therefore to fight tooth and nail to remain true to that agreement, ward off outside influences, and keep intact the divine legacy received from Abraham, Moses, Isaac and Jacob. Through misfortune or destiny, however, the chosen people were not safely installed in some inaccessible corner of the world, but on a piece of land that every conqueror – Persian, Chaldean and Greek – wanted. The Greeks were seen as one of the most dangerous, perhaps because their luminous culture had succeeded in seducing the Romans themselves. Greek had replaced Latin as the international language, Greek architecture was copied, the Greek cult of the body was aped. And, in the end, the man-made Greek gods were worshipped.

Three centuries earlier, Alexander the Great had conquered Palestine. The wealthiest Jews had quite quickly adapted to the Greek way of life. Indeed, the High Priest, the highest religious authority in Israel, would later compromise himself to the point of allowing the evening prayers to be shortened so that the officiants could go to athletic competitions – modelled, of course, on those of Olympia.

It was important, therefore, to react against this contagion. And when Herod undertook the building of the Temple, things were extremely tense. The greater the temptation to merge into the outside world, the more the Israelites receded into their own world and formed a buttress in defence of their faith, their Law and their rules. There were interminable discussions between the priests and the king. But Herod was clever. He had access to good architects, could dip at will into the state coffers: they would come to some arrangement. The Temple, though Greek in aspect with its sumptuous Corinthian columns, fulfilled every demand of the Law.

At the top of Mount Moriah, the very site that David had chosen for the first Temple, Herod's architects had marked out a vast strip of land,[6] surrounded by white stone walls, forty feet high. Ten thousand men, according to some estimates, or eighteen thousand according to others, went to work. Among them were a thousand lower-caste priests, specially trained in masonry, who were to build the Holy of Holies: no ordinary mortal could approach the sacred place, even during its construction. That teeming horde of workers on a building site worthy of Pharaoh was a godsend for the small city and its merchants. But such a mass of people worried the priests, the king and the Romans. They knew how prone the proletariat was to occasional restlessness.

Peace never really reigned in Jerusalem – a town in which so many beliefs, creeds and interests collided. Always anxious to please the occupier, Herod decided to erect a sculpture of the Roman eagle above the portal of the Temple. Blasphemy! The night before he died, Jews demolished the statue. Herod still had enough clarity and strength to have those responsible burnt alive and certain key figures executed. But the eagle was not replaced. At that period, the Romans were anxious to avoid causing religious offence to the Jews, and would not insist on the imposition of Roman culture. Indeed, they even occasionally executed legionaries who, through drink or stupidity, were guilty of doing so. Later, Pilate, a hard, provocative man, would be less careful, and the mad Caligula would even demand that his own statue be erected in the middle of the Temple ... But that is another story.

The year the boy came to meet the scribes, the works were proceeding apace, but were not yet finished – and would not be until AD 64. Nonetheless, the Temple already looked magnificent. Its architects are thought to have been trained at the school of architecture in Alexandria They had used the Greek technique of building a cube – with proportions similar to those that, centuries later, would be used for the black stone of Mecca. There, white stones were alternated with strips of gold. The white, according to one source, was so white that 'the superb edifice, when seen from afar for the very first time, looked like a snow-covered mountain', and the strips of gold so thick that 'as daylight began to pour over them, they appeared as brilliant as golden rays of sunshine'. Around that cube were huge courtyards, separated by powerful columns in the purest Corinthian style.

Let us go back again, and follow the boy in his discovery of the Temple, one of the most sumptuous and imposing monuments of the then-known world. It must have left a young Nazarene speechless with awe and admiration.

First, he crosses through the Courtyard of the Gentiles – the non-Jews or pagans. It is a gigantic esplanade where the tourists from the empire and the east congregate, with the blind and the traders, and crippled beggars, who are considered impure and so not allowed to proceed further. A colourful and noisy crowd surges around the money-changers – better set up here, with their little pulpit-shaped tables, than on the Mount of Olives. The crowd flows around the stalls where some of the 20,000 or so priests in the service of the Temple sell incense and oils for sacred offerings. They also sell 'seals' which the pilgrim, if he has not already done so, can exchange for a dove, a sheep, or even a bull if he is wealthy or has much to give to or ask of the Eternal. It is a scene of general tumult: the traders shout, the priests noisily extol their sacred wares, and the animals moo, bleat, bray, coo, cackle and chirrup.

The formalities over, the tax paid to the priests for the soul of each member of the family, the pious Jews, prayer shawls over their heads, cross the colonnades and climb the stone steps that have been trodden by thousand upon thousand of pairs of sandals before them. Mary, of course, stays behind in the Courtyard of the Women, and the boy does too, because he has not yet reached the age of religious majority.

Going through the Nicanor gate, where a choir of Levites are singing psalms, Joseph enters the Courtyard of Israel, the area set aside for the male faithful. He perhaps takes with him a lamb. He is a pious man, according to all the evidence, and the knowledge of the sinfulness that separates him from God pains him. He wants to be reconciled with Yahweh.

Approaching the sacrificial altar, he stretches his hand over the head of the animal which is to die, thereby identifying himself with it. The animal dies in his place, for wickedness results in death and he himself merits only that end. After the animal has been taken to the sacred abattoir, the priests bring the sacrificial blood to the Courtyard of the Priests, the closest to the Holy of Holies, and lay out the lamb's body on the raised altar, over twelve feet high. This is a sign that the pardoned sinner has offered his whole being to God. And then the pious Jew invites his relatives and companions to eat the animal's remains with him. This meal signifies that, having been reconciled with God, he now wants to be reconciled with his fellow men.

It is not usual to travel from Nazareth to Jerusalem, enduring the fatigue and the danger of the journey, only to go home again immediately. In any case – another boon for local trade – every pious Jew has to spend a tenth of his income in the town. Jerusalem's economy, largely conducted or controlled by the priests, is therefore almost exclusively supported by religion. And so, devotions and purchases made, Joseph and Mary doubtless choose to spend several nights in their tent outside the city walls.

On this first day in Jerusalem, the boy perhaps goes to one of the study rooms that flanks the synagogue, where the scribes teach, quibble and pronounce. He likes it, goes back the next day with his parents, and when the time comes to go (in Luke's words, 'the feast was ended'), when Joseph, Mary and their Nazarene companions started on the return journey, he stays behind at the Temple.

It is hardly surprising that they do not notice his absence at once, since the outgoing crowd is as huge as the incoming one has been. The tents have been taken down, and everything packed – the utensils used to prepare the meals, the souvenirs, the clothes bought in Jerusalem. The children run on ahead, as impatient to leave as they had been to arrive; the donkeys, also impatient to move off, bray. Jesus is a serious child whom no one would suspect of running off. He must be with the other children, they think.

When the Galileans break their journey to rest, his parents still cannot see him anywhere; they presume he is with his uncles, cousins and neighbours. At nightfall, however, when they stop to put up the tent, they have to face the fact: he is missing. No one has seen him. Perhaps he has got lost – the Judaean roads are surrounded by holes and caves into which he may have wandered. He is not in the habit of going off by himself like that, but who can tell? Since earliest childhood he has been as independent of spirit[7] as he is well-behaved. Or perhaps he has encountered some unsavoury character.

So Mary and Joseph react as all worried parents in their situation. They turn back to Jerusalem, where (says Luke) they find him only after three days of searching – quite plausible, in such crowds. (The figure three, frequently used in the rest of the gospel, is perhaps no more than symbolic. Like their contemporaries, the evangelists were fond of symbols, as we shall see.)

The details of the search are not important. What matters is what they find. The boy is sitting in the middle of the scribes, asking questions and listening, as they in turn put questions to him. As usual, they are discussing passages from the Torah, the Law. The scribes are struck by his questions, comment to each other on this remarkable child, who seems so bright, so aware, so knowledgeable. In short, he is a prodigy, who also exhibits an impressive faith. They are awestruck, astonished; some are filled with tenderness for this gifted child. A crowd mills around him, including someone who has come to ask a scribe if it is indeed true that one may not eat a new-laid egg on the Sabbath,[8] beggars, and the faithful who want to atone for some wrongdoing. There is no doubt – this one will be a rabbi. He certainly deserves to be admitted, if he has not already been, into the Courtyard of Israel.

When his parents catch sight of him, they are filled neither with awe nor tenderness. They already know that the child has an aptitude for learning, is gifted with a radiant intelligence, and is filled with a deep faith. What drives them now is their frantic worry, mixed with relief and a degree of irritation. As usually happens when worried parents find a missing child who seems to have totally forgotten their existence, it is the mother who speaks first, doubtless in a bid to stem the father's recriminations – with men, one never knows – and because she has been paralysed with fear and is now, although she does not let it show, shaking with joy at having found her child again.

'Son, why have you done this to us?'[9]

And the reply comes:

'Why were you looking for me? Did you not know that I must be in my Father's house?'

This reply, the evangelist tells us later, they do not understand, but considering the angel's annunciation to them before his birth, this is strange. They should have been prepared for unusual behaviour, extraordinary words. But anyway, having said it, the child does return home with them.

Let us now move forward again to consider these events from today's viewpoint. This episode of Jesus' life has been disputed by theologians, who believe that it is a text inserted later; this theory is supported by the purity of the Greek in which it is written. The episode is in no way implausible, however. It would have been customary for pious people like Joseph and Mary to go to Jerusalem for Passover, and to take their son with them – certainly when he was approaching his thirteenth birthday. That he was advanced for his age is, given the ensuing events, likely.

I have chosen to begin the book with this story because it is charged with meaning for me – though not that usually attributed to it. I have heard dozens of sermons and homilies on this passage from the gospel whose author we know as Luke. These preachers usually emphasise the consciousness that Jesus had of his destiny and mission, the necessity that he felt from then on to be harsh ('seemingly', they add) with those closest to him, and the sacrifice of normal family ties that Mary and Joseph had already accepted, and so on. These are all acceptable interpretations. But I have never come across a preacher expressing surprise at the scribes' reaction. These scribes were people who, at that time of the year, spent most of their day in the Temple. They arrived first thing in the morning to find that the boy who had been there late the pre-vious evening, when the courtyard was emptying and the priests keeping watch for the night were coming to their posts and light-ing their oil lamps or their torches, was still there. Yet these scribes seem not to have wondered, even for a moment, where the boy was sleeping, or concerned themselves with what his parents must be thinking – and he evidently had parents, for he was not begging like so many others, who had to be chased away like irri-tating flies. He was so knowledgeable about the Law, so pious: per-haps they thought that he had accompanied a rabbi from Galilee, for the child's accent unmistakably identified him as a Galilean, in which case, this rabbi, if he had had the slightest sense of respon-sibility, should have been looking for him everywhere.

But no. These learned doctors of the Law had got hold of a prodigy of a rare piety, and they were fascinated, delighted, astonished – that was all they wanted to know. The idea that his parents must have been worried was, as we can deduce from the fact that Luke makes no mention of that aspect of the affair, of lit-tle importance. Again, I emphasise that this worry has been of similarly little importance to most preachers and to ancient or modern commentators – at least those that I have read or heard. These are nonetheless fine men. So, doubtless too, were those scholars who voluntarily spent hours in the Temple, speaking to the faithful and perfecting youngsters' religious education. I sometimes feel – and this is my point – that Jesus is always to some degree (let us not exaggerate: it is only to *some* degree) in the hands of the scribes; they, in their passion for him and for the Law, are not interested enough in the Marys and the Josephs of this world. Not interested enough, in other words, in people like us.

I shall try to explain this further, in order to clarify the subject of this book.

Not many people today, at least among serious historians, deny the existence of a person called Jesus, or rather *Ieschoua* (Joshua, translated into Greek as *Iesous*), whom his disciples saw as the Messiah (in Greek, *Christos*, from which 'Christ' is derived) and who appeared to be the founder of a new religion. Whether or not one believes that he was God Incarnate, one has to admit that he played a decisive role in the history of humanity. The words attributed to him still resonate as words of fire and absolute love – despite the distortions, dilutions and expurgations to which his disciples, followers or those simply disturbed by his words have sometimes subjected them. For all these reasons, many people want to know more about him, how he lived, his actions and his words, and the extent to which the texts that recount his life, the gospels, are historically accurate.

Without any doubt, these texts have been disputed, dissected and analysed more than any other documents of that period. The rare allusions to Jesus' existence in other, non-Christian, texts have also been put under the microscope. Eminent scholars, exegetes, historians, archaeologists and linguists have carried out intense and painstaking research in an attempt to verify the most minute details, and to give the best evaluation of the authenticity of what for centuries was accepted as fact. And they are making headway. We continually know a little more about this person called Jesus, about who he truly was and what he truly did – and also about who he was not and what he did not do.

However, the findings of these scholars are usually published in specialist journals or written in language inaccessible to the general reader. They are sometimes used by cranks or poets to build fantastic hypotheses about Jesus' life or borrowed by more serious authors who make their own selection, choosing some, discarding others, without ever explaining the reasons for their choice. The research also serves to fuel the arguments of writers who claim that the gospels are merely legends, myths. These historians enthusiastically home in on anything in the gospels that expresses something of the transcendent or the supernatural. Now, whilst it is appropriate to distinguish between the original texts and what has been added to them by tradition or piety, we must also beware of going to the other extreme. Like picture restorers cleaning the accumulated dirt of centuries from a masterpiece, we must avoid using overly strong materials that would eat into the painting itself and destroy its very substance.

So the findings of the work carried out by scholars in this field are too often the province of scribes – very respectable people as I have pointed out, but people who nonetheless dare not get to the truth of the texts. Some of them, or the authorities on which they depend, are terrified of disturbing the 'weak' – as these authorities sometimes put it – by saying, for example, that while the nice story of the Three Wise Men has almost certainly no basis in fact, it can usefully be seen as having a symbolic reality, in the sense of a story or a parable that points to a profound truth. In other words, it did not happen as the text says it did, but it nevertheless deserves the most careful attention because it means something extremely important.

It seems to me that any reasonable person could respect and understand this kind of explanation. But from fear of upsetting the 'weak', which is doubtless a very worthy motive, the gospels are still often treated as though they were dealing, from beginning

23

to end, with historical truths. That does not alter the fact that few people are fooled. Those with any insight can see that alongside indisputable or likely elements lie disputable and unlikely ones. The most devout church-goer has no problem admitting that while, according to Mark, Jesus went only once to Jerusalem, according to John he went there several times, that John's version of how the disciples were recruited is different from that of the other three evangelists, that Matthew occasionally sees double with his 'two blind men' or 'two men possessed by demons', where Mark is content with only one, and so on.

It is quite possible to tackle these questions head on. In doing so, one finds that the similarities between the gospels far outweigh the differences. One could also argue that in the earliest centuries the Church actually proved its honesty by its willingness to disclose the complete 'Jesus file', allowing these discrepancies to stand in texts that they had proclaimed authentic. But in general people prefer to act as if there is now less thirst for historical truth.

The aim of my book is therefore simple: to recount the life of Jesus as completely, clearly, vividly and respectfully as I can, while taking account of the latest research and hypotheses of academics of all disciplines. The notes, placed at the back of the book, cite my sources and give further information and analysis for those who want to know more, and in an Appendix of Sources I attempt to summarise what we know today of the available texts and of the conditions in which the gospels were written.

Chronological sequence now dictates that I begin with the passages that have raised the most questions: these that are usually called the infancy narratives and deal, in particular, with the birth of Jesus. Many doubts have been cast on the historical accuracy of these stories.

2

Birth

THE precise circumstances of Jesus' birth remain, not surprisingly, mysterious and controversial. The infant Galilean was not one of those princes whose arrival in the world is greeted with a fanfare. Who amongst his contemporaries could have predicted that his words and actions would have such an impact on the world? As Teilhard de Chardin says in the context of the origins of life itself:

> It is the same *in every domain*: when anything really new begins to germinate around us, we cannot distinguish it — for the very good reason that it could only be recognised in the light of what it is going to be. Yet if, when it has reached full growth, we look back to find its starting point, we only find that the starting point itself is now hidden from our view, destroyed or forgotten.[1]

It is difficult for a very young child looking at a seed to imagine the fruit it is going to produce, so difficult that he doesn't even notice the seed. And later, when he is captivated by the beauty and the taste of the fruit it is too late to rediscover its origins.

The circumstances of Jesus' birth, later the subject of endless paintings and stories as well as the origin of the most widely celebrated festival in the world, did not concern his contemporaries very much. Even his first disciples were interested only in his message and, later, in his Resurrection. The apostle Paul, whose testimony is the oldest and therefore the closest to the time of the crucifixion, wrote to the Christians living in Corinth:

> I taught you what I had been taught myself, namely that Christ died

for our sins, in accordance with the Scriptures; that he was buried;
and that he was raised to life on the third day, in accordance
with the Scriptures; that he appeared first to Cephas and secondly
to the Twelve. Next he appeared to more than five hundred of the
brothers....[2]

The enumeration of the witnesses goes on – but there is not a
single allusion in Paul's letters to the birth or the childhood of
Jesus. Nor are they mentioned in Mark's gospel, which is probably
the oldest of the four, nor in that of John. What is worse, the two
gospels that do refer to them, Luke and Matthew, contradict each
other more than once.

All the same, it is impossible to ignore or discount these accounts, as so many writers do. Perhaps hoping to avoid potential
pitfalls, they confine themselves to what might be called Jesus'
'public life', which begins with his baptism by John the Baptist.
They are wrong to do so. These birth stories reveal much about
the times in which Jesus lived, the way those who came after him
saw him, and what aspects of him they wanted to pass on to other
people. It is useful to re-examine those accounts without being
frightened of the difficult question they may raise or of analysing
the answers that have been suggested to them.

The first difficulty to be resolved is that of the date of Jesus'
birth. Several historians have set out to establish it by carefully
analysing all the surrounding evidence. This approach has not
proved very fruitful. Luke states: 'When he started to teach,
Jesus was about thirty years of age ...',[3] but according to John,
the Jews – or more precisely the inhabitants of Judaea – expressed surprise to Jesus, not long afterwards, that 'You are not
fifty yet, and you have seen Abraham!'[4] People do not speak like
that to a man of about thirty. What is more, Irenaeus, one of the
Church Fathers, affirms, on the basis of the testimony of John's
disciples, that when Jesus died he was nearing fifty.[5] This does
not make things any easier. (Irenaeus was Bishop of Lyon in the
second century; I shall return to him in the appendix.)

Examining the clues given by Luke and Matthew does not help much either: Matthew states that Jesus was born before the death of Herod the Great, the builder of the Temple, Luke that Jesus was born well before Herod's death but at the time of a census of 'the inhabited world' ordered by Caesar Augustus. This was the 'first census' and Quirinius was then 'governor of Syria'. The problem is that Herod died in 4 BC and Quirinius did not come to Syria until AD 6 – ten years later.

Scholars have racked their brains trying to solve the problem and have come up with various answers. Some have suggested that Luke was mistaken and had confused Quirinius with another Roman, an imperial legate named Saturninus, who, according to Tertullian, had organised a census in 6 BC. But this argument does not hold much water, given that Tertullian, the first Christian author to write in Latin, lived two centuries after these events. In any case, the census under Quirinius is well documented, and it is difficult to imagine how, given the organisational difficulties involved, two such complex operations could have been carried out so close together. And finally we must wonder why, if that were the case, Luke would speak of the 'first census'. Some commentators have suggested an error in translation, arguing that the Greek adjective *prote* ('first') can also be used as an adverb, in which case the census to which Luke refers would not be the 'first', but would have occurred 'at the beginning' of Quirinius's government – meaning that others could have taken place earlier. But the sleight of hand that transforms an adjective into an adverb has had far from universal acceptance.

In short, as one of the best contemporary scholars, Charles Perrot, of the Catholic Institute of Paris, has said, 'the question remains open'.[6] Most commentators incline to the view, however, that Jesus was born before Herod's death – a point on which Matthew and Luke agree. To be more specific, if one dare use the word, Jesus would have been born between 6 and 3 BC. The monk Dionysius Exiguus, who lived in Rome in the sixth century, made a mistake in the calculations and fixed the birth at the year

752 in the Roman calendar, which became year 1 in our calendar.

To fix the day is obviously even more difficult, not to say impossible. The gospels give no clue on the subject other than that Jesus was not born in December. Even in Palestine, it was too cold then for shepherds to be sleeping outside with their flocks. Now, the earliest organisers of the Christian Church thought that the new religion would be better accepted if it did not break with the ancient customs and rituals. The Romans celebrated the winter solstice on 25 December, and the early Christians found it easy to compare Jesus with the sun: St Augustine would later use the biblical expression 'the star in the sky' to describe him. Since symbols play such an important role in this area, it is also interesting to note that the feast of John the Baptist is celebrated on the day of the June solstice, from which time the sun in the northern hemisphere begins its descent, while Christmas is fixed near the moment at which the sun begins its ascent. In the same way, the light spread by the forerunner, John the Baptist, gradually dims until the day the glorious light of Jesus appears. That light takes over and outshines the light that prepared the way.

Luke and Matthew did not go so far. What the authors of these gospels wanted to do when they produced this tangle of dates[8] was to show that they were speaking of a God who had entered human history. The Second Vatican Council would translate this concept, some twenty centuries later, by the phrase 'And the Word was made flesh and entered into history.'

And this, according to the accounts in Luke and Matthew, is how it happened. The principal role is at first taken by an angel, Gabriel. 'Gabriel' means 'God is strong', and 'angel' means 'messenger' (the Hebrew *malak*, 'messenger', translates into the Greek *angelos*, from which Latin derived *angelus* and French *ange*). These pure spirits had only one aim: to make God's desires and wishes known to men. 'They are angels only when they announce something,' declared Pope Gregory. The Jews had such an elevated notion of God that they could not imagine Him appearing here, there and everywhere to communicate with humans, and so intermediaries were used – except during Jesus' 'public life', when the angels disappeared from the scene, and God did His own work, so to speak.

Despite their habitually smiling portrayal in church architecture and religious pictures, angels initially strike terror into the people to whom they appear. The Bible frequently testifies to this, and Gabriel's first appearance, to the elderly priest Zechariah, is no exception. He announces the birth of a son, John, who 'must drink no wine nor strong drink' but will 'bring back many of the sons of Israel to the Lord their God'. Fear, says the evangelist, 'fell' on the old man, and the angel reassures him, 'Do not be afraid ...' But – and this is also typical – the person receiving the message refuses at first to believe it. 'I am an old man,' Zechariah explains and then, with the tact of a gentleman, 'and my wife is getting on in years.'

Mary is also 'deeply disturbed' when she sees Gabriel coming into her house, and he has to repeat his reassurance, 'Do not be afraid.' Then, when he announces that she will bear a boy, 'Son of the Most High', she is, like Zechariah, incredulous, as she would be. 'How can this come about, since I am a virgin?' He explains that 'the Holy Spirit will come upon you', and then gives her proof: her kinswoman, Elizabeth, who was believed barren, and who was no longer young, had conceived a son. Indeed, she was already six months pregnant, 'for nothing is impossible to God'. After which, Mary goes to Elizabeth – 'as quickly as she could', Luke tells us, although he does not say whether she goes to congratulate the older woman, to help her in what must have been a tiring pregnancy, or to make sure that the whole thing had not been a dream.

Contemporary commentators have another theory. From the beginning, problems (to which I shall return) ensued between the disciples of John the Baptist, who was the first to appear in public, and those of Jesus. It was therefore important to the evangelists to make Jesus' pre-eminence clear by emphasising that even whilst still inside his mother John had recognised Jesus' greatness: 'the child in my womb leapt for joy,' Elizabeth tells Mary after the customary greetings.

To return to the messages brought by Gabriel;[9] all the annunciations, in the Old and the New Testaments, are made in this way. They end with some proof that the message is true: for Mary, Elizabeth's pregnancy; for Zechariah, a punishment ('Since you have not believed my words, which will come true at their appointed time, you will be silenced and have no power of speech until this has happened').[10] The annunciation concludes with the recitation of psalms – though not for Zechariah, of course, since the poor man had been struck dumb. In her Magnificat, Mary repeats almost word for word the prayer spoken by Hannah, centuries earlier. Like Elizabeth, Hannah had been barren and had eventually, after much prayer – women in the Bible were completely obsessed with the idea of becoming a mother – had a son, the prophet Samuel. We should note, however, that while Mary repeats Hannah's prayer, she uses more forceful language: 'The bow of the mighty is broken but the feeble have girded themselves with strength'[11] becomes 'He has pulled down princes from their thrones and exalted the lowly.'[12] She also adds a phrase of her own invention: 'He has ... the rich sent empty away.'[13] This speaks volumes about the character that Luke assigns Mary. It is one that bears little relation to her customary meek and mild image.

The annunciations by the angel Gabriel of the successive births of John the Baptist and Jesus are therefore modelled on other biblical annunciations. As such, they belong to a literary genre that contains five elements: appearance, fear, prediction, proof, recitation of psalms or prayers – just as classical theatre observed the rule of the three unities: time, place and action. In other words, it is not a question here of history, but of literature, not of reporting what actually occurred, but of giving a flavour of the event.

In Matthew's version, 'an angel of the Lord' (that is, God, in the language of the Bible) appears to Joseph 'in a dream' to tell him what has happened. Engaged to Mary, he already knows that she is pregnant and has resolved to 'send her away quietly'. Dreams are frequently used in the Bible as a means of communication. Another Joseph, the son of Jacob, who was sold by his brothers before becoming Pharaoh's prime minister, was in the habit of dreaming. First he was granted dreams which predicted his brilliant future, and then he began to interpret the dreams of the Egyptian officers and of Pharoah himself, which, needless to say, did no harm to his career.

Gabriel and the 'angel of the Lord' have a single purpose: to make it clear to the reader that Jesus was sent by God, charged with His mission. Joseph does not hesitate. Despite the likely scandal, he brings Mary to live with him. Joseph was a person of note in his village, since for the Jews, all manual work was sacred. The greatest rabbis, the greatest scribes, had never been too proud to get their hands dirty, and had been woodcutters, cobblers, bakers, etc. 'The craftsman need not get up when the greatest doctor enters the room,' said the rabbis. And carpenters were particularly valued. Some even claim that the term 'carpenter' meant, in local languages as well as in Greek, a small builder. In any event, a man like Joseph would not have been happy simply joining tenons and mortices. With the tools at his disposal, hammers, scissors, gouges and saws, he would have made many things. A century later, the Greek Christian Justin, a philosopher who taught in Rome before being martyred there, would assert that Jesus made ploughs and yokes in Joseph's workshop and that his workmanship was still being talked about in Palestine. Whether or not this is true does not matter much. What does matter is Justin's commentary on this: Jesus, he says, used ploughs and yokes 'to teach the symbols of justice and of the active life'.[14] The word 'justice' is interesting. A carpenter is forced by the nature of his trade to follow rules, to measure things exactly. He would become such an expert that his opinion was sought on matters of justice. It is not just in passing that Matthew calls Joseph a 'just man'. The Talmud, the commentary on the Law, relates how, when a tricky point of law arose in a trial, the question was sometimes asked: 'Is there a carpenter or the son of a carpenter present who can answer that question?'

So that is Joseph: a respected and influential figure in his community who suddenly learns that his fiancée is pregnant, knowing, as he has every reason to, that the child is not his. 'Fiancée', however, did not mean what it does today: then, she had almost the same status as a wife. Marriage was a two-stage process. First, the mutual engagement, a sort of contract which laid down, among other things, the financial arrangements. Later, the woman went to live in the man's house, to share the marriage bed. There was a considerable gap between these stages, but the woman was, from the first, thought of as married. Were she to have an affair, for example, it would be an act of adultery carrying the death penalty. It was therefore really very brave of Mary to sing the Magnificat when Gabriel told her of God's plans for her. She must have prayed that the Lord would send an angel to Joseph, posthaste, to tell him too – which is indeed what happened. This was not before time, as the carpenter had already decided to break off the engagement and to send Mary away secretly, so that she would not be put to death. Forewarned, he took the other option and brought her to live with him, concluding the marriage arrangements although, as Matthew tells us, 'he knew her not until she had borne a son' – in other words, they had no sexual relations. In the eyes of the world, however, they were man and wife.

Mary had got off by the skin of her teeth – which is not to say that there was no gossip. That came later, after Jesus had died and been resurrected and his fame had spread. After, in fact, he had become disturbing. We need to examine this gossip, however unpleasant it is, because it perhaps provides a partial explanation of why Matthew and Luke were so anxious to spell out the details of Jesus' birth. A rumour aimed at discrediting the first Christian communities was circulating in certain circles in Jerusalem. The story was that Mary had actually been the mistress of a Roman legionary called Panthera, and her bastard son was thus the offspring of a pagan father – which would obviously mean that he

could not have been the long-awaited Messiah.[15] The Jewish texts
that reproduced this calumny were not contemporary with Jesus,
but seem to have been widespread from the first century onwards.

It was also important for Matthew and Luke to refute the notion that the Jewish people, particularly the Pharisees, were still
dreaming (even if without real conviction) that a 'son of David'
would come to deliver them from the Romans and from the dynasty of Herod, just as King David had conquered the Philistines,
taken Jerusalem and established it as his capital, made the
covenant with God, and then built the first Temple. The evangelists therefore set about establishing that Jesus was the 'son of
David'.

Matthew drew up a list of three sets of fourteen names beginning with Abraham and ending with Jesus, Luke a list of seventy-
seven names beginning with Adam. The two lists contradict each
other, and in any case historians cannot take them seriously. On
the other hand, they are teeming with symbolism. Luke places a
certain Jesus forty-ninth in the list of seventy-seven. Why?
Because seven is the most sacred number, denoting completeness,
the number of days in the creation. And seven times seven is
forty-nine. And the fact that the other Jesus, the real one, the
one who counts, is seventy-seventh on the list is clearly not acci-
dental. Similarly, Matthew stresses (by playing around with the
figures a little) that 'The sum of generations is therefore: fourteen
from Abraham to David; fourteen from David to the Babylonian
deportation; and fourteen from the Babylonian deportation to
Christ.'[16] Fourteen is of course a multiple of seven, but it is also
half a lunar month, the moon being the symbol of Israel, which
was continually renewing itself. The three cycles of fourteen generations also correspond to the three periods in Israel's history:
the patriarchs, the kings and post-Exile.

The whole of antiquity, in search of laws that would explain
the world and its history, loved to use numbers and symbols like
this. They do not, however, give the historian much to go on – as
far as we know, the line of David had ended with Zerubbabel, one

of his descendants. Moreover, according to the genealogy, the line reaches back through Joseph and it is through Joseph that Jesus was descended from the great king of Israel, which hardly fits in with the angel's message.

The two evangelists saw the problem, but did not solve it. Jesus, says Luke, was 'the son, as it was thought, of Joseph',[17] while Matthew, after having repeated ad infinitum 'the father of' finally arrives at the end of his genealogical tree: 'Jacob was the father of Joseph the husband of Mary; of her was born Jesus who is called Christ.'[18]

Joseph is therefore reduced to the role of adoptive father – the legal or 'putative' father, as a now-forgotten but pretty carol expresses it. And Jesus is not of David's blood.

Scholars have put forward another explanation of Matthew's genealogy: while, line after line, it names fathers, it does not use the word in the case of Jesus, the most important figure in the list. Why? Because Matthew's text was Jewish in origin and aimed at a Jewish readership. And, for the Jews, the name of God must never be spoken. Silence as to the identity of the last father on the list was therefore extremely eloquent.

The only snag is that a contradictory text exists, and it is not just any old one. The apostle Paul – whose writings, it is worth restating, are the oldest, and so the closest in time to the life of Jesus – writes that Jesus, 'according to the human nature he took, was a descendant of David ... who, in the order of the spirit, the spirit of holiness that was in him, was proclaimed son of God in all his power through his resurrection from the dead'.[19] If Jesus were descended from the line of David, 'according to the human nature he took', that could only mean through Joseph. Here, then, we are dealing with one of the most controversial questions in Christianity, that of the 'immaculate conception' announced by Gabriel and the 'angel of the Lord'.

What is more, Paul seems never to have heard of any miraculous birth. He writes to the Galatians, the descendants of the Gallic tribes that had emigrated to the region called Cappadocia

34

(in modern Turkey), that 'God sent his Son, born of a woman'.[20] He uses the term *gune*, 'woman', rather than *parthenos*, 'girl' or 'maid'. Now virginity is no incidental matter for Paul, but quite the reverse. It is reasonable to assume that if this champion of virginity had known about the virgin birth, he would have shouted it from the rooftops.

It seems that Paul was not the only one to be ignorant of it. Apart from a few sentences in the gospels of Matthew and Luke, no clear mention of the virgin birth of Jesus is made anywhere else in the New Testament – including the Acts of the Apostles, which tells of the apostles' tribulations and evangelism after Jesus' death and resurrection. The first Christians were also apparently unaware of the virgin birth, or were simply not interested in it. They, and particularly Paul, were entirely ready to believe that Jesus was both human and divine, but were quite unconcerned about the circumstances of his birth. Indeed, even Matthew and Luke, who talk of the virgin birth as though it were unassailable fact, do not make anything out of it. Jesus himself never speaks of it. And it is hard to understand the episode of the boy Jesus in the Temple if Mary and Joseph had already known of the miraculous, divine, indescribably extraordinary nature of his birth. As we saw, they are worried and anxious at his disappearance and, when they find him, ask him at once why he has behaved in such a way. To which he replies, 'Did you not know that I must be in my Father's house?' 'But,' Luke adds, 'they did not understand what he meant.'[21] When two angels come to tell you that you are expecting a child who is none other than the Son of God, it is unlikely that you would be surprised by anything that such a child might do.

Were the two evangelists inspired, as has sometimes been suggested, by ancient stories of gods who had sexual intercourse with human girls? A stack of such stories has been uncovered. In ancient China, for example, a certain Pei Han, a supernatural being – although human in appearance – gave a luminous object to the king's wife, telling her that she would have a son.[22] But the wife in that story was not a virgin – and China is a very long way away. Nearer to home, Perseus, the Greek hero who had to cut off the head of the Medusa, the Gorgon whose look would kill, was born of the virgin Danaë, impregnated by Zeus who had come to her in the form of a shower of gold. But the sober tone of the evangelists' testimonies bear little relation to the rather licentious character of Greek mythology.

Others have seen an Essenian influence in the claim that Jesus was born of a virgin. We shall return to the Essenes later. They were the pious and extremely ascetic people made famous by the discovery in 1947 of the Dead Sea Scrolls, and they prized virginity highly. In one of these scrolls, the *Testament of Joseph* (not Mary's husband but one of the twelve sons of Jacob), we find the sentence, 'And I saw that from Judah a virgin was born, wearing a robe of linen, and from her issued a lamb without blemish.'[23] But the Essenes constituted only a small minority of a Jewish world which, St Paul and a few others aside, did not hold virginity in particularly high regard. This world had such a sense of the transcendence of God that it did not, could not, maintain that the Eternal, the Infinite, had degraded Himself with a mortal being. Rabbis recommended marriage as young as possible: 'Any man who is unmarried at twenty will be subject to sin for the rest of his life,' and enjoined a man to 'honour his wife above himself'.[24]

The rabbi Trypho, writing in the second century to St Justin in Rome, upbraids him severely: 'You should blush at telling the same stories as them [the Greeks]. It is better to say that Jesus was a man among men.... If you do not want people to say you are as mad as the Greeks, you must stop speaking of these things.'[25]

Was that the common feeling at the time? The gospel attributed to Matthew was written, say scholars, in such a way that the Jews would be convinced that Jesus' words and actions fulfilled certain promises that God had made in the Old Testament, and that he was therefore the Messiah they were waiting for. And this is what he does here: 'Now all this took place to fulfil the words spoken by the Lord through the prophet: "The virgin will conceive and give birth to a son, and they will call him Emmanuel." '[26]

The first thing to say is that this text is a kind of parenthesis in the narration of Joseph's dream, almost as though it had been added afterwards. The prophet to whom the evangelist refers is Isaiah — but the Hebrew of Isaiah's text spoke of Emmanuel's mother as a 'young woman'. It was the translators of the Septuagint (a Greek translation of the Old Testament written between 250 and 130 BC, for the Jews who had been dispersed throughout the Greek world and who did not speak Hebrew) who mistranslated that by 'virgin'.

Matthew might be accused of protesting too much, especially as the gospel attributed to John has the disciple Philip saying, without any qualifications: 'We have found the one Moses wrote about in the Law, the one about whom the prophets wrote: he is Jesus son of Joseph, from Nazareth.'[27] C. H. Dodd, one of the best of the recent commentators on the gospels, stresses that the words 'the son of Joseph' occur

> in a formal confession of Christ by Philip, one of the first disciples, and can hardly have been intended to be entirely erroneous. The intention appears to be to identify Jesus as the son of Joseph from Nazareth and then to designate him as the Messiah of whom Moses and the prophets wrote, as Son of God, and as King of Israel.[28]

In Dodd's analysis of John, therefore, nothing prevents the Son of God *also* being the son of Joseph, and the belief in the virgin birth is therefore not essential to the Christian faith.

A problem nevertheless remains: why do Matthew and Luke insist on the extraordinary nature of the birth when they must know that it would not easily be believed and that it would be unacceptable to their Jewish readers? Zealous propagandists, anxious to convince, would have been very careful about swimming against the tide in this way. We must therefore conclude that the authors of the gospels did not *want* to adulterate the truth. This does not mean that what they write *is* the truth. Historians cannot follow them down that path. They cannot, in fact, draw any conclusions at all. But people are free to believe that, as Gabriel said, 'nothing is impossible to God'.

Equally, however, the virgin birth can be regarded as a *theologoumenon*, an academic word that I hesitate to use but which will help us more than once. A *theologoumenon* is a kind of image that helps us understand an aspect of faith. In other words, we are dealing not with historical truth, but with a symbol that expresses a profounder truth. An example of a *theologoumenon* is the adoration of Jesus by the Magi (which we shall examine later and about which historians have very good reasons to be sceptical), which demonstrates the vital point that through Jesus God revealed himself not only to the Jews but to the Gentiles – in other words, to the whole world. To consider the virgin birth as a *theologoumenon* does not diminish its meaning. Rather, it shows that Jesus, like Adam, owed his life to the direct intervention of God. Jesus was therefore a gift from God and began a new era in the history of humanity.[29]

3

The First Witnesses

LUKE'S census (whose existence we have seen to be very contro-versial) would not have gone down well with the Jews. First, because it had been ordered by the Romans, who must, as usual, have had some ulterior motive, like the introduction of a new tax, up their sleeve. They did not count their subjects for the fun of it. Also, there was an old superstition that a census of the Jews would bring misfortune unless it had been commanded by Yahweh Himself. When the great King David had forced Jacob to count all the tribes of Israel, the Lord had been so angered by this 'sin' that in retribution he had unleashed a terrifying plague that had killed 70,000 men.[1] But the edict of Caesar Augustus ordered everyone, not just the Jews, to be counted, and that had perhaps appeased Yahweh's anger. And, in an attempt to sugar the pill and to pacify these rebellious people, the Romans had allowed them to return to their native towns to be registered, since this was appar-ently their custom (though again this is controversial).

If we accept Luke's account, we can imagine Joseph's irritation at all this. As if the fact that Mary, hardly more than a child, was pregnant – which had set the tongues of Nazareth wagging – were not enough! Now he had to take her to Bethlehem, by poor roads, on a journey of at least four days by caravan, because that was where the family of David had originated. This also meant, of course, that he had to stop work, close the workshop and turn down several orders, all when his wife was about to give birth. If 'the angel of the Lord' who had visited the carpenter in a dream had spoken the truth – and he had no reason to doubt it – this miraculous event had occurred at a very awkward time.

* * *

They set off. They are not alone. Most Nazarenes will be registered on the spot, but the Jewish people, who have suffered so much, have been scattered far and wide, and some Judaeans have settled in Galilee. So a caravan has formed to travel south – it is wiser to travel in a group. As the donkeys bray and the little bells worn by the camels tinkle, the men go on ahead, with the women and children following a little way behind. From time to time, they sing blessings. At night, they stop at caravanserais where, amid the crowd of people and animals, women run to the wells to fill the goatskins with water and prepare the food, while the men look after the animals, ensuring that the donkeys drink at the water trough before the camels – which would empty it in seconds to stock up for the journey ahead if they got the chance. And the children are like children the world over. They run around, playing, shouting, getting in people's way.

And Mary? Even though she is riding on a donkey, she is exhausted. The child in her womb moves ceaselessly – perhaps he is disturbed by the journey. As long as he is not about to be born before— Before what? Bethlehem? The return to Nazareth? How could she know what to expect? She is still virtually a child herself? Of course there will always be an older woman around, only too ready to give advice – but then there would always be another to say the exact opposite.

Finally, they reach Bethlehem. It is a tiny white town perched on the side of a hill, surrounded by fields of wheat ('Bethlehem' means 'house of bread') and by orchards (it was nicknamed 'Ephrathah', 'rich in fruits'). The caravanserai is overflowing, because those who claim descent from David are numerous. The natives are not very welcoming. They like this wretched census no more than other Jews, and their town is being overrun not only by the Roman officials who have come to do the registering, but also by this dusty crowd of men and women, newly arrived from all over the country, who mingle with their usual customers, the nomads coming to barter material and cheese for cereals and fruit.

Joseph and Mary eventually find shelter in a stable.[2] She

knows, instinctively, that her time has come and the child is about to be born.

Let us now turn to the account of these events in the Bible. Luke says, 'She gave birth to a son, her first-born. She wrapped him in swaddling clothes, and laid him in a manger.' One could not have a more stark description of the event. There is no sense of the supernatural here, but rather an evocation of loneliness. Elsewhere in the Bible, there are detailed descriptions of the rituals following birth: the cutting of the umbilical cord, and the salt sprinkled on the child's belly before he is washed and then wrapped in swaddling clothes – i.e. bound tightly in strips of cloth so that he could not move arms or legs. This process was thought to make him stronger, and went on for six months, although the clothes would be removed daily so that the infant could be washed and rubbed with olive oil and myrrh, a sweet-smelling resin. Luke's gospel does not bother with such details. The child is born. That is the important thing.

The first witnesses of that significant event were poor, insignificant people, shepherds. Shepherds were thought to be dishonest and thieving. Indeed, they were held in such low regard that there was a saying: 'One does not rescue from pits *goyim* [Gentiles] and those who breed and pasture small cattle.'[3] From the very beginning, therefore, Jesus' companions were not the most desirable. And the shepherds did not come across the infant by chance. An angel had sent for them. This angel has no name but, as usual, he frightens the people he has come to speak to. Also, as usual, he reassures them, announcing the birth of a Saviour and then giving them, in the classic model, some proof: 'Here is a sign for you: you will find a baby wrapped in swaddling cloths and lying in a manger.' Finally there is the prayer, although here it is said by a whole army of angels, 'a great throng of the heavenly host'.

The annunciation to the shepherds is therefore firmly in the literary mould, as outlined in the previous chapter. There is one significant difference. These good people do not utter a single expression of disbelief (although it is true that a whole choir of angels singing at the tops of their voices and floating in a sky exploding with light would probably have convinced the most hardened of sceptics), but go off in search of the child, leaving their flocks unprotected. (Quite apart from thieves, wild bears, leopards and jackals were rife in the region.) But then, the poor were no strangers to risk. They went to see, as the gospel has them saying rather oddly, 'this thing that has happened which the Lord has made known to us'. 'This thing' had been announced by a heavenly host. Again, there is the same contrast between the magnificent and glorious, and the anonymous and humble. The author of this account leaves nothing to chance; his composition is perfect, and the message that he wants to get across is clear.

Eight days later, as demanded by the Law, the child is circumcised. This rite, practised by numerous peoples at the time (although usually at puberty), had a particular significance for the Hebrews. It symbolised their Covenant with God. Performed with a flint, which evoked the time of Abraham, when the covenant had been made, it cut the infant and drew 'the blood of the covenant'. Any baby thus circumcised became from that moment an ally of God. Comprehension of this key idea is central to an understanding of Judaism, and then of Christianity, which would replace circumcision with baptism.

Luke's description of Jesus' circumcision is nonetheless perfunctory. This is perhaps unsurprising, for he doubtless realised that it was a little odd that it should have been performed at all, since the Covenant which it signified was in this case between God and Himself. At the same time, by undergoing this rite Jesus clearly demonstrates both his belonging to the Jewish people and his solidarity with them. The evangelist's attention is, however, elsewhere. 'When the eighth day came,' he writes, 'and the child was to be circumcised, they gave him the name Jesus, the name the angel had given him before his conception.' It is therefore the name that is important, doubtless because it had been ordained by the angel, but also because a name was always of great significance to the Jews since it expressed a vocation. Jesus himself, in Mark's gospel, changed the name of some of his disciples: 'And so he appointed the Twelve; Simon to whom he gave the name Peter, James the son of Zebedee and John the brother of James, to whom he gave the name Boanerges or "Sons of Thunder" '.[4] To name someone was to mark out his destiny. Remarkably, naming was often the privilege of the woman, or even of the group of older women who were present at the birth, as in the case of David's grandfather: 'And the women of the neighbourhood gave him a name, saying, "A son has been born for Naomi ...", and they named him Obed. This was the father of David's father, Jesse.'[5] After Elizabeth has given birth, her relatives and neighbours want to give the child his father's name, Zechariah, but she protests. ' "No," she said, "he is to be called John." '[6] They object that no one in the family bears that name, and appeal to the still dumb father. He, however, confirms his wife's choice by writing on a tablet and – divine reward, promise kept – regains his speech as he does so.

In fact, it is not surprising that Zechariah should confirm the choice of name, because it was to him that Gabriel had said, 'You must name him John,' just as the angel who had gone to Joseph in a dream to tell him of the coming birth had commanded him, 'You must name him Jesus.' And Matthew repeats, 'He named him Jesus.' The maternal privilege has been overturned. Cynics might interpret that as a kind of consolation prize for Joseph, who has been given something of a rough deal by the divine will. But there is another interpretation. Although it was usually the mother who named the child, this was not invariably the case; Abraham and Moses, for example, had chosen their sons' names. The choice can therefore be seen as something that denotes a remarkable person.

The name Jesus is not, however, remarkable. The Bible has a dozen Jesuses, the first of whom, Josue (Joshua), was Moses' second-in-command and his eventual successor. The Jewish historian Josephus cites twenty or so people of that name. In other words, the child is the Saviour, but a saviour who has taken on the common condition of his people. Once again, we are to understand that he is both human and divine. When the parents go to the Temple to purify the virgin and to present the baby, the child is placed in the arms of the pious old man Simeon, who frequents the place. By this single gesture the child is being entrusted both to God and to humanity.

Every woman had to be purified after she had given birth. For forty days if she has had a boy, eighty if a girl (the ancient world was quite brutal in its attitude towards women), the woman was considered impure, preventing her from, among other things, entering the Temple. To be purified, she had to take a lamb – male of course – to the Temple entrance. The lamb would then be entirely burnt, unlike the pilgrims' offerings, on the altar. She also took a dove or turtle-dove, whose head would be cut off, and if the woman were poor, the lamb could be replaced by another bird. The young couple took advantage of this dispensation, from which we can infer that Joseph, although a carpenter, was not very well off.

Most commentators refrain from drawing attention to the inconsistency: did Mary, presented as virgin, as mother of the Son of God, need to be purified? Of what? There is no plausible answer, except, perhaps, that she wanted to obey the common law. The author of Luke's gospel seems, however, to have recognised the problem. He speaks of the purification, when he could, like Matthew, have drawn a veil over it. For him, evidently, this rather awkward event occurred, and he feels obliged to mention it. Such scrupulousness on his part should be acknowledged, especially since Matthew is so often accused of taking certain liberties with the facts. Luke has to solve the problem somehow, and he does so by dealing with it in the same way as he dealt with the circumcision: 'And when the time came for their purification according to the law of Moses, they brought him up to Jerusalem to present him to the Lord.'[7] Suddenly, through this clear differentiation of main and subordinate clauses, it is no longer the rite of purification that matters. That is only the context, the pretext. The central episode is the presentation to the Lord.

Luke's 'their purification' is another marvellous sleight of hand, implying that Joseph also needed to be purified. Of course, translators have puzzled over this strange plural. Some of the less scrupulous (of whom there have been plenty, including a fair number of monastics, in days gone by) have made it into a singular. But it is a plural, a plural that contradicts the notion that Mary alone was impure. We should perhaps feel sorry for Joseph, although we can also draw the more agreeable conclusion that, in the author's eyes, Mary and Joseph are truly a couple.

In any case, this rite of purification holds little interest for the evangelist. He is far more concerned with the presentation of the infant at the Temple, which took place to observe 'what stands written in the Law of the Lord: Every first-born male must be consecrated to the Lord.'[8] He is even more concerned with what happened while they are there – the prophecies of the old man Simeon, to whom they had entrusted the child on entering the sacred place, and of the prophetess, Anna. Simeon, who has moreover received a direct revelation from the Holy Spirit (Gabriel and his fellows having been replaced by greater emissaries, perhaps because the Temple is involved), does not doubt for an instant that he is holding the Messiah in his wrinkled arms. Now, he says in summary, I can die, for the child is born as 'a light for revelation to the Gentiles'. Once again, Mary and Joseph are astonished by these words. And yet, as we have said, after having been visited by angels and doubtless told by the shepherds of the heavenly chorus and a sky lit up like the aurora borealis, they should not have been astonished by anything. The author of the gospel is obviously not afraid of seeming to contradict himself, or at least of being illogical. Does he mean to suggest that, despite all the annunciations, the truth – so overwhelming, so incredible – only sank in to them little by little? Is he suggesting that they received a kind of divine tutelage, a gradual revelation? What happens next allows such an interpretation.

Simeon, this man who has been charged with a mission by the Holy Spirit, in a sense completes Gabriel's annunciation. The child, he says to Mary (Joseph moving into the background), 'is destined for the fall and for the rising of many in Israel, destined to be a sign that is rejected – and a sword will pierce your own soul too.'[9] Mary has been forewarned. Gabriel had given only the rosy side of the picture. But one can also see the whole of this narrative, from the census to the presentation, as a *theologoumenon*, an image designed to help us understand that Jesus was born and lived among the poor, and was recognised at the Temple only by slightly eccentric – certainly powerless – old people.

The infant is also acclaimed by the very elderly Anna, and Luke gives us a complete run-down of her marital status, as though he had been with her when she was registered in the census. In fact, he gives us more detail about her than about anyone else in the gospel: prophetess by profession (not unusual in Israel at that time), she is eighty-four years old and had been married to her husband for seven years, and her father was called Phanuel ('in front of God') and belonged to the tribe of Asher. This forest of details is all the more surprising since Anna speaks neither to Mary nor to Joseph but, having seen them in the Temple, speaks of the child 'to all who were looking for the redemption of Jerusalem'. That is all. So many uncharacteristic details leading up to that one simple sentence. Why? The scholars have told us to look at the numbers, of which Luke is so fond. The seven is there: the number of years Anna was married. And the years she was widowed or unmarried: eighty-four minus seven equals seventy-seven. As many years as generations that have been, according to Luke, waiting, alone in a pagan world, for the Christ. One could obviously theorise at length about the significance of the old meeting the young, but the numbers give us more clues. Once again we are not in the realm of history but of symbolism (which does not mean of lies but, as we have seen, of a profounder kind of truth).

* * *

Let us move now to the other gospel that covers Jesus' childhood, Matthew. As in Luke, Jesus is born in Bethlehem, which is similarly specified as being 'in Judaea'. That detail was not put in by chance or to help those contemporary scholars who have wondered whether this Bethlehem was not the one of the same name a few miles from Nazareth and therefore in Galilee. The fact that Matthew and Luke specify the district means that they were aware that there was another Bethlehem, and what they want to show is that the birth of Jesus fulfilled the Scriptures, in which God had promised the people of Israel that a Messiah would be born in Bethlehem.

One such prophecy was made through Micah, a 'minor' prophet who lived not far away at the time of Isaiah and who generally predicted terrible events. He had written: 'But you, Bethlehem Ephrathah, the least of the clans of Judah, out of you will be born for me the one who is to rule over Israel.'[10]

Matthew, however, seems to have considerably distorted Micah's text in his version of it. The other promise of God concerning Bethlehem is found in the biblical books of Samuel, which cover a long period in the history of Israel. In them the Lord says to Samuel: 'Fill your horn with oil and go. I am sending you to Jesse of Bethlehem, for I have chosen myself a king among his sons.'[11] This second prophecy is not overwhelmingly clear, but the first seems to have been fairly well known by the Jews.

This is confirmed by a passage in the gospel of John, although he makes no mention of Bethlehem as Jesus' birthplace. The scene takes place in Jerusalem in the third decade of the first century AD, during the Jewish Feast of Tabernacles. This feast commemorates the wandering of the Jews in the desert as they returned from Egypt to the Promised Land (where they had lived in tents or shelters, also called tabernacles). Celebrated after the autumn harvest, it was also an occasion of giving thanks to God.

Many Jews have gathered at the Temple for the festival. Jesus, the gospel of John tells us, also 'went up' to Jerusalem. There he preaches, says that he is sent from God, announces that he will soon leave and exhorts the crowd, 'If any one thirst, let him come to me and drink'. All of which, as one can imagine, caused quite a stir. Some accept him: 'He is the Christ!' But others ask, 'Would the Christ be from Galilee? Does not Scripture say that the Christ must be descended from David and come from the town of Bethlehem?'[12] This confirms the idea that the Jews were waiting for a saviour who would come from Bethlehem. Surprisingly, John does not have Jesus or the disciples replying that he had, in fact, been born in Bethlehem, which would seem the natural response. He simply comments that 'the people could not agree about him'. It therefore seems reasonable to presume that the evangelist knew nothing about Jesus' birthplace.

According to Luke, the shepherds and then the elderly prophetess, Anna, had spoken of Jesus' birth everywhere, yet no one seems to have any memory of it. It is true, of course, that what unimportant people say is not always heard, especially when what they are saying is literally incredible. Anna and the shepherds must have been dismissed as mad. Nonetheless, not every scholar accepts the birth in Bethlehem as historical fact.

Let us return to Matthew. The birth in Bethlehem causes fewer problems than does his claim that Joseph and Mary lived there and were still there two years later, at the time of the visit of the Magi, whereas, according to Luke, they had returned to Galilee forty days after the birth. In Matthew's version, the infant was born not in a stable but in a 'house',[13] and it was there that he would receive the strange visitors from the East. 'On what precise facts is the ancient Christian tradition of this story [of the adoration of the Magi] based? We will never know with certainty' declare the authors of *La Bible du peuple de Dieu*.[14]

The story is nevertheless a very beautiful one. First, a star appears in the sky. To have a star accompany their birth was the privilege of 'great men' in the ancient world. Alexander had one, as did Augustus and Abraham, while in China a star greeted the birth of the Buddha, and the *Bhagavad Gita* mentions one at

Krishna's birth. The people who discovered those stars must be given due credit. As Daniel-Rops points out, they were looking at the sky with the naked eye or with rudimentary instruments, and thus lacked the basis that even the smallest telescope gives to modern astronomy. In trying to establish information about the star seen by the Magi, many specialists, including astronomers, have drawn comparisons with the famous Halley's Comet, which was seen in Jerusalem in 1910. This comet, which travelled from east to west, took the same route as that indicated by Matthew, although it could not have left its path to indicate a precise spot, as did the star that took the Magi to Jesus. Now Halley's Comet appeared in the region in 12 BC, which hardly corresponds to the likely date of the birth but is close enough to be of interest. And Kepler, the German astronomer who lived in the sixteenth and seventeenth centuries, and who therefore could not know that modern scholars would fix the date of Jesus' birth at around 6 BC, established that a conjunction of Jupiter and Saturn in Pisces occurred in that very year. The evangelist had perhaps been inspired by the memory of such things, transmitted by word of mouth from generation to generation in a world that loved this kind of marvel.

The light, then, was seen by the Magi. These were not kings,[15] but interpreters of dreams and of remarkable events and, in addition, astronomers – 'astrologers', said the detractors. The Jews had long hated astrologers because God and the prophets had condemned them,[16] and what is more, these came from the East (from which precise part is never specified), as had the Chaldean troops who had frequently invaded Judaea, pillaging and murdering. But opinions had altered somewhat. Astrology was so seductive, and the desire to know the future so strong. As we know from the discovery at Qumran, even the highly ascetic Essenes, respectful of the Law as they were, knew of or even themselves drew up a horoscope of the promised Messiah. Over the years, and especially at the time that Matthew's gospel was composed, astrologers of every sort had begun to get a better press.

So the Magi set off. Perhaps they knew that Israel was expecting a Messiah. We know that they came from afar, because when the star eventually led them to their destination they found not a new-born infant, but a young child (*pais* in the Greek of the gospel). The crib scenes that one sees today in churches or in people's homes bear little relation to the historical reality, since these good astrologers cannot have coincided with the shepherds.

They were a little too good – or perhaps a little naive, or at any rate ignorant of what was happening in Judaea – because they had no hesitation about paying Herod a courtesy call on their way through Jerusalem. (He, incidentally, gave them a great welcome, which shows how much the image of astrologers had improved.) There were many reasons to be wary of Herod, for as everyone knew, he was a collaborator, and an imposter to boot. In 63 BC, the Roman general Pompey had taken Jerusalem, after conquering Syria, at a cost of thousands of lives. He had stayed to rule or – as it was later put – to 'pacify' the natives. This was not an easy task, with the Jews so restless. The Romans had employed their usual method, and sought out locals who would help with their dirty work. And that is why the Roman Senate had decided to proclaim Herod 'king of the Jews, friend and ally'. But Herod was not truly Jewish, since his mother was an Arab. No sooner had he been elevated to this status than he went off to the Capitol in Rome to offer a sacrifice to Jupiter in thanks. Knowledge of this had soon circulated throughout the villages of Judaea, but Herod was unconcerned and went on to build pagan temples at Caesarea, the Roman headquarters. For him, all gods were alike. The important thing was to ingratiate himself with the occupier, who would then leave him alone to lead the life that he pleased.

Sex, money and blood. In the eyes of his contemporaries, these were Herod's gods. He wiped out the family of one of his wives, beginning with his mother-in-law and ending with the wife herself and two of the children he had had by her; he stole treasures, at night, from the tomb of David at Jerusalem; he appropriated land at will. In short, it would be pretty difficult to find a worse example of unprincipled tyranny.

But Herod was also cunning, an arch politician who pretty well succeeded in pacifying the country. When famine, epidemics and earthquakes hit the people, he lowered taxes and sold off some of his goods to give money to the afflicted. His successors would not do as much. He also launched huge building programmes, the biggest being the Temple in Jerusalem (even if, according to some, his own palace was more sumptuous). This project had put ideas into his head. The first Temple had been proposed by David and built by Solomon, but he, Herod, had done both, even if the work was not yet finished. In his own eyes he was therefore greater than David, and he even attempted to claim that he was the Messiah. This pretension would exacerbate the desire for the coming of the *real* Messiah, which by the time of Jesus had become even more fervent.

And so this was the character to whom, according to Matthew, the Wise Men from the East went to pay their respects. And these innocents tell him, without a second thought, that the king of the Jews has been born, and that they are looking for him so that they can pay him homage. It is not difficult to imagine Herod's expression – *he* is King of the Jews! And then the worry that overtakes him – a wise tyrant is always on his guard. Practically everyone in Judaea knew that the King promised by the prophets would be born in Bethlehem, but Herod, whose religious knowledge is obviously distinctly shallow, has to consult the highest ranking clergy of Jerusalem to discover this. Duly informed, he recalls the Magi to him: if they go to Bethlehem and find the infant, would they kindly let him know – 'so that I too may go and do him homage'?

This story is really very implausible. In all common sense, a tyrant of Herod's stamp would have sent one of his men hurrying off to Bethlehem to find out if the story were true. He would not have entrusted the task to these boobies. It is very difficult to believe that he would have been so naive, and we must conclude therefore that it is the evangelist who is naive and who is ignorant of the machinations and tactics of powerful men.

And so the Magi set off again, the star duly reappearing to guide them to the dwelling of Joseph and Mary. They see the child 'with his mother Mary' (again no mention of Joseph) and give him, according to Matthew and the 'apocryphal' gospels – those rejected by the Church – gold, incense and myrrh. These were well-known symbols: gold for sovereignty, incense for God, and myrrh, which was used to embalm corpses, for mortality before resurrection. The contrast, no doubt deliberate, between these gifts and the poverty and ordinariness of the people who received them is astonishing. The example set by the circumstances of this birth is not, incidentally, one that the dignitaries of the Church have always followed, dazzled as they have sometimes been by material riches.

The Magi then depart, having been warned – not before time, 'in a dream' – to beware of Herod. And then Joseph, always there in a crisis, learns from an anonymous angel that he must leave: 'Get up, take the child and his mother with you, and escape into Egypt, and stay there until I tell you, because Herod intends to search for the child and do away with him.'[17] Egypt is indeed the only safe place if they are to flee from Herod, but the strands of three great civilisations are symbolically joined in the 'East', from where the Magi, the Jews and the Egyptians had come. There is also a clear parallel with the history of Israel and its exile in Egypt, particularly Moses' return from Egypt in the book of Exodus after the death of Pharaoh. And what is most important to Matthew, always concerned to convince the Jews that Jesus is indeed the promised Messiah, is the fact that all the prophecies have been fulfilled. He makes no secret of his aims: 'This was to fulfil what the Lord had spoken through the prophet: "I called my son out of Egypt." '[18]

Herod, needless to say, is furious at having been double-crossed by the Magi who, now cautious, had not returned through Jerusalem. Here is another mystery. How is it that such a cunning and unscrupulous strategist as Herod had failed to have these three foreigners followed? If the evangelist is to be believed, Herod then decides to have all the infants in Bethlehem below the age of two killed (which does, incidentally, confirm that the visit of the Magi occurred well after the birth). But this 'Massacre of the Innocents' is mentioned nowhere else. Josephus, the great Jewish historian who detailed the deeds and misdeeds of Herod with the meticulousness of a court reporter, is unaware of it. That such an event could pass unrecorded by anyone other than Matthew must cause doubt about its historical truth – which is just as well, because otherwise the first consequence of Jesus' arrival on earth would have been a frenzy of infanticide.

The anomaly of this story has naturally not escaped the commentators. Some have drawn a discreet veil of silence over it. Others have emphasised the diabolical wickedness of Jesus' enemies, and several have commented that Jesus himself would later say that his coming would destroy and divide. Many have sought an escape route by arguing that we must not judge it with our modern minds (for a long time, a relatively small value was attached to the death of young children because so many died of natural causes in the first months of life), or by saying that all births are bloody.

Let us picture the scene, however: the infants torn from their mothers and run through with a dagger or a sword; the bodies smashed against walls or beams; the shattered skulls ... What a beginning for a saviour! Fortunately. the story is in all probability untrue, and serves rather, once again, as a symbol or as a reference. The death of the innocents of Bethlehem marks the beginning of the new Covenant between God and men, just as the death of the Egyptian children had marked the beginning of the Covenant with Moses; because Pharaoh had not allowed the Hebrews to leave Egypt, the country to which they had been exiled, the Lord inflicted nine plagues on his land:

Moses said, 'This is Yahweh's message, "Towards midnight I shall pass through Egypt. All the first-born in the land of Egypt shall die; from the first-born of Pharaoh, heir to his throne, to the first-born of the maidservant at the mill, and all the first-born of the cattle." '[19]

So the Jewish Passover was instituted. On the fourteenth day of the first month of the year, between three o'clock in the afternoon and the setting of the sun, a lamb was sacrificed and its blood smeared on the two doorposts and the lintel before the meat was eaten:

It is a passover in honour of Yahweh. That night, I will go through the land of Egypt and strike down all the first-born in the land of Egypt.... The blood shall serve to mark the houses that you live in. When I see the blood I will pass over you and you shall escape the destroying plague.[20]

We are therefore once again in the realm of symbols. The authors certainly had it in mind to scotch the gossip concerning the circumstances of Jesus' birth that had circulated after the crucifixion. And their stories probably have their basis in some measure of historical fact; those facts were, however, embroidered and twisted by those who told and retold them to teach the Christian communities who Jesus really was.

The chapters in Matthew and Luke devoted to the birth narratives are today considered by most scholars as a poetic introduction to the life of Jesus. If one accepts the view of Charles Perrot, at whose works the religious authorities have barely batted an eyelid, this part of Matthew was a later addition to the original text. Referring to the circumstances of Jesus' birth, Perrot talks about 'indications that the Matthean text is older'.[21] For a long time, the accounts of Jesus' life that circulated among the early Christian communities seem to have begun, as in the gospels of Mark and John, with the baptism of the adult Jesus by John the Baptist.

As to the Magi, Jean Martucci, a professor of theology at Montreal University, summed up the fairly widespread academic opinion when he said, during an interview on Radio Canada:

> There is every reason to believe that what we are dealing with here
> is the development of a story whose historical base cannot be
> verified.... And if we did accept it word for word, it is astonishing
> that people did not say later on in Jesus' life, 'Oh, but listen! The
> wise men came from the ends of the earth to visit Jesus! His birth
> put Herod's palace into total panic!'
>
> But we have nothing like that. And so we must be very cautious
> about its historicity.[22]

As the English scholar C. H. Dodd, who admittedly has occasionally upset the authorities, says: 'He would be a bold man
who should presume to draw a firm line between fact and
symbol.'[23]

So let us not be bold. Let us instead concentrate on the
symbols. First, the visitors. The shepherds are poor, powerless and
despised, the kind of people who according to the gospels Jesus
would later have as companions. And the Magi, who are not kings
but astrologers, about whom opinion was divided and sometimes
hostile, are, above all, foreigners whose principal role in the story
is to demonstrate that Jesus came for all men.

And then, Jesus was born at night, into a world of shadows
and uncertainty, in a town that had kept only the vestiges of its
glorious past. The people who counted were elsewhere, at
Jerusalem or Caesarea. He was born impoverished and under
threat. The light that shone at his birth was seen only by the
poor, foreigners and outcasts – although the men of power were
alarmed and would stop at nothing, including a massacre of
weak and defenceless innocents, in their attempts to remove him
and silence his voice before he could proclaim his message. This
man Jesus, starting life in a manger or a hovel and ending it on a
cross like a common criminal, succeeded in getting the whole
world to listen to him. Indeed, he altered the course of human
history. Never has a revolution been accomplished with less – or
at least with *outwardly* less, because in reality he had at his

disposal the greatest and most powerful of weapons: the Word. This is what the birth narratives of the gospels mean.

After they had returned to Nazareth, Luke says, 'the child grew to maturity, and he was filled with wisdom'. With this he repeats a biblical phrase,[24] but also indicates that the story, the revolution, is not completed – that it is written in time and space, and has not ended.

4

Childhood

NAZARETH was a dump. It was such a dump that the Bible and the rabbis had never before mentioned it. Some people have even wondered if the village existed outside the evangelists' imaginations before it became a town and a place of pilgrimage in the Christian era, although that is doubtless a view that takes scepticism to extremes.

In fact, there was a spring at Nazareth, which meant that caravans arriving from arid areas stopped there. It also attracted settlers, who could water their cattle, irrigate their land and sell handicrafts and food to the travellers. Caves were hollowed out of the side of the hill to serve as stores for provisions or as dwelling places. Later, houses in the usual style were added – rudimentary, low constructions made from mud bricks with a flat roof of woven branches placed on top of beams and then covered with clay. The inhabitants could climb up to these terraces by means of a ladder or an outside staircase, to sleep on warm nights, eat meals, or to dry washing or fruit. They were so frequently used that Deuteronomy, a biblical book that combines theology with practical advice, enjoined the Israelites to build a parapet around the roof, 'then your house will not incur blood-vengeance through anyone falling from it.'[1]

The interior of the house was the small kingdom of the woman, of Mary. This was where she wove wool or linen on a primitive loom: men wore tunics drawn in at the waist by a leather or fabric belt and a kind of cape on top. In the house she used a handmill, two stones between which grain was ground, to produce the flour that would become bread. An essential foodstuff, bread also served as a plate on which to eat meat. Food was eaten with the hands.

There was not much meat, in fact, except for special occasions when people feasted on fatted calf or the sacrificial lamb; fish was more usual. Of course, it would be unthinkable to eat anything other than kosher (pure) meat. This prohibition originated in the commandment that the Eternal had given to Noah and his sons after they had been saved from the flood: 'You must not eat flesh with life, that is to say, blood, in it. I will demand an account of your life-blood. I will demand an account from every beast and from man. I will demand an account of every man's life from his fellow men.'[2]

Blood was life. It was therefore forbidden not only to eat animal blood but also to spill man's blood – although the first injunction was of course better observed than the second. The blood of every slaughtered animal and bird had to be immediately drained away and covered with sand or earth, and any blood remaining in the beast was then removed by immersion in water, using a special bowl. The Hebrews appreciated wine and celebrated it in lyrical terms. It accompanied every meal and was similarly kosher. Only Jewish hands had been involved in its production.

Jesus did not question these customs. In the Acts of the Apostles, Peter has a strange vision. A great white sheet knotted at the corners descends from the sky, 'filled with every possible sort of animal and bird, walking, crawling or flying ones', and a voice commands the apostle to kill and eat them. To which he replies, 'Certainly not, Lord; I have never yet eaten anything profane or unclean.'[3] It is therefore reasonable to think that Jesus, with whom he had shared many meals, followed the same rules.

That would hardly be surprising. He had been brought up to follow them. His family was Jewish, in a region where many Gentiles also lived: 'Galilee' meant 'land of Gentiles'. Like all others of their race and religion, his family observed the rites and customs all the more strictly so that their identity, their uniqueness and their faithfulness to the Eternal were clearly delineated.[4]

Phoenicians, Syrians, Arabs and Greeks had settled in the region – some, it seems, having been forcibly converted and circumcised – to cultivate the land and, in particular, to trade. The local olives were highly prized, and their oil exported to the four corners of the Mediterranean for Jews of the Diaspora who were thus assured that it had not been polluted by non-Jewish hands. Galilean wheat had a similar reputation. This abundance led to an influx of immigrants but also, as we shall see, to a certain amount of tension.

The fertility of the Galilean soil, especially in comparison with the aridity of Judaea, would inspire people, like the nineteenth-century writer Ernest Renan, to flights of praise. After visiting Galilee, he described it as 'a green, shady, pleasant region, the real land of the Song of Songs, of hymns to the beloved. During the months of March and April the countryside is a carpet of flowers, an incomparable medley of colour.'

Even the 'extremely gentle' animals had seduced him: 'Elegant, lively turtle-doves, blackbirds so light that they could perch on a blade of grass without bending it, crested larks who come so close that they almost get under the traveller's feet, little river turtles with soft, shining eyes, swans that have a sombre, modest air about them and are fearless, letting people draw close to them, seeming, indeed, to call them hither.' What is more, 'in no other country of the world do the mountains spread out with so much grace or inspire such elevated thoughts.'[5] It was, in short, a kind of paradise.

The social reality was less magical. This same writer describes the austerity of houses whose only opening was a door, and which consisted of only a single area that served as stable, kitchen and bedroom, and had as its only furniture 'a mat, several cushions to sit on, one or two clay vases and a painted chest'. He also talks of the poverty of the villages: 'a confused mass of huts, terraces, and press-houses hewn out of the rock, of wells, tombs, fig and olive trees.'[6] And he does not underestimate the political tensions at the time of Jesus, which were many and severe.

* * *

The life of Herod, who reigned over the four provinces of Palestine (Judaea, Samaria, Galilee and, least known, Peraea, east of the Jordan), ended in violence and madness. Suffering, it is said, from ulcers and gangrene, he believed that his entourage consisted entirely of enemies bent on his assassination. This paranoia began with his own family, inspiring the Roman emperor Augustus to remark, 'Better to be Herod's swine than his son.' Three years before his death, Herod had two of his sons strangled – although it is true, if hardly a justification, that they were already brazenly and openly fighting over their eventual inheritance.

Herod's funeral was an opportunity for his remaining family to demonstrate their magnificence and ambition by equalling the splendour of the Roman emperors. The tyrant's corpse, wearing a crown, was carried in a jewel-encrusted golden coffin from his palace in Jericho to the Herodium, the luxurious citadel that he had had built south of Jerusalem. Following behind, in an enormous cortège, came mourners, relatives, flute-players, mercenaries primed for action and finally, Josephus tells us, 'five hundred men, household staff of the deceased king, bearing perfumes'.

Over-weaning ambition, great disappointments. Under Herod's will, his son Archelaus – who had organised the funeral – would reign over the largest part of the territory. But the Romans were wary of him and Augustus refused to grant him the title of king. This proved to be a wise move, for almost immediately a revolt broke out against Archelaus. It spread like wildfire from Jerusalem to Jericho where the palace (the second home that Herod had built for himself, to escape from the frenetic restlessness of the capital) was destroyed. The army killed some three thousand people without managing to quell the uprising and the Romans had to intervene, sending in two legions (12,000 men) and four cavalry regiments under the command of Varus, governor of Syria. Finally, in AD 6, Augustus decided it would be wisest to send Archelaus to Vienne in Gaul, at the other end of the Mediterranean.

From then on, Judaea, like Samaria, became a province of the Roman Empire, under the command of a high-ranking cavalry officer, the procurator,[7] who was in turn answerable to the governor of Syria. The most famous of these procurators, Pontius Pilate, will soon come into the story. Herod's other two sons, Philip and Herod Antipas, received respectively the territory east of the Jordan (where Philip did not manage too badly, or at least was barely remarked on) and Galilee, where Antipas took the title of tetrarch, or viceroy.

And so the Roman presence, embodied in low-ranking, mediocre officials, since the emperor was hardly going to send his best men into these far-flung, remote countries, became even heavier – and was even less tolerated. Some locals, it is true, adapted to it without too much difficulty. There are always people who will accept the seemingly inevitable, discover good qualities in those in power, and do business with them. On the other hand, some several thousand men, mostly those of some reputation – scribes, artisans and merchants anxious for religious reform – decided that they had to observe the Law with the utmost rigour and follow its tiniest commandments meticulously. This was, they felt, a form of resistance, a way of saving Israel's soul. These people were called Pharisees, or 'separated ones'. Their resistance increased, and sometimes took surprising forms. Some Pharisees went as far as to say that all land outside Israel was impure and that every foreigner would infect everything he touched with this impurity. They would debate for hours, engaging in interminable and passionate squabbles, to decide whether one could eat bread cooked in an oven fired by wood cut by non-Jews, or whether a weaver could use a shuttle made from foreign wood. And since the scrolls of sacred texts did not provide clear-cut answers, they pored over them for hints, allusions or precedents that might furnish the smallest clue to the desires of the Eternal on these questions. It was inevitable that such an obsession with purity – although this had begun to be less marked by the time of Jesus – would cause them to despise the Galileans, who were somewhat racially suspect, infected as they were by the presence of pagans.

The Galileans, for their part, had hardly submitted quietly to the Romans. On the contrary, shortly after AD 6 and the census under Quirinius, a certain Judas the Galilean, from the town of Gamala on the western bank of Lake Tiberias, decided that he had had enough of Roman harassment and taxes, and incited his compatriots to revolt. Taxes were too heavy (representing between 20 and 25 per cent of income from the land, on top of which there were religious taxes to be paid to the Temple and to the priestly caste) but that was not the main bone of contention for this Judas and his principal collaborator, a Pharisee named Zadok. Their complaint against these Roman levies was that they were a form of sacrilege. Man should recognise only one master, God, and to pay tax to a profane overlord, the Roman emperor, was in effect to put him in the place of God.

'From this', writes Josephus, who had no love for Judas and his companions, 'were born uprisings and political assassinations, of their fellow citizens ... as well as of their enemies.' He adds that famine pushed 'the most restless to extremities', without saying whether this famine, in a fertile region, was caused by damage wreaked by these conflicts or by some climatic disaster. And he is amazed by 'the invincible love of liberty' displayed by Judas's mostly very young followers. These followers would later be confused with the Zealots (zealous servants of the Law) or the *sicarii*, so called because of the dagger – the *sica* – that they wore at their belts. 'The most extreme forms of death, the supplications of their relatives and friends, left them indifferent,' writes Josephus, 'all that mattered to them was not having to call any man master. Since so many people have borne witness to the unshakeable fixity with which they bore all these trials, I will not speak more of it, for I fear ... that my words would give only an inadequate idea of the scorn with which they accepted and tolerated pain.'[8]

Here, the Jewish historian, with his hatred of the Zealots, is no longer talking about the revolt of Judas the Galilean in AD 6, but has jumped ahead to the Jewish insurrection of 66. But the two campaigns are not really comparable. Unlike the Zealots, the dissidents of the earlier uprising did not display excessive respect for the religious Law, and they derived from their faith a real aspiration for political freedom. The 'revolt' – it barely merits the term – was quickly quashed. Jesus was ten or twelve at the time, and must have retained some memory of it; he would enjoin his disciples, for example, not to call themselves 'masters'. Peace, however, did not reign absolutely.[9] Several dissident groups still campaigned for political freedom – and their movement was given impetus by the tears in the social fabric.

Indeed, it had not been by chance that the prophets, since Amos (who had first been a herdsman, around 750 BC), had ceaselessly condemned the monopolisation of land and capital and the propensity of the rich to excessive consumption of goods, to injustice and hardness of heart. Nor was it by chance that Jesus, in many of his parables, spoke of the large estates that city-dwelling owners had left in the management of a steward. Similarly, the author of the book of Job provides his hero, before a terrifying onslaught of misfortunes falls on the poor man's head, with seven thousand sheep, three hundred camels, five hundred yoke of oxen and five hundred she-asses. It was true that every seven years loans to the poor were remitted and crops given to the destitute, but, as with most such well-intentioned measures, this had the opposite effect. As the fatal year approached, the rich simply stopped lending to the poor.

As in most villages, the peasants of Nazareth were small landowners, but they also worked as paid employees, along with a few slaves[10] (usually foreign, sometimes Jewish) on large properties. Getting hired in the first place was by no means automatic. The famous parable of the eleventh-hour labourers[11] shows that work was not always easy to find, and that there was some unemployment. The householder who needed labourers for his vineyard finds some 'standing round' in the market-place at the third, sixth and ninth hours. Finally, at the eleventh hour, he asks those who are still waiting why they have been idle all day long. This question shows a blithe ignorance of social conditions, for the simple answer is that 'no one has hired us'. In short, the 'average' peasant in Nazareth could barely make ends meet after paying the tax to the Romans, the tithe (a tenth of the crop) to the priests, the 'first fruits' of each harvest to the Temple, the 'first-born' of the herd for sacrifices and so on.

These peasants, and also certain craftsmen, were called *am-ha-rez* by city-dwellers, doctors of the Law, scribes and priests who looked after the Temple. *Am-ha-rez* literally meant 'people of the country' but it had come to mean 'yokels' or 'country bumpkins'. These poor people were suspected of being slipshod about the rules of the Torah. The rabbi Hillel, president of the Sanhedrin (a sort of Jewish High Court of Justice), a learned man whose authority at the time of Jesus was considerable, said that 'an *am-ha-rez* is incapable of piety'. According to the rabbinic tradition, an *am-ha-rez* also cared little about his children's education, neglected the laws of purity and impurity, and could be excluded from eternal life.[12] In John's gospel, when Jesus is preaching in the Temple on the Feast of Tabernacles, the Pharisees revile his audience – 'this crowd knows nothing about the Law.'[13] The rabbi Aqiba, who was an *am-ha-rez* in origin, said that he had held such a grudge against the doctors of the Law that, had he had one at his mercy, he would have bitten him like a donkey and broken his bones. Certain rabbis felt the same way about the *am-ha-rez*, as they recommended these peasants be slit in two, like fish. In short, Daniel-Rops was right in his estimation that 'there existed an active class hostility in Israel'.[14] But Renan's description of Galilee as 'a vast furnace in which the most diverse factions simmered and boiled'[15] was nonetheless an exaggeration.

It was in this troubled world that Jesus grew up. He learned his father's craft, as was customary. 'Just as you have a duty to feed your son,' said the Talmud, 'you have a duty to teach him a manual trade.' And, stronger still: 'He who does not teach his son a manual trade as good as makes a criminal out of him.' This prescription applied to all the social classes, even the priests of the

Temple. For it was said: 'He who makes himself useful through work is greater than he who knows God.'

Jesus also learnt to read – later, in Nazareth itself, the gospel of Luke describes him reading a passage from Isaiah[16] at the Temple. He could also write. When a woman 'caught committing adultery' is brought to him at the Temple and he is asked what should be done with her, he begins writing 'on the ground with his finger' and repeats this mysterious action after he has responded.[17] He also learnt about the Jewish religion. His parents may have been, in the eyes of the doctors of the Law, *am-ha-rez*, but, as we know, they were very pious. Joseph therefore soon began taking Jesus to the synagogue.

There, he might have found a line of youngsters, enthusiastically singing and brandishing scrolls of the Law, running through the synagogue. This joyous dance, a kind of farandole, is the *simhat torah*. The children would not need to be coaxed to join in when the rabbi started off the dance – the morning of the sabbath, spent almost entirely at the synagogue, would have dragged for them. To begin with, they would have understood almost nothing of what was said, because everything would be in Hebrew, the language of the law and, above all, of religion. They would know only the local dialect and then, as they get older, Aramaic – something of a lingua franca in that part of the east, but ill-suited to the expression of abstract concepts. The most affluent and the sons of merchants would also hear a little Greek at home. This was the language of business, of the upper classes, and occasionally of townspeople. Hebrew was kept for the synagogue. In the end, from going there three times a week, the children of pious families would get some idea of it.

The synagogue was not a place of formal worship or sacrifice. That happened only in the Temple, the One Temple, in Jerusalem. The synagogue served rather as a kind of community hall, for schooling, prayers and the reading of the Torah on Mondays and Thursdays. It would have been a small, rather austere building, sparsely decorated with palms and with stars of David. At the far end would be the ark, in which the scrolls of the Scriptures are kept, and in the middle, a wooden chair where the rabbi would sit; he would not be a professional priest, but a pious man who had been trained in knowledge of the Law. He would alternate benedictions, readings and commentaries, calling on one or other of the male faithful (women were admitted only to an upper gallery) to participate. Like him, they would be wearing the *tallith*, the prayer shawl, a rectangular strip of material whose sacred character is conferred by the fringes, the *tzitzit*.

Joseph would undoubtedly have explained the meaning of these *tzitzit* to Jesus. Four white threads, woven only by Jews, were fixed at the four corners of the shawl then twisted seven times, knotted twice, and twisted again before another double knot was added. In the end, there were thirty-nine gaps and five double knots per *tzitzit*. And among these white threads — white being considered the synthesis of all colours — a single, bright sky blue one was introduced.

Let us consider the significance of the numbers. It is of course not by chance that the threads are twisted seven times, and the total number of twisted and retwisted threads and knots is 613. This corresponds to the commandments of the Law: 365 prohibitions and 248 recommendations. A man was also said to have 365 tendons and 248 organs. The process was carried out in obedience to the word of God:

> Yahweh spoke to Moses and said, 'Speak to the sons of Israel and tell them to put tassels on the hems of their garments, and to put a violet cord at this tassel at the hem.... The sight of it will remind you of all the commands of Yahweh. You are to put them into practice then, and no longer follow the desires of your heart and your eyes, which have led you to make wantons of yourselves.'[18]

This, then, was the kind of ritualism, charged with meaning, to which pious Jews adhered. In the synagogue, people stood to hear the sacred texts and to sing all the benedictions, their heads

turned towards Jerusalem. These benedictions were very beautiful, all beginning with the same invocation: 'Blessed be You, Lord,
King of the universe ...' They were the continually renewed links
that bound man to God; that is why each Jew had to recite dozens
of them between sunrise and sunset.[19] Recited one after the other,
however, they would have seemed interminable to the youngsters
– and perhaps to many others, whose boredom could not be so
visible and who were not able to let off steam by dancing the
simhat torah.

It was at the synagogue that Jesus learnt to say *amen* – 'that is
true' or 'so be it' – after each benediction. The Talmud explained
that when a child began to say *amen* he attained part of his future
salvation. It was there, within that intimacy with God and warmth
of community, that for thirty years or so Jesus prepared himself. It was also there that he became acquainted with the
Pharisees, for while the Sadducees kept the Temple, the Pharisees
ran the synagogues.

The Pharisees were the prime movers in their religion, and it
would be due to them that monotheism, the belief in a single God,
was preserved when the people of Israel were scattered and persecuted and the Temple destroyed. Later, Jesus would berate them
for their ritualism and by doing so would come into direct conflict
with the religio-economic institution of the Temple and its
priests. But he would never attack the synagogue.

A question about Jesus' childhood remains: was he an only child,
or did he have brothers and sisters? The question, raised by several passages in the gospels, the Acts of the Apostles and the
Epistles of Paul, has caused, and still causes, the fiercest
debates.

Let us look at the texts first.

Mark. Jesus has returned to Nazareth after having performed
several miracles, notably the raising from the dead of Jairus'
daughter, and is teaching in the synagogue. His audience marvel
at the miracles and at his wisdom. A local lad, no less! 'This is the

carpenter, surely,' they say, 'the son of Mary, the brother of James and Joseph and Judas and Simon. His sisters, too, are they not here with us?'[20]

Matthew. In a practically identical text, Jesus is teaching in the synagogue of his village and his audience asks, 'This is the carpenter's son, surely? Is not his mother the woman called Mary, and his brothers James and Joseph and Simon and Judas? His sisters, too, are they not all here with us?'[21]

Mark again. Jesus, having gathered his disciples together, is preaching. The crowd tells him, 'Your mother and brothers and sisters are outside asking for you.'[22]

John. As the Feast of Tabernacles approaches, Jesus' 'brothers' tell Jesus, as a sort of challenge or trap, to go and show himself in Judaea. 'Since you are doing all this,' they say, 'you should let the whole world see.' And John adds: 'Not even his brothers, in fact, had faith in him.'[23]

Acts. Luke recounts that after Jesus' resurrection and ascent into heaven, while the apostles were waiting for the descent of the Holy Spirit, they assemble to pray. He adds: 'All these joined in continuous prayer, together with several women, including Mary the mother of Jesus, and with his brothers.'[24]

Letter of Paul to the Galatians. After telling his audience 'how merciless I was in persecuting the Church of God', and how he had been touched by grace on the road to Damascus, Paul tells how he had gone to Arabia and returned to Damascus. Then, he goes on, 'I went up to Jerusalem to visit Cephas [Peter] and stayed with him fifteen days.' But, 'I did not see any of the other apostles; I only saw James, the brother of the Lord.'[25]

Enough quotations. It must be emphasised that, apart from Matthew and Mark, these passages do not refer to the same episodes, and Paul's letter is earlier than the gospels. In another text,[26] Paul refers to the 'brothers' of Jesus – who had, as we have seen, begun by seeing him as a crank or even a threat to their welfare.

Other sources also allude to Jesus' brothers. According to

Josephus, one such brother, James, was condemned to death by the High Priest in AD 62.[27] According to the Greek prelate Eusebius of Caeserea, author of *History of the Church* – admittedly written well after the events, at the end of the third century – the grandsons of Judas, brother of Jesus, were suspected by the Roman emperor Domitian of being pretenders to some sort of sovereignty over the Jews, and were arrested. They were released, however, after he found them to be nothing more than simple peasants – although despite these humble origins they went on to become leaders of Christian communities, probably in Galilee.

The Catholic Church refuses to acknowledge that Jesus had brothers or sisters. Its principal argument is derived from a passage in John where he refers to a sister-in-law of Mary, also called Mary, who was at the crucifixion: 'Near the cross of Jesus stood his mother and his mother's sister-in-law, Mary the wife of Clopas, and Mary of Magdala.'[28] This other Mary would be the mother of James and Joseph. In addition, Mark and Matthew also refer four times to a Mary who is the mother of one or other, or both, of these two men. What the gospels call Jesus' 'brothers' would therefore be his cousins.

This argument should obviously be respected. But it has to be noted that in the episode at the synagogue recounted by Mark and Matthew, the four brothers (not just James and Joseph, which were very common names) accompanied Mary the mother of Jesus (and not the wife of Clopas). Most readers would naturally assume that these brothers and sisters, mentioned directly after Mary, were her children.

The Greek texts of the gospels use the word *adelphoi*, which unquestionably means 'brothers', not 'cousins' (*anepsioi*). Nowhere else in the New Testament is *adelphoi* used to mean 'cousins'; why should it be so used solely in regard to Jesus' family? The defenders of the Catholic tradition have another argument. In fact, they say, the Greek term is something of a mistranslation. There is a Hebrew word *ah* which designates a blood link, including that of cousins, and it was this word that was wrongly translated by the Greek text. It is therefore legitimate to speak of 'cousins'.[29]

However, when Paul writes to the Colossians, a Christian community installed in the north-east of Ephesus, in modern Turkey, he uses the precise Greek word *anepsios*, not *adelphos*, to refer to 'Mark, the cousin of Barnabas', who was another apostle for a time. There is no confusion there between 'brother' and 'cousin'.[30]

It is also remarkable that all the authorised Catholic commentaries allow, without any debate, all the other brothers in the gospels. They do not claim that what is meant there is really cousins, or a blood link. In these cases, they happily accept that *adelphoi* should be translated as 'brothers'. Only the existence of Jesus' brothers and sisters is called into question. This is for a serious reason: if he were the eldest of seven or eight brothers and sisters, his mother, a virgin at his birth, could obviously not have been a virgin after it.

Now, two sentences in the infancy narratives raise doubts about Mary's perpetual virginity. We have already encountered both of them. One is from Luke, who says that Mary 'gave birth to a son, her first-born',[31] which leads us to think that she subsequently had other sons. The other is from Matthew. He explains that, after the angel had told Joseph what had happened to Mary, 'he took his wife to his home and he did not know her until the day she gave birth'.[32] Which, again, allows us to presume that he 'knew' (i.e. had intercourse with her) afterwards.

The theological scholar France Quéré emphasises in this regard that

> Jews, in the ancient world, believed that sexual relations in pregnancy heartened and strengthened the foetus. Matthew highlights the fact that Joseph desisted from this sanitary recommendation in order to emphasise that the child was divine and had no need of ordinary masculine fortification.[33]

In her book, published in a Catholic collection (although

Joseph Doré, lecturer at the Catholic Institute of Paris, makes
several qualifications to her theories in his preface to the book[34]),
France Quéré continues in passionate vein: that Mary was a virgin
at the time of Jesus' birth did not mean she remained one

> as if she were the embodiment of virginity and femininity, virgin-
> ity and maternity! We do not know its origin but that strange pro-
> priety has since been used against women; their natural – that is,
> culpable – womanhood has been held against them.

She wonders at 'this strange ideal of marriage caught in the
grip of virginity' that is held up for our admiration, and points
out that 'the dogmatic tradition of Ephesus' (the Council held at
Ephesus in 431) sees Mary's primary role as the mother of God
and not as Virgin of virgins. 'It is because she has the honour of
being the mother of a God that she is blessed among women, not
because she is, under the frowning gaze of men, Virgin above all
others.'

The theory that Jesus had brothers and sisters is supported by
the fact that the Jews approved of 'normal and lawful' sexual ac-
tivity, as André Chouraqui puts it: 'Sexuality was not … dissociated from the couple's emotional life and no Hebrew word exists to
differentiate it. The Jews were quite free of complexes about sexual life.'[35] Jewish people adored large families and hordes of children. Fertility was always exalted, and a barren couple were
considered to be unloved by God. In Genesis, Rachel says to
Jacob: 'Give me children, or I shall die!'[36] This sentiment is more
lyrically expressed in the Psalms:

> Your wife: a fruitful vine
>   on the inner walls of your house.
> Your sons: round your table
>   like shoots round an olive tree.
> Such are the blessings that fall
>   on the man who fears Yahweh.[37]

Even Paul, that great champion of virginity (although he

conceded that it was a personal view, unsupported by 'directions from the Lord'[38]), enjoined couples: 'Do not refuse each other except by mutual consent, and then only for an agreed time, to leave yourselves free for prayer; then come together again in case Satan should take advantage of your weakness to tempt you.'[39]

Paul's championship of virginity does nonetheless seem to show that it was an ideal that had begun to spread in that restless world. Philo of Alexandria, a Jewish philosopher of the period, speaks of elderly women who had kept their virginity through love of wisdom. The Essenes, to whom we shall return, had some influence in this respect, and the Qumran documents show that some Jews wanted to remain celibate within marriage. Nonetheless, this remained the exception rather than the rule.

There are several reasons why the Catholic Church has traditionally believed that Mary had no other children and thus remained a virgin. Some are practical. It was doubtless necessary to prevent Jesus' family from establishing some sort of dynastic claim after his death (a possibility hinted at by certain passages in the Acts of the Apostles). But the real reasons lie elsewhere.

Many religions seek to exempt their founders, or their heroines, from the common human condition. Christianity, unlike most other religions, is a religion of Incarnation, and from its beginnings it proclaimed vigorously that Jesus was 'true God and true man'. For a long time, however, it refused to accept the consequences of the second half of that declaration, as if to do so would somehow be degrading to Jesus' status. The Gnostics of the second and third centuries claimed to have had personal revelations that there were two opposing forces at work in the world: a good, transcendent God and a bad spirit that had created the world and the flesh. The Gnostics were excommunicated as heretics, but the idea that the flesh was bad nonetheless became implanted in people's minds and took root. Ascetics, numerous in these centuries, did not preach such ideas, but the self-denial and the renunciation they practised involved them in what can only be described as competitive mortification and encouraged them to despise the body, which was considered a hindrance to the elevation of the soul. The pagan world surrounding the early Christian communities preached and practised the exact opposite, and the great Fathers of the growing Church let themselves, as France Quéré puts it, 'be enchanted by virginity. [The Church] allowed the Ambroses and the Jeromes to declare that virginity liberated women from the vicissitudes of an unbridled sexuality.'

There is not space here to show how, over the centuries and right up to the present day, a whole cult and theology of the perpetual virginity of Mary has grown up. They are undoubtedly ideas to be respected. But they cannot be attributed to the text on which the Catholic Church considers it is based: the New Testament. The Orthodox Church believes, based on the 'apocryphal' gospels, that Jesus was surrounded by half-brothers and half-sisters, Joseph's children from a previous marriage.[40] Other than the apocrypha, however, there is nothing to confirm such a theory.

It is impossible to make definitive statements about this. It is true that several passages in the gospels give a sense of Jesus being alone with his parents or with Mary: his visit to the Temple as a boy, the wedding at Cana, the crucifixion where, before he dies, he entrusts his mother to John. But others refer plainly to his brothers and sisters. It therefore seems probable, even if shocking, that Jesus had brothers and sisters and that, as a real human, he belonged to a real family which would, as was the custom, have been large.[41] It is also probable that he was the son of a real woman, even though a whole body of literature on Mary has made her not only a perpetual virgin, but an ethereal, inhuman creature.

There is nothing in that to diminish Mary's greatness or seriously disturb someone who is confident in his or her faith. The Catholic Church has, however, so elevated the cult of Mary that anything that questions the image traditionally given to her will upset some believers and throw the very essence of their faith into doubt. Yet that essence lies elsewhere and cannot be threatened by such details.

It is to that essence that we now come: Jesus' ministry and message.

5

Baptism: the Voice from the Sky

T HE river twists then twists again through the red hills and the lush plains, as though it will never find its true path. If it ran straight, the Jordan would join the Sea of Galilee to the Dead Sea in less than a sixty-five miles. But it changes course twice more and sometimes, after the spring floods, changes its mind altogether and forges another route amid the tamarisks, the clumps of reeds, the mass of brambles and the tangle of oleander intertwined with vines. Finally it hurtles down the six hundred yards between the levels of the two seas. It is a whirlwind, a brute force that sweeps along mud, branches and every kind of rubbish. At times it also takes with it those bold or foolish enough to have thought that they could cross its shallow waters in safety.

There are, however, four or five fording places where the water calms down and affords some respite. Here, caravans stop at the rough caravanserai where small rooms, home to bugs prettily named 'summer season beasts', have been built to make money out of the travellers. Those who stop here are always assured of someone with whom to talk and grumble.

It was on the banks of the Jordan that John (or Johanan or Yokanaon, a very common name that meant 'blessed by Yahweh' or 'favoured by Yahweh') preached. We know almost nothing of what became of him after Elizabeth had given birth to him, and his father, the old priest Zechariah, had recovered his power of speech. Except, that is, for the fact that John had refused to follow

75

in Zechariah's footsteps by becoming a priest (the priesthood was principally a hereditary institution).

The community of priests – in effect the clergy – was divided into twenty-four classes. Dispersed throughout Judaea and Galilee, they were called in turn to Jerusalem to perform sacrifices at the Temple. Below them existed a lower clergy, the Levites, who were in a sense jacks of all trades: singers (to them the most prestigious function), sacristans, Temple police and so on. The priest Zechariah belonged to the Abia class, eighth in the hierarchy of twenty-four, which was no more than an honourable rank. He was probably not very rich. In theory, every priest received a tithe of the produce of his village, but in practice the peasants were apt to skimp on what they gave. In addition, the permanent priests at the Temple in Jerusalem, the priestly aristocracy, would often go over the heads of their lowly colleagues and appropriate the tithes for themselves. This did not, needless to say, help relations between the two groups.

This priestly aristocracy, the highest-ranking clergy, had a terrible reputation. They lived in Jerusalem and had allowed themselves to fall under Greek influence, adopting Greek dress and Greek names, collaborating freely with the Roman occupiers – while claiming, of course, that they had the dispensation of the Eternal for this behaviour. Ordinary priests such as Zechariah were not slow to criticise them for their lax morals, laziness and corruption. But there were also theological differences between the two camps. These men of Jerusalem, the Sadducees (a name probably derived from Zadok, a priest in King David's time), mocked the popular belief in eternal life: in their view, all that mattered was this earthly existence. They taught that if the sons of Abraham led their lives with wisdom and honour, they would find their reward here on earth, in prosperity and reputation. Material success therefore became the sign of respect for the Law. This greatly displeased the most pious Jews, including, of course, the Pharisees. Those essentially intellectual religious and lay leaders advocated religious reform and a greater adherence to the Law.

They believed in the immortality of the soul and the resurrection of the body. For a hard-line Pharisee, the word 'Sadducee' was synonymous with 'materialist' and 'epicurean'.

John was not a Pharisee, but the Sadducees had nothing that could attract this young man of whom, according to Luke, the angel Gabriel had said: 'He must drink no wine, no strong drink. Even from his mother's womb he will be filled with the Holy Spirit and he will bring back many of the sons of Israel to the Lord their God.'[1] To become a priest like his father would not automatically have made him a Sadducee, but it would have bound him, like it or not, to the Temple of which they were masters. By refusing to follow Zechariah, John had broken with the Temple, which was also the main economic power of the time.

And then he suddenly appeared on the banks of the Jordan, with its muddy and fast-flowing waters, looking like a hermit, rather wild and unkempt, his skin tanned by the sun that beats down ten months of the year, dressed in camel hair and wearing 'a leather belt round his waist'.[2] Matthew does not describe him in this way by accident. The prophet Elijah wore 'a hair cloak ... and a leather loincloth'.[3] Camel-hair clothes had the advantage of being both impermeable and hard-wearing (the best were made in Anatolia and Cilicia). The girdle – or belt – represented human freedom, the power that each man had over his destiny: 'The traveller would wear one to give him the power of going where he chose.... Among the nomads of the steppes, to untie one's belt at the same time as removing one's headgear was to acknowledge vassalage, dependence.'[4] John lived on honey gathered from tree trunks where bees had made their nest, and on locusts, raw, or cooked on four branches over an evening fire. There was nothing surprising in that, for many poor bedouins had occasionally to subsist on that kind of food.

The times were favourable to those who announced the arrival of a new era. The Mediterranean basin, which for over a century had been the theatre of many disturbances and conflicts, was enjoying a degree of harmony, a relative peace. The Roman emperor had given people 'bread and circuses'. They were now vaguely hoping for the dawning of the golden age. Israel shared in that hope, but more dimly and in its own way. These were a people who felt that God had given them a mission, who bore the heavy burden of being the sole ally of the Eternal in this base world. They were waiting for the Kingdom of God to be established on earth, first in their own land, and then in other nations. Caesar in Rome, who was considered divine by many of his subjects,[5] including some from the east, could be in Jewish eyes only a rival, a usurper who was wrongfully playing the part of 'son of David'. The real son of David would, when he came, establish a Jewish empire as powerful and as widespread as that of the Romans. And because the Jews longed so much for the coming of this Messiah who would put God's great plan into effect, it began to seem imminent. It could happen any day.

They could not take any more. They repeated, on their own account, the words attributed to Isaiah, eight centuries earlier:

> No one makes just accusations
> or pleads sincerely.
> All rely on nothingness, utter falsehood,
> conceive harm and give birth to misery....
> We looked for light and all is darkness,
> for brightness, and we walk in the dark.
> Like the blind we feel our way along walls
> and hesitate like men without eyes.
> We stumble as though noon were twilight
> and dwell in the dark like the dead.
> We growl, all of us, like bears,
> and moan like doves....[6]

When John began preaching, written and spoken messages of comfort and hope abounded. They assured the Jews that the day was finally coming when God would help them. These texts were called 'apocalypses', a word which did not carry the pejorative sense that it does today. Prophets went from town to town, village to village, spreading the idea that the time had now come, that it was about to happen. Hoaxers and madmen did the same, proclaiming themselves to be the Saviour promised by God, who would found a new society and abolish all injustice. As that injustice became more blatant and as the gap between social classes widened, people listened more readily to these claims. Although they had been specially chosen by God, the Jews feared that they had become unfaithful to Him. Were not the priests of the Temple setting a bad example? Had not King Herod built Greek gymnasiums, theatres and stadiums? Were not obscene Greek comedies and Greek tragedies, ones celebrating the exploits of pagan heroes and gods, put on at the theatre in Jerusalem? The more these people feared for their identity, the more they were disposed to listen to those who predicted that everything was about to change, that D-day was just around the corner.

But the hairy prophet called John who preached on the banks of the Jordan did not proclaim a golden age of sweetness and light. On the contrary, he abused his listeners, called them a 'brood of vipers', a term that Jesus would also use, and warned them of the 'retribution that is coming'.[7] And instead of focusing their fears and resentments on the foreign occupying pagan, he told them that the fact that they were Jews conferred no special privileges on them. 'Do not presume to tell yourselves "We have Abraham for our father", because, I tell you, God can raise children for Abraham from these stones.'[8] They are like others, they will be judged by the same standards, with the same severity, and without delay: 'Even now the axe is laid to the roots of the trees, so that any tree that fails to produce good fruit will be cut down and thrown on the fire.'[9] This John is therefore the exact opposite of an agitator or demagogue. He was rougher than Jesus was to be, seeing in his listeners hardened sinners who would respond only to the threat of divine judgement, whereas Jesus, though occasionally severe, would speak readily of forgiveness and of God's grace.

But then John lived as an ascetic, an outsider. To find him, one

79

had to leave towns and villages, shake off an evil society and discover the desert. Jesus, on the other hand, would go from town to village, would attend social gatherings, and his companions would fast no more than he did (indeed, he would be labelled a 'glutton'). They had their reasons: 'Surely the bridegroom's attendants would never think of fasting while the bridegroom is still with them?'[10] The anxious period of waiting would be succeeded by a time of joy.

But when John began his impassioned, almost terrifying speeches, Jesus had not yet appeared in public. Surprisingly, these less than reassuring harangues did not deter the crowds. Just the opposite in fact. John impressed them so much that Josephus mentions him, describing him as 'a good man who commanded the Jews to practise virtue and to be just to one another and devout towards God'.[11]

Everyone crowds around John, bombarding him with questions. 'What must we do, then?', they ask; they are told, 'If anyone has two tunics he must share with the man who has none, and the one with something to eat must do the same.' Tax collectors also come and ask the same question. To them, he says, 'Exact no more than your rate' – in other words, do not collect taxes dishonestly to line your own pockets. And to soldiers, presumably legionaries, he enjoins: 'No intimidation! No extortion! Be content with your pay!' – which tells us much about their practices.[12]

This troubling, demanding prophet is so successful that his fame travels as far as Jerusalem. The important people decide to send out a commission of inquiry, made up of priests and Levites. He spells out to them who he is not: he is not the Messiah, the Christ, nor is he the reincarnation of Elijah the prophet. They respond impatiently: 'Who are you? We must take back an answer to those who sent us.' These interrogators are not the ones pulling the strings; they are nothing but obedient puppets. All they care about is not having to return empty-handed, which would not do their careers any good. So John answers:

'I am, as Isaiah prophesied:
a voice that cries in the wilderness:
Make a straight way for the Lord.'[13]

The evangelist John, who is the only one to include this appearance before a commission of inquiry, says no more than that. But the priests' questions and doubts can easily be imagined: is this really a visionary, as the talk running round the country has it? What does he mean by saying he is preparing the way for the Lord? They soon decide he is nothing more than a harmless crank. Except for one thing: he baptises. And this constitutes another rupture with the Temple, the second challenge that John had issued to it.

In almost every religion, water is a symbol. And it has a particular significance for people like the Jews who live in, or have crossed, the desert. One of the benedictions that the pious Jew had to recite throughout the day thanked 'God, King of the universe ... who commanded us to wash our hands'. Heavenly, or simply pleasant, places in the Bible are watered by springs of fresh water. Judaism had multiplied rites of purification with water. Before entering the Temple and before and after the ceremonies, priests had to wash with fresh water (in Hebrew, *mayim hayim*, 'living waters'), that is, rainwater or water channelled from a spring, but not drawn with a receptacle, for then it would lose its purifying properties.[14]

At the time of John and Jesus, when Israel was preoccupied with preserving an identity that was being threatened by foreign influences, the desire for purification with water had become almost obsessive, particularly among the Pharisees, who were especially anxious to defend the integrity of their religion. Most of the synagogue rabbis, who were under the Pharisees' influence, had begun admonishing the faithful to follow the same scrupulous purification rites as the priests. If a pagan had touched an object or a garment, it had to be plunged into water. It was therefore

through water that the Jew distinguished himself from the impure non-Jew – but he did not attain the promised salvation of
God through this purification and it had to be repeated again and
again.

The prophet's innovation of a confession of sins followed by
baptism with water that saved once and for all was therefore startling. John also baptised in public, whereas the customary purification rites were performed in private, by the pious Jew himself.
John was offering forgiveness of sins without the need to go via
the Temple, its rites or its men, and that was a powerful challenge
to the religious hierarchy. Someone who wanted to demonstrate
faith and profound allegiance to God no longer had to undergo the
enormous trouble and expense of a journey to Jerusalem, where
he would have to take offerings to the Temple and pay taxes to the
priests. It was enough to show a sincere repentance and a strong
desire to change (which was, admittedly, quite a lot) and to be dipped in the swirling waters of the Jordan. Clearly, the Temple hierarchy would not have regarded John's success with equanimity.

Such a revolution never, as history demonstrates, erupts in a
single moment, at a single place, as though by magic. Other groups
which could be called baptising sects existed in Israel. For example, there was a strange group called the 'Morning Divers', who
took a bath every morning, thereby combining hygiene and spirit-
uality. They were in disagreement with the Pharisees, whom they
accused of invoking the divine Name in the morning without having bathed. To which the Pharisees retorted that the Morning
Divers pronounced the Name with impure lips.[15] Obviously, this
baptism by immersion in water was not truly comparable to what
John was doing, because it had to be repeated daily. The Essenes
also performed numerous ritual baths. It has even been claimed
that John, who had certain ideas in common with them and who
baptised not far from their monastery at Qumran, belonged to this
very sect and that he had received his religious training from
them.

This is a good moment to describe the customs and beliefs of the Essenes. Although scholars were aware of their existence, they did not become well-known until 1947 when a young Bedouin discovered the Dead Sea Scrolls in a cave in the Judaean desert. Most Essenes lived in the desert, in tents, or occasionally in caves. They led a communal, monastic existence and scrupulously followed the demands for religious and moral purity laid down in biblical texts. These saintly men were, as the Roman Pliny wrote, 'a solitary tribe remarkable beyond all others in the whole world'. However – and contrary to popular belief – they had not all left society for good. 'They do not live in a single town but are found in great numbers in every town,'[16] said Josephus, according to whom some were even married – not having discovered any other way of propagating themselves.

Those who like colourful details will want to know that a good Essene was not supposed to spit in public, but in private and to the left, the side of evil and impurity. He also had to relieve himself in private, after having dug a hole for the purpose, always with the same tool, a small hoe, while wrapping his garments about him so as not to offend the sun. He could not, however, relieve himself on the sabbath, since that would have been a profanity. He had to get up every day before dawn and observe silence before praying to the Eternal to make the sun rise.

There were many other such rituals, for the whole of Essene life was structured by an almost military discipline. Those who had completed their two years' novitiate immersed themselves in water every day before the common meal, which was, it seems, quite a cheerful occasion. Every new member had also to give up his property. After three years of training, they preached for a living. In the case of a serious misdemeanour, they were expelled from the community. This was a terrible punishment, for one of the vows they had taken was not to eat any food produced by non-Essenes. For an outburst of anger they were excluded for a year, and for an 'excessive' word, three months, during which time they had to make do with a diet of herbs and roots.

But the important thing to remember is that the Essenes – then some four thousand men and women strong – believed to all intents and purposes that they were the true elect of the chosen people. They did send occasional offerings to the Temple, but they disagreed with the sacrifice of animals practised there and thought the priests infidels. They also believed other Jews to be children of darkness (even though, strangely, they had at one time been quite close to Herod). They awaited the imminent arrival of the great day when God would establish His sovereignty over the earth and would smite the pagans and the heretical Jews. They would then re-establish the real worship of the Eternal in the Temple, the elect would live in peace and joy while the others would be consigned to the flames of hell.

John probably knew of and had contact with the Essenes. Some people have a theory, based on an allusion in Luke to his childhood, that he was brought up by them, but that is very debatable. John, says the evangelist, 'grew up and his spirit matured. And he lived out in the wilderness until the day he appeared openly to Israel.'[17] It is true that according to Josephus, the Essenes often adopted children to indoctrinate them,[18] but we can also conclude from the text that it was only in the years before he 'appeared openly to Israel', that is, after he was twenty, that John lived in the desert, where Essenes were not the only inhabitants of the caves. And would Zechariah, who belonged to the priestly caste, willingly have entrusted his son to these people who believed that all priests were corrupt and worthless?

In fact, John's baptisms had little similarity – apart from the physical immersion in water – with those of the Essenes. Their ablutions were only for purification, were repeated daily and could be performed only after two years of novitiate, whereas, as the British writer John Drane observes, 'John baptized people who wanted to change their way of life. The community at Qumran accepted only those who could prove that they had already changed their way of life.'[19] No one had, therefore, ever done precisely what John the Baptist was doing. He was breaking new ground. But this revolutionary was not working on his own account, but announcing the coming of Jesus, whom he already knew for the very good reason, if Luke is to be believed, that they were cousins.

'I am nothing,' John says in so many words to the crowds who throng around him. 'Another is coming soon, and "I am not fit to undo the strap of his sandals."' Now here is a remarkable, because rare, fact: with the exception of one or two words, all four gospels use that exact same phrase – as did the philosopher Justin, born in AD 100 and martyred in Rome in 164 or 165, who left several texts on Jesus. It is as if that allusion to sandals had struck them all as important.

Sandals were the usual footwear, except among the rich, who preferred soft boots of hyena or jackal skin, or red shoes with raised toes, or the Romans, who considered sandals effeminate. But who undid sandals? When the master came home tired in the evening, one of his servants or slaves would kneel down to take them off. John's declaration therefore has two meanings: 'He who is coming will not behave like an overlord,' and, 'However, he is so much greater than I – whom you all think so important – that I am not even worthy to behave like his servant or his slave.' His listeners, unused to such paradoxical statements, must have been bemused.

But John the Baptist himself did not yet realise Jesus' extra-ordinary destiny. Indeed, he declares, according to the evangelist John, 'I did not know him.' In other words, 'I did not really know him, I did not really know who he was.' John the Baptist did not suspect the true meaning of the message that Jesus would preach. For him, the coming of the Messiah would result in harsh judge-ment, in condemnation. He uses peasant images to convey this: Jesus would have a 'winnowing-fan ... in his hand to clear his threshing-floor and gather the wheat into his barn, but the chaff he will burn in a fire that will never go out.'[20] Since we have largely lost our knowledge of the land, I should explain that the chaff is the fine husk in which the cereal grain is enveloped.

The Saviour promised by God was therefore, in John's eyes,

someone who would burn the useless chaff that has been separated from the useful wheat, and the society he would usher in would be founded on judgement and damnation. But Jesus would preach a message based on love and forgiveness – a message that his contemporaries, and even people today, find hard to comprehend. So it is not surprising that the Baptist did not immediately cross that threshold of understanding.

He would not do so until he saw Jesus walking towards him, when he cries, 'Look, there is the lamb of God, who takes away the sin of the world'.[21] The world would no longer be condemned. The expression 'lamb of God' has inspired many commentaries and interpretations, the most common of which identifies Jesus as the sacrificial lamb. Thousands of pages have been written, thousands of sermons given, explaining to people that God sent Jesus to undergo the worst sufferings and death to 'wipe out original sin and appease His Father's wrath', in the words of *Minuits chrétiens* – an old song which evokes pleasantly nostalgic memories but which has contributed to the dissemination of this nonsense. Can one really imagine a God of love, the Father of the prodigal son in the famous parable, agreeing to forgive men for the stupidity of their earliest forefathers only by sending His Son as a sacrifice to Him? That vision of God as blood-thirsty barbarian so drunk with a desire for revenge that he would sacrifice His only Son was a terrible one. It is a vision that has no relationship to Jesus' message. Jesus never spoke of original sin, only the evil of the world, which is completely different.

So how should we interpret this 'lamb of God'? Much more simply, according to the Jesuit commentator, Fr Xavier Léon-Dufour.[22] The Jewish people were continually sacrificing animals, most frequently lambs, to maintain contact with the Eternal and to re-establish their link with Him. The coming of Jesus rendered these rites unnecessary, since he himself established a direct contact with God. He was the lamb sent by God for that purpose. There is another interpretation. Just as the Passover lamb played a part in the liberation of Jews captive in Egypt, so Jesus was a liberator of the people. Indeed, a Jewish tradition compares the history of Israel to the struggle between wolves and a lamb which is protecting the flock that the Eternal had placed in its care.

And so Jesus decides to follow the crowds that are streaming to John the Baptist. This young man from the country, of whom no one has yet heard, goes to the renowned prophet; according to Matthew, John recognises him at once and marvels, 'It is I who need baptism from you ... and yet you come to me!' To which Jesus replies, 'Leave it like this for the time being; it is fitting that we should, in this way, do all that righteousness demands.'[23]

John was not the only one to marvel at this. Why should Jesus, who was, according to the evangelists, free from all sin, want to be baptised? He was surely the one person for whom baptism was unnecessary. This question would torment the evangelists and Jesus' disciples. Some early Christian writers quoted something known as the Gospel of the Hebrews, a text which circulated among the first Christian communities, in which Jesus *himself* asks the question:

> The Lord's mother and his brothers said to him: 'John the Baptist baptizes for the remission of sins; let us go and be baptized by him.' But he [Jesus] said to them 'In what have I sinned, that I should go and be baptised by him?'[24]

The officially recognised gospels do not relate this scene, but the problem did not escape their attention. John, who describes the meeting between Jesus and the Baptist, resolves it by not uttering a word about baptism. After informing us that John had been imprisoned, Luke mysteriously mentions Jesus' baptism: 'Now when all the people had been baptized and while Jesus after his own baptism ...'[25] Who was his baptiser? Matthew, for his part, forgets to mention that John baptised for the remission of sins. Many scholars think that, by seeking baptism, Jesus wanted to associate himself with the movement that was taking people to John in droves and make a first gesture to demonstrate that the new age had begun. In any case, that gesture tells us something about Jesus' intentions. As soon as Jesus appears on the scene, he moves into John's camp, sanctions what the Baptist is doing and, by extension, the break away from the Temple and its religio-economic power.

The Baptist does not prolong the discussion but baptises Jesus without further ado. And that is when, the evangelists tell us, the Holy Spirit descends on Jesus 'like a dove'. The four gospels all have this episode, but in Matthew and Mark, Jesus alone sees the dove, whereas in John it is the Baptist who sees it.

Doves often appeared in Jewish literature, playing various roles, and this incident has naturally intrigued scholars. According to Fr Léon-Dufour, 'there are at least seven different interpretations of the dove at Jesus' baptism.'[26] We shall not linger in that labyrinth, however. Another exegete, Jacques Guillet, wrote, with the approval of the religious authorities (the imprimatur) that the gospels did not intend to describe 'an external objective form' but rather 'a spiritual experience, a vision'. It is a question, he insists, of 'an internal experience of our Lord seeing the Holy Spirit and hearing the Father's voice'.[27] And when the gospels add that 'heaven opened', it is of course a beautiful image that signifies that the link has been re-established between the sky, where the ancients traditionally situated God or the gods, and the earth.

The sky opens and the Eternal speaks. The evangelists have different versions of this, and John makes no mention of the sky opening. For him, it is the Baptist who speaks, saying that 'he who sent me to baptise with water' (the Eternal) had led him to recognise in Jesus 'the Chosen One of God'. According to the Jewish writer David Flusser, professor of Religious History at the Hebrew University in Jerusalem,

> echoing voices were not an uncommon phenomenon among the Jews of those days.... Endowment with the Holy Spirit, accompanied by an ecstatic experience, was apparently no unique

experience among those who were baptised in John's presence in the Jordan.[28]

But Flusser and many other scholars believe that the words reported by the evangelists are not exactly accurate. For them, the 'voice' was simply echoing the words of Isaiah:

> Here is my servant whom I uphold,
> my chosen one in whom my soul delights.
> I have endowed him with my spirit,
> that he may bring true justice to the nations.[29]

To complicate the matter further, Luke has the voice saying 'You are my Son, today I have become your father',[30] which is taken from a psalm[31] and which, centuries earlier, had been applied to the kings of Israel. The Messiah awaited by the Jews at the time of Jesus was also to become their king.

The debate is critical because it centres on the sense that Jesus had of himself and of his mission. Who did he think he was? And what did that 'spiritual experience' reveal to him? If one agrees with David Flusser (who declares that 'nothing we have learned casts any doubt upon the historicity of Jesus' experience at his baptism in the Jordan'), Jesus must from then on have considered himself a prophet among others. But did he consider himself much more than that – the Son of God? If so, did he think this before he went to the Baptist? Did he think it from the moment he heard the voice? Or did he only gradually realise the significance of his mission? The question has provoked much research and controversy.

Whatever theory you go for, one thing is certain. After the message from the heavens, Jesus has a sharper consciousness of his particular relationship to God and of the role he must play, at least for the Jewish people. He would say, later, that he had been sent 'only to the lost sheep of the House of Israel'.[32] What happened that day on the banks of the Jordan was therefore what might be called the annunciation to Jesus. The early Church considered it so important that at the beginning of the fourth century the birth and the baptism of Christ were celebrated simultaneously on 6 January.[33] A hymn was sung that bound the two events together closely:

> All creation proclaims him,
> The Magi proclaim him,
> The star proclaims him:
> See, the Son of the King.
> The heavens open,
> The waters of the Jordan flow,
> The dove descends:
> This is my beloved Son!

Later, the two celebrations would be dissociated, to avoid a confusion that had been judged heretical: certain people, particularly in the East, had claimed that God had not Himself been born as a man, but had temporarily entered Jesus after his baptism. In other words, Jesus was nothing more than a man to begin with, and God did not take on human form, did not enter Jesus' body, until the moment when the dove descended on him. At the Council of Nicaea in 325, the Church rejected that theory and affirmed that Jesus was 'fully divine and fully human' from his birth. But the controversy demonstrates the importance of the baptism to the Church.

Luke gives us several clues about the date of the event. 'In the fifteenth year of Tiberius Caesar's reign', he says, John began baptising. Tiberius' predecessor had died on 19 August AD 14, and the first year of the emperor's reign was counted as beginning on 20 August. The following years were counted from 10 December, the date of the renewal of the emperor's 'tribunician' power. The fifteenth year therefore began on 10 December 27.[34] Born between 4 and 7 BC, Jesus was thus between thirty-one and thirty-four when John began preaching. But it is possible that the baptism occurred later, since it would perhaps have taken some time for John's popularity (which was such that it would provoke Jerusalem into sending out a delegation to investigate him) to establish itself.

So Jesus was now almost – but not totally – ready for his mission. First he had to decide his strategy and priorities and also to receive another annunciation.

6

The Beginnings: Choice of Strategy and Men

JESUS crossed the Jordan and went east, to the desert: a plain glistening with salt, spiked with chalky rock and limestone formations and frequented by eagles and jackals – and by men, because hermits and ascetics have a real passion for these desolate spots. Political dissidents also sometimes sought refuge there.

For the Jews, the desert had two aspects. It was an empty space in which men, freed from distractions and worldly obligations, could more easily find God. This had been Moses' experience in Exodus. Then the exiled Jews had crossed the desert on their return from Egypt, and the Eternal had manifested His goodness and His care for the chosen people by sending them manna from heaven, 'a thing delicate, powdery, as fine as hoarfrost',[1] to nourish them.

But the desert had a darker side; it was also a cursed place where the ground 'is in mourning'[2] and 'a place unfit for sowing, it has no figs, no vines, no pomegranates, and there is not even water to drink!'[3] Animals avoided these lonely expanses. The desert was synonymous with death, with curses and demons. It was a place of temptation, of spiritual combat.

It is entirely plausible that Jesus should feel the need to retreat there after the mystical experience of the baptism and that he should need time alone to assimilate the shock he had received. There is no reason to question this. But what happened then, according to Matthew and Luke (whose 'devices and desires' we have seen in the infancy narratives), is more mysterious.

Jesus stayed forty days and forty nights in the desert, fasting and praying. Forty: again, this is not a number plucked out of the air at random. It features in many ancient legends and determines the length of funeral rites of many African and Asian peoples; the Buddha and Mohammed both began preaching at the age of forty; in Judaism, the waters of the flood had covered the earth for forty days, David and Solomon both reigned for forty years, Moses stayed on Mount Sinai for forty days and forty nights. The use of the number forty should therefore alert us to the symbolism of this passage. We are entering a domain that is undoubtedly more literary than historical. We are, once more, dealing with a *theologoumenon* – though that is not to say that nothing actually happened.

The account of the three temptations of Jesus is well known. The Devil begins by challenging Jesus to change stones into bread to prove his divinity, to which he replies with the biblical quotation: 'Man does not live on bread alone but on every word that comes from the mouth of God.'[4]

The Devil, not in the least discouraged – that is not his style – then takes Jesus to the pinnacle of the Temple (from which there is a drop of five hundred feet to the Kidron valley floor) and, again, challenges him: this time, to jump off. 'Scripture says,' he says,

> He will put you in his angels' charge ...
> and they will support you on their hands
> in case you hurt your foot against a stone.

The Devil obviously knows his Scriptures; here, he is quoting a psalm.[5] And Jesus replies with another quotation, from Deuteronomy: 'You must not put the Lord your God to the test.'[6]

Third temptation: the Devil, indefatigable, takes Jesus to the top of a very high mountain to show him 'all the kingdoms of the world and their splendour', which he promises to give him if Jesus will fall down and worship him. To which Jesus replies with the unambiguous 'Be off, Satan' and another biblical quotation: 'You must worship the Lord your God and serve Him alone.'[7]

This abundance of biblical quotations confirms what the symbolism of the numbers had led us to suspect: this is a kind of

parable. And since there were no witnesses to this triple temptation in the desert, we would have to assume that Jesus talked to
his disciples about it. Yet when that is the case, the evangelists
make it clear by showing us Jesus saying it to them – which does
not happen here.

Does this mean that the passage, added later like the birth and
infancy narratives, has no basis whatever in historical fact? We
cannot be sure that this is the case, since the story is embarrassing
rather than helpful to Jesus' followers, who wanted to convert as
many people as possible, both Jews and Gentiles, to their faith. In
effect, it shows a God subjected, like any common miscreant, to
temptation by the Devil. For the Jews, and of course many others,
that was scandalous, totally unacceptable. If Matthew and Luke
still recount it, it can only be because something really did happen, confirmed by Mark in a single sentence ('Immediately afterwards the Spirit drove him out into the wilderness and he
remained there for forty days, and was tempted by Satan') and because they want to emphasise Jesus' humanity. They also, it seems,
wanted to answer the Pharisees' accusation that they were in
league with 'Beelzebub, the prince of devils'.[8] Finally, it forms a
kind of preface to Jesus' life and teaching: this is what he will not
be, should not be.

First, he is not a magician. At that time, miracle workers were
two a penny in Israel. Jesus, in the gospels, also performs miracles
– but he does so reluctantly. It was not the main feature of his
ministry. He does not perform them in order to prove anything,
even if he is occasionally tempted to do so and even if his followers take the miracles as signs and proof.

Paul would later write to the Corinthians that 'Jews demand
miracles'.[9] We could add that this trait is shared by many others
even today. So the story makes it clear that Jesus' strategy – even
if it was formulated later by Matthew and Luke rather than decided beforehand by Jesus himself – did not lie predominantly
in miracles and wonders but in words. His first appeal is to his
audiences' intelligence.

And then Jesus does not want to be a king, which was exactly what the Jews expected the Messiah to be. Indeed, many Jews believed that the coming King would supplant the Roman emperor and exercise temporal power over the entire universe. Jesus' refusal of this role in this episode is of course made easier by the fact that to accept it would mean submission to the Devil (which raises the obvious question of whether the evangelists believed there was something diabolical in all worldly power).

There is another possible interpretation of the story of Jesus' temptation. It is not Jesus who decides, after having fasted and prayed, what he does not want to be; it is the Eternal who reveals to him what he should be and do. In this interpretation, the period in the desert constitutes another stage, after the baptism and the divine annunciation to Jesus, in the revelation of his real nature and mission. Jesus would not, however, be alone in that mission.

The four gospels do not give the same version of the beginning of Jesus' teaching. Matthew, Mark and Luke all have him preaching in Galilee, admonishing crowds: 'Repent, for the Kingdom of God is close at hand.' He goes for a walk along the Sea of Galilee where he meets some fishermen, two sets of brothers, Andrew and Simon and the sons of Zebedee, James and John. He asks them to follow him, which they do at once. This happened, the three texts say, after the other John, the Baptist, had been arrested by Herod Antipas's men.

The evangelist John, who is normally careful about chronology,[10] has a different sequence of events. The day after the baptism, he says, John is with two of his disciples (Andrew and another, unnamed) when Jesus passes them. The two decide to go after him, apparently prompted by John's pronouncement: 'Look, there is the lamb of God.' Jesus sees that he is being followed and turns round to ask them: 'What do you want?' They address him as 'rabbi', 'master': 'Rabbi, where do you live?' He takes them to the place – unspecified – and they spend the day with him. That evening and the following day, a chain begins. Andrew goes to his brother, Simon, to tell him, 'We have found the Messiah.' Andrew then recruits a friend and fellow Galilean, Philip[11] (the two would often appear together after this[12]). Philip in turn recruits Nathanael, who is initially sceptical – Jesus comes from Nazareth; can anything good come out of there? But Nathanael is won over when Jesus says that he saw him 'under the fig tree' before Philip called him. In the rabbinical tradition, the fig tree was the tree of knowledge of good and evil, and Jesus' curious words therefore seem to mean that by studying the Law, Nathanael had been preparing to meet him.[13] In any event, Nathanael is completely persuaded and becomes the first disciple to proclaim Jesus as the King of Israel. To which Jesus responds with: 'You believe that just because I said: I saw you under the fig tree. You will see greater things than that.' In other words, this is just the beginning.[14]

The two versions, of John and of the other three evangelists, are not completely contradictory. It is possible that, having met these men in John's entourage, he meets them again by the Sea of Galilee. It is certainly likely that he would have recruited his first companions from among those of his cousin.

These were simple men, some of whom certainly could not read or write. But none of Jesus' disciples, including those who would become closest to him, the apostles, could be said to have been poor. There were plenty of fish in the Sea of Galilee (one of the best being St Peter's fish, or John Dory). They were caught in little round nets or dragnets fastened between two boats – and fishing boats were not tiny smacks. In the episode of the calming of the storm,[15] Jesus was with several of his disciples in the boat and still had room to leave them and go to sleep. The fisherman Zebedee, father of James and John, had employees. Among the 'land people', the tax collector Matthew was certainly very comfortably off, and Judas would not have been entrusted with the group's finances if he had not had some experience of managing money.

They chose, however, to live unorthodox lives, albeit with some breaks. The gospels give the impression that the apostles were not always with Jesus. Peter, for example, continued to fish, at least to start with, and then after the resurrection. But for months at a time these young men, some of whom were pillars of their community, became homeless wanderers.

They were not alone in doing so. As we have seen, that troubled period saw a proliferation of prophets, visionaries and soothsayers roaming the land, carrying in their wake groups of faithful followers, all, in various ways, waiting for the Messiah. This phenomenon was not limited to Israel. In other parts of the Roman Empire itinerant cynic philosophers (so called after Diogenes, nicknamed the dog – *kuon* in Greek – when he was living in his tub), bearded and unwashed like hippies, were choosing to live on the fringes of society. But these rootless people were more common in Judaea and Galilee. According to the Roman Pliny the Elder, the 'hordes of people' who went to Qumran to live with the Essenes were 'tired of life and driven there by the waves of fortune'.[16] There were, Josephus tells us, as many wealthy people among these refuseniks as there were poor. Such people also took refuge in political campaigns (principally, but apparently a little later than this period, that of the Zealots), although the ranks of these resistance fighters were composed mainly of debt-ridden and destitute peasants, unable to pay their taxes. Then there were the beggars, the cripples, the handicapped, the deranged who were thought to be possessed by demons, the outcasts. We meet these people on practically every page of the gospels, including in the parable of the 'dishonest steward' who is sacked by his master on a charge of wasting goods. Not strong enough to undertake manual work, he thinks of begging (but 'I should be too ashamed'[17]), as though he has no brothers or family to help him, as though that phenomenon of social isolation were common and there were little community support to fall back on.

This little world – apart from beggars, who were attracted to Jerusalem, as they always are to places of pilgrimage – kept away from towns, the centres of politico-religio-economic power. Towns, for their part, did not welcome such people but closed ranks against them. City-dwellers and country people are usually, in any case, suspicious of each other. When Jesus arrived in Jerusalem on the occasion called Palm Sunday, it was groups of pilgrims from the country who welcomed him, and at the time of his trial it was apparently the townspeople who called for his death and who hurled insults at him.

Jesus and his group mostly kept to the countryside. Towns like Sepphoris, Jotapata or Gischala, important at the time, are now unknown simply because they were never mentioned in the gospels; what figure are minuscule Galilean locations, not found in any other source. Or else Jesus and his group go to the outskirts of towns. Mark's gospel has them going to 'the villages of Caesarea Philippi'[18] or 'the region of Tyre'.[19] Admittedly, these towns were very much under Greek influence and Jews, who were sometimes in the minority, were often relegated to the suburbs.[20]

These wandering prophets had a pretty miserable life. When Jesus said he had 'nowhere to lay his head', he was not just using a figure of speech. When he enjoined his listeners, in the Sermon on the Mount, not to 'worry about your life and what you are to eat, nor about your body and how you are to clothe it',[21] these were not words picked at random. He had to raise the spirits of young men who were sleeping rough, wrapping their capes around them at night for a blanket, after having walked for miles on bad roads, shaken by the wind, burnt by the sun or drenched by rain. He had to rekindle the enthusiasm of disciples who usually had nothing more nourishing or substantial to eat than bread and dates, and who had to endure the gibes of sceptics or opponents, respond to hecklers, and watch out for the numerous bandits who, like hoodlums the world over, had no scruples about preying on those poorer than themselves.

Little by little, however, a sort of support network grew up. From certain passages in the gospels,[22] it is clear that the group were knocking on doors not only to preach but also to ask for food and shelter. Jesus and his followers were also sometimes welcomed into sympathisers' houses, to the home of a member of the group (with Peter's family, for example, where, according to Matthew, Jesus heals the mother-in-law[23]), of Martha and Mary[24] or of rich tax collectors. They were also provided with hospitality like the large meal offered them by the Pharisee (for which these vagabonds loll on couches, in the manner of good bourgeois diners), where a woman – 'a sinner', Luke assures us – disturbs them by anointing Jesus with ointment.[25] Women play a large part in this support network. Luke gives us a list: Mary Magdalene, others 'who had been cured of evil spirits and ailments'[26], one Susanna, and notably Joanna, the wife of a very high official – Chuza, Herod's steward – who cannot have been short of either money or connections in means or contacts. Finally, if Judas looked after the group's finances, it means that they had some – from collecting alms, from some other source of funding or from working at their own jobs between preaching tours.

Jesus would soon structure this group. First he chose his closest followers. This was contrary to the Jewish tradition, in which a rabbi is chosen by young people who become his pupils (the first meaning of the word 'disciple'), are initiated by him, and eventually become rabbis themselves. Jesus did not work like that. Here, it is the master who calls, 'Follow me!'[27] And those called should not be under any illusions: 'A disciple is not superior to his teacher.'[28] They would not succeed him, overtake him, or be promoted. 'You ... must not allow yourselves to be called Rabbi, since you have only one Master, and you are all brothers.'[29] But they would be handsomely rewarded, nonetheless: 'If you make my word your home you will indeed be my disciples, you will learn the truth and the truth will set you free.'[30] So there would be no career path, but something much better: freedom.

Jesus takes his men from many places: conformist country people and less cautious fishermen, Galileans and at least one Judaean (Judas), a tax collector, and a declared opponent of the system (Simon). They do not always get on very well, suffer fits of jealousy, seem wary of one another and have often to be called to order: 'You are all brothers.'

These were the inner circle, the ones we call the apostles. But the gospels show that Jesus' 'movement' (others would call it his 'party') had three layers. At the base were the sympathisers, who were more or less faithful. They stayed at home with their families, remained in their jobs and were occasional providers of refuge. In Jesus' view, they were numerous: 'Anyone who is not against us is for us.'[31] Some of them were even among his intimate friends – most famously, Lazarus. The next level were the disciples. Much was demanded of this group. First, they had to follow him unhesitatingly. One aspirant, for example, had wanted to go and bury his father before accompanying Jesus and was told to 'leave the dead to bury their dead.'[32] Another wanted to say goodbye to his family before following the rabbi, and was upbraided sharply: 'Once the hand is laid on the plough, no one who looks back is fit for the Kingdom of God.'[33] The general rule was that 'If any man comes to me without hating his father, mother, wife, children, brothers, sisters, yes and his own life too, he cannot be my disciple.'[34]

Jesus knows that to place such a demand on those who want to pledge their allegiance to him is harsh, almost unacceptable. 'From now on a household of five will be divided; three against two and two against three'.[35] And, 'You will be hated by all men on account of my name.'[36] These words were undoubtedly based on experience. His own family, says Mark, even 'set out to take charge of him, convinced he was out of his mind.'[37]

These disciples could find themselves entrusted with a particular mission. Luke says that as Jesus is making his way to Jerusalem, he sends a vanguard of missionaries to announce the Kingdom of God. 'The Lord appointed seventy-two others, and sent them out ahead of him, in pairs, to all the towns and places he himself was to visit.'[38] The figure seventy-two should doubtless not be taken too literally, for it was the number of ancient sages of Israel that Moses had assembled in the desert to help him govern the people,[39] and also the number of descendants of the sons of Noah given in the book of Genesis.[40] It simply means that there were quite a lot of disciples.

Finally, at the top of the pyramid – or rather at the heart of the nebula – were the apostles. The Greek word *apostolos* is a translation of the Aramaic *chelilah*, which meant 'envoy' and was used for the official representatives sent out by Jerusalem to the provinces. The apostles were not organs of government or a board of governors but Jesus' closest companions, the people in whom he confided. Yet when he chose them, it was 'to be sent out to preach with power to cast out devils'.[41] In other words, they were given exactly the same mission and the same powers as the other disciples. The distinction between apostles and disciples is not, in any case, always very clear.[42]

This assembly of twelve is primarily a symbol of the twelve tribes of Israel descended from the sons of Jacob. The gospels of Mark, Matthew and Luke at first call them simply 'the Twelve'. It is only after they have been sent out on missions to the surrounding villages that they are given the name apostles[43] or envoys. After Jesus' death they take on a new role. The gospels do not give the apostles the same names, and John does not have a total of twelve: he omits, for example, Matthew (also called Levi) the tax collector, and Simon. On the other hand, he mentions a Nathanael whom the three others omit. Only Andrew, Peter, John, James son of Zebedee, Thomas and Judas Iscariot appear in all four gospels. If all the names are counted, they actually add up to fourteen. This has given rise to endless debates and computations, but can in fact probably be explained by the few forenames in use with the Jews at the time, the frequency of namesakes and the resulting preponderance of nicknames, all of which created confusion. It is likely that there were only twelve, given that number's powerful symbolic meaning. By choosing it, Jesus wanted to demonstrate his authority in Israel and his desire to re-cast the people of God in their original role.

7

Cana: the Sign of the Wine

WHAT a party! The procession has set off: in front, almost running, the groom with his friends and cousins, all bearing torches that form a sea of light in the dusk. Following behind comes the main body of the crowd, the older neighbours and the family, walking as fast as they can so as not to miss the arrival at the bride's house, when the celebration will really begin.

She has waited, quietly, with her parents and several bridesmaids. They all wear embroidered dresses, but the bride's forehead is decorated with sparkling jewels, below which hangs a veil. Her bridesmaids carry small terracotta lamps and each has a little flasks of spare oil tied to a finger. Nervous, excited, she listens to the growing murmur of the approaching group. It *is* them; it *is* him. He arrives, asks permission to see her, lifts her veil, declares his happiness to everyone. And then, amid general hubbub, shouts and laughter, the procession sets off again, carrying the bride on a sedan chair. A vial of ointment is broken, and, the vows exchanged, the party begins.

What a party! Galilean peasants adore weddings, an opportunity for family and friends to gather and forget the daily grind of work, worries and wants. Usually they wait until the end of harvest to celebrate weddings. Then the wheat lofts or bins are full, toil is over and people can enjoy a short patch of prosperity which may or may not last until the following summer. But to hell with penny-pinching! It will be soon enough to worry about things when they happen; it is not every day that one marries off one's son. The father of the groom, at whose home the wedding will be celebrated, is in any event quite pleased with himself. He has negotiated well with her family, and this new daughter-in-law has not cost him too much. So there is no question of stinting: they will celebrate until the sabbath. And since the wedding takes place on a Tuesday,[1] they have three full days ahead of them.

That first evening, nothing is lacking. Things have got under-way after the rites of the wine: 'Blessed the Creator of the fruit of the vine!' The wine has not been diluted with water, even though its alcohol content is high. Anything, or almost anything, is al-lowed on a wedding day. The stone jars, filled with water, are there only for the many purification rites. Wine will accompany and wash down the meats, the fish stuffed with walnuts and pista-chios, the chicken stew with black olives, the game liver paté and the grilled dates.

And so it happens that on one of these three days of the wed-ding feast at Cana, a large village on a hillside, the wine begins to run out. Perhaps the date liqueur, too. Mary, who has been there from the beginning and who is doubtless rather more sober than most of the guests, is the first to notice; women have a gift for such things. She tells Jesus, who has just arrived with his new companions. His answer, translated literally, is, 'Woman, what to you and to me?' This seems at first glance a strange reply, and has given rise to many interpretations. Why doesn't Jesus call her 'Mother'? He calls her 'Woman', a title he will use on other occa-sions to strangers or friends, because from then on he wishes to abstract the bond that links them. His mission is greater than fam-ily ties. As for this 'What to you or to me?' (usually rendered by 'What have you to do with me?' or 'Why turn to me?'), it is an ex-pression still common in modern Aramaic and in several African languages; it means simply, 'This matter does not concern us'.[2] To which Jesus adds, 'My hour has not come yet.'

Mary, unruffled, orders the servants to do what he tells them. First, he commands them to refill the six stone jars with water – now empty, because there have been many purification rites. This was not the first day of celebrations, and the marriage has been consummated. The blood-stained sheet, proving the bride's virginity, has been shown to the cheering guests. The fact that Jesus uses these jars is curious, because wine was usually stored in amphorae. Water jars were enormous, each holding between fifteen and twenty-five gallons of water, so in this case six soon held a hundred gallons or so of the very best quality wine.

The party can go on. Nobody notices a thing. Boys and girls dance on the swept threshing-floor, which a few days earlier had been covered with wheat. The older people watch their glasses being refilled, too tipsy to notice any difference between this wine and the last lot. Only the wine waiter, or the master of the banquet or the steward (choose whichever translation you like; they all show that this was no cheapskate occasion, but that things were being done in style) appreciates that it is far superior, and is a little resentful that it has been kept hidden from him until now – he would have served it on the first night, when people's palates were fresh enough to distinguish between nectar and plonk.

This is how John's account ends. (None of the other evangelists mention the episode.) He remarks in conclusion: 'This was the first of the signs given by Jesus; it was given at Cana in Galilee. He let his glory be seen and his disciples believed in him.'[3]

It is up to us to decipher it.

This was, in the words of the evangelist, a 'sign'. For John, the function of a miracle was primarily to demonstrate something. Towards the end of his gospel, he writes, 'There were many other signs that Jesus worked and the disciples saw, but they are not recorded in this book. These are recorded so that you may believe....'[4]

But this miracle was different from the subsequent healings and exorcisms. First, it had very few witnesses, apart from the servants, the groom, Mary, and the disciples, of whose loyalty Jesus is now certain. And then, contrary to the pattern of most other miracle accounts, the beneficiaries of the miracle – because certainly it would have been awkward for the newly-weds and their families if the wine had run out – are not identified as such. The bride is at the centre of every wedding, but here she does not appear, and the groom has only a small non-speaking part at the end. Their silence is all the more remarkable because John is voluble about certain other details, such as the six water jars and their contents.

What is more, neither the beneficiaries of the miracle nor their relatives had asked for anything, unlike the widow of Nain, the blind man of Jericho, or Martha and Mary who were so devastated by the death of their brother Lazarus. And their plight was not one that particularly inspired compassion. 'It is from the cry of pain as Creation and man are born that miracles are produced,' writes the Jesuit priest Georges Chantraine, who doubts neither that the miracles of the gospels happened nor that miracles can happen today.[5] Clearly, this miracle has little to do with the birth pangs of either creation or creatures. If these people, who were not asking for anything, had not suddenly been given this extra wine, they would not have behaved any worse: indeed, it is tempting to say that they behaved worse because of it. This, then, was a free miracle, a gift-miracle, performed by Jesus at his mother's instigation, and which primarily constituted a 'sign' for his intimate circle and the servants.

These servants should not go unnoticed. Normally, Jesus made little use of intermediaries. Later in this gospel he would take the active role himself, in the feeding of the five thousand ('Then Jesus took the loaves, gave thanks, and gave them out to all who were sitting ready; he then did the same with the fish....'[6]), the healing of various sick people and the raising of Lazarus. Why does John elaborate here on the role of the servants and their obedience? And why do they not go and explain to the wine waiter (or the *maître d'hôtel*) how the water had become wine? And why does he make no mention of their appreciation after the miracle, as in similar episodes?

So many comments and questions mean that this miracle needs special attention. In a book already mentioned,[7] sanctioned by the imprimatur, Fr Léon-Dufour observes calmly that 'the inescapable conclusion is therefore that the episode at Cana is not of the bio-graphical kind.' And that is the view of most scholars.

So we are dealing with a symbol, or rather with several sym-bols, into which some literal elements are mixed. Let us begin with these. What the story reveals straightaway is that there has been some kind of break with the Baptist. It is impossible to imag-ine the wild-looking hermit who preached on the banks of the Jordan going to the marriage feast at Cana or staying there until the wine laid on by the organisers begins to run low. That is not his kind of thing. A little later, Luke and Matthew tell us, Jesus himself emphasised this difference. Reproaching his audience for their disbelief, he says,

> For John came, neither eating nor drinking and they say, 'He is pos-sessed.' The Son of Man came, eating and drinking, and they say, 'Look, a glutton and a drunkard, a friend of tax collectors and sinners.' Yet wisdom has been proved right by her actions.[8]

In other words, there are different ways of doing God's will.

Not everyone, however, felt that way. Little love seems to have been lost between John's and Jesus' followers. These words of Jesus are in fact preceded in Luke and Matthew by an episode that reveals much about these differences. John the Baptist had apparently had an image of the Messiah in mind, to which Jesus did not conform, and he had begun to doubt. His remaining disci-ples must have encouraged his growing scepticism; this Jesus was rivalling their master! They needed to persuade themselves that, unlike their companions who had deserted them to follow Jesus, they had made the right choice. And John allows himself to be in-fluenced. So although he had officially recognised his cousin's supremacy at the time of Jesus' baptism, he now sends two of his disciples to ask him: 'Are you the one who is to come, or have we got to wait for someone else?'[9]

The Gospel of John recounts another scene. When the Baptist is baptising 'at Aenon near Salim, where there was plenty of water', Jesus was doing the same in Judaea. The Baptist's disciples did not appreciate this: 'Rabbi, the man who was with you on the far side of the Jordan, the man to whom you bore witness, is baptising now; and everyone is going to him.' He calms them down, somewhat impatiently. 'You yourselves can bear me out: I said: I myself am not the Christ; I am the one who has been sent in front of him.' And he launches into a beautiful discourse, full of poetic language and imagery, to make them understand that which they refuse to understand:

> The bride is only for the bridegroom;
> and yet the bridegroom's friend,
> who stands there and listens,
> is glad when he hears the bridegroom's voice.
> This same joy I feel, and now it is complete.
> He must grow greater,
> I must grow smaller.[10]

The Baptist, then, had initially been overjoyed (although not everybody was as enthusiastic), but had begun to suffer from doubts and so sent his two emissaries to get reassurance from Jesus, which is duly given: 'Go back and tell John what you hear and see: the blind see again and the lame walk, lepers are cleansed and the deaf hear, and the dead are raised to life, and the Good News is proclaimed to the poor.' This substantial list of marvellous miracles is what, it seems, is needed for these people to be convinced – 'so that you may believe', as the evangelist says. And then Jesus begins, just as John the Baptist had done, to sing the praises of the other. John is, he says, 'more than a prophet' and, 'of all the children born of women, a greater than John the Baptist has never been seen.' He makes it clear, however, that great though he is, John is only a precursor: 'He is the one of whom scripture says: "Look, I am going to send my messenger before you; he will prepare your way before you."'

The leaders of the two groups, if one may put it like this, are thus clearly concerned to define their respective roles, acknowledge the merits of the other, and persuade their disciples and the crowds that they are not rivals.

A little later, John is put in prison. The tetrarch of Galilee, Herod Antipas, has proved no better than his father King Herod. If anything, he is worse. His crimes are multifarious, he is a puppet of the Romans and, to cap it all, he marries Herodias, who was a granddaughter of Herod, and therefore his own niece, with whom he was madly in love. This was too much for John. He left the Jordan and went to the tetrarch to tell him that the Law did not permit such a marriage.[11] Herod Antipas is furious, and his first thought is to have John's head cut off. But the Baptist's popularity is such that the tetrarch changes his mind and simply has him thrown into jail – into the huge fortress of Machaerus, Josephus tells us.

Antipas would let him out only to have him executed. The story the evangelists tell is well-known, though it should be approached carefully. The Galileans hated Herodias and it is possible that the disciples exaggerated a little. The story is that Herodias, who felt that the Baptist had cast aspersions on her reputation, has revenge on her mind. She wants him dead. At a party celebrating the tetrarch's birthday, her beautiful young daughter, Salome, dances for him. He is entranced. He has had the mother; now he wants the daughter. She flirts, seems to promise much. He, doubtless drunk, swears that she can have whatever she wants, and Herodias, seizing her opportunity, whispers to the young dancer to ask for the head of John on a plate. Matthew continues:

> The king was distressed but, thinking of the oaths he had sworn and of his guests, he ordered it to be given to her and sent and had John beheaded in the prison. The head was brought in on a dish and given to the girl who took it to her mother. John's disciples came and took the body and buried it; then they went off to tell Jesus.[12]

He, undeterred, retires to the desert for a time. The tetrarch, for his part, never totally got over this execution, hardened though

he was. When later he is told about Jesus, he thinks it is a resurrected John.

John's disciples were deprived of their master, but they did not
all automatically rally round Jesus; various clues indicate that
their group continued separately. And when the evangelist John,
after the events, underlines in his preamble that 'He was not the
light, only a witness to speak for the light',[13] it was obviously to
dispel a confusion that already existed.

To return to Cana and its symbols. By going to the wedding
feast, Jesus was not only breaking with the tradition of John. His
attendance also clearly separated him from the Essenes, with
whom some commentators – especially since the discovery of the
Dead Sea Scrolls – have tried to connect him. At the feast, Jesus
violates several dietary taboos. Deuteronomy, in many respects a
kind of guide to civil law, cites the case of a 'rebellious' son who
not only disobeys his parents but 'is a glutton and a drunkard'.[14]
As we have seen, Jesus' opponents would level this same accusation at him. But Jesus was not seeking to be provocative by such
behaviour, since it happens at a wedding – and concerns some
wine.

Wine was symbolically charged at several levels. The historian
Jean-Paul Roux, director of research at the CNRS in Paris, explains that 'vinification was a recent agricultural discovery and it
still had something of the mysterious, even slightly disturbing,
about it – mainly because it could lead to drunkenness. For a long
time, the classical world had drawn parallels between what they,
like the Jews, called the blood of the vine and the sap which ran
through the veins of men and animals.'[15] The grapes were trodden
and put into a winepress before being turned into a scarlet blood-
like liquid. They go through a kind of death before being reborn
in a different form. Now when the evangelist recounts the episode
at Cana, he has in mind two different events: the last supper that
Jesus took with the Twelve, during which he gave them wine to
drink, saying it was his blood; and his death and his resurrection
in a different form.

Another obvious symbolic meaning of wine was that of joy. It is true that Job, that upright and decent man, thinks that his sons and daughters may be polluting themselves by drinking and making merry at each other's homes, and that Noah's sons are ashamed of their father who, having planted the first vine in the world, then partakes so liberally of its fermented fruit that they find him lying naked in a drunken stupor – though, according to Genesis, this did not stop the old patriarch living another 350 years. But Ecclesiastes said that 'wine gives joy to life',[16] and Psalm 104 that the Lord had given wine to men 'to make them cheerful'.[17] Just so long as it was consumed in moderation, cautioned another biblical book, Sirach (a prominent figure in Jerusalem) or Ecclesiasticus: 'Drunk at the right time and in the right amount, wine makes for a glad heart and a cheerful mind.'[18]

Finally, and above all, wine is, as in the Song of Songs, a symbol of sexual union. And it will flow in rivers at the heavenly banquet, at the marriage between God and man, at the end of time. The prophets had predicted these things:

> ... the mountains will run with new wine,
> and the hills all flow with it.[19]

And

> On this mountain,
> Yahweh Sabaoth will prepare for all peoples
> a banquet of rich food, a banquet of fine wines ...[20]

What marriage was the author of the episode at Cana thinking of? The strange non-appearance of the bride has already been pointed out. The principal role is played by Mary, who is not mentioned by name but simply as 'the mother of Jesus'. Most scholars feel that the mother of Jesus stands here for Israel or, some feel, for the Church.

So the story represents the marriage between Israel the bride and God the husband, brought about through Jesus. The whole can therefore be interpreted in this way: Israel points out the problem as she sees it (the lack of wine), but Jesus is not persuaded. His mission is more important and universal. Israel, however, refuses to be discouraged but puts her confidence in him, without appropriating him to herself (Mary does not say, 'Do what *my son* tells you', but 'Do what *he* tells you'). Jesus then turns to the jars that have been emptied of the water used for the rites of purification during the feast, signifying that Israel had done her duty (although not perfectly because there are only six jars rather than seven, the sacred number of completion) and had responded to the will of God as they had interpreted it. And it was on that basis that Jesus acted.

The Italian Dominican Thomas Aquinas believed that the use of water highlighted the perseverance of a teaching God who had prepared men throughout the period of the Old Testament for the message that Jesus would give them. Jesus, he says,

> did not want to make wine out of nothing but out of water, showing that he did not want to introduce a totally new doctrine or reject the old but rather to fulfil it. 'I have not come to destroy, but to fulfil ...' What the old Law had imagined and promised, the Christ revealed and manifested.[21]

Finally, when the servants had placed their trust in Jesus and therefore obeyed him (once more in this gospel, it is the poor who do God's will; they are rewarded by witnessing the miracle), a new age begins, marked by the word 'now'. When the servants have filled the jars with water, Jesus says: 'Draw some out now ... and take it to the steward.' The author of the gospel could have done without this 'now', but in texts of this kind we must weigh up each word very carefully. That 'now' is not there by chance. It is *now*, through the presence of Jesus, that the new Covenant between God and humankind begins. All men of good faith will become allies of God, just as the servants in the story were the allies of Jesus. His mission is accomplished by this fulfilment.

The episode at Cana is rich in other meanings. This first 'sign', to use John's word, is given at the behest of a woman; when Jesus replies to Mary he calls her 'Woman'. In other words, her femininity is here more important than her maternity. Another interpretation involves the quality of the wine. The wine that was served first represents the gradual revelation of the identity of the one God and His will for Israel, set out by the prophets, but Jesus brings a total revelation, represented by the superior quality of the wine his miracle produces – a quality that surprises the steward, although the guests are initially unaware that there is any difference.

And finally, of course, the transformation of water into wine prefigures the Eucharist and the Last Supper.

Although it is not,therefore, 'of the biographical kind', the episode at Cana deserves detailed analysis. For John, the only evangelist to recount the story, it is a preface, the second chapter of his gospel. It is as though he wishes to repeat, in a different way, what he had said in the first:

> ... though the Law was given through Moses,
> grace and truth have come through Jesus Christ.
> No one has ever seen God;
> it is the only Son, who is nearest to the Father's heart,
> who has made Him known.[22]

Significantly, this episode makes it clear from the outset that Jesus' ministry was to be characterised by joy. Renan makes the point, although it is typically exaggerated, that Jesus 'wandered through Galilee in the midst of a perpetual celebration.'[23] This idea is one that, over the centuries, those calling themselves Jesus' disciples have often forgotten.

8

The Miracles

JESUS performs a total of over forty miracles in the gospels: twenty-two in Matthew, nineteen in Mark, fourteen in Luke, and seven in John. Obviously, some of these are the same, some are different – of the seven related by John, six are found nowhere else. But all of them say that there had been other miraculous events – 'many', according to John.[1] Most of them involve the healing of the sick: the blind, the paralysed, the leprous, the deaf and dumb, a woman with chronic haemorrhaging. The other miracles constitute a total reversal of natural laws: Jesus calms a storm, multiplies bread for the crowd in the desert, restores the dead to life.

The gospels and the Acts of the Apostles[2] are our only sources of information about these miracles, although a Jewish text, the *Babylonian Talmud*,[3] states that Jesus was executed because he practised 'sorcery', which could at least confirm that he was doing the same sort of things as the healers and the exorcists.

To judge by the space they devoted to them, the evangelists attached some importance to the miracles. This is particularly true in the case of Mark. Apart from the chapters on the Passion, descriptions of miracles take up 47 per cent of his text. It is interesting, however, that the evangelists never use the Greek word *terata*, 'amazing wonders', to describe them. Rather, they use the more modest *dunameis*, 'acts of power', or, in John, *semeia*, 'signs'.

The evangelists certainly amplified and multiplied these acts of power. The healing of a blind man and of a man possessed of evil spirits in Mark becomes in Matthew the healing of two blind men and of two possessed men; four thousand people fed on bread and fish in one becomes five thousand in the other, and the leftovers increase from seven baskets to twelve. All this leads us to suspect that the faithful made certain additions to these texts as they were being copied.

The gospels portray Jesus himself as having an ambiguous attitude to the miracles. On the one hand, he tells John the Baptist's envoys that he is indeed 'he who is coming' and proves it by giving a list of miracles (the lame walk, the blind see, and so on) which is in part a quotation from Isaiah.[4] On the other, these miracles almost have to be wrung out of him – certainly he never undertakes them on his own initiative. He never acts like a magician or a conjuror encouraging the crowd: 'Roll up, ladies and gents! Come and see the marvellous miracles!' On the contrary, he plays them down. They brought him 'a deaf man who had an impediment in his speech', and he 'took him aside in private, away from the crowd'[5] to heal him. At Bethsaida, people bring a blind man and beg Jesus 'to touch' him – in other words, to heal him. He does so, but only after leading the man into the countryside and then sending him back home with the injunction, 'Do not even go into the village.'[6] When a leper goes down on his knees and begs Jesus to heal him, he does so, but orders him to 'say nothing to anyone'.[7]

When asked to perform a miracle, as an ambassador is asked to present his credentials, or a suspect to prove his identity, Jesus often responds impatiently. After the second miracle involving the multiplication of bread and fish, Mark has the Pharisees demanding that Jesus give them a 'sign from heaven' (as if the miracle they have just witnessed is not enough, or they refuse to believe it, or see in that sudden appearance of bread a sign, not from heaven but from somewhere else – from Satan, for example). Jesus, 'with a sigh that came straight from the heart', says, 'Why does this generation demand a sign? I tell you solemnly, no sign shall be given to this generation.'[8] Which could also mean: because you stubbornly refuse to believe, you can be sure that I will not perform a miracle just for you – I resort to miracles only when it is useful. Jesus had spoken in similar vein to the Devil himself when challenged to turn stones into bread in the desert. He expresses the same irritation in Matthew's version of the 'second miracle of the loaves', although with rather a more threatening edge:

> In the evening you say, 'It will be fine; there is a red sky,' and in the morning, 'Stormy weather today; the sky is red and overcast.' You know how to read the face of the sky, but you cannot read the sign of the times. It is an evil and unfaithful generation that asks for a sign! The only sign it will be given is the sign of Jonah.[9]

The sign of Jonah is undoubtedly a reference to the destruction of the town of Nineveh and the scattering of its inhabitants, which the hapless fellow had ceaselessly prophesied after his escape from the whale. Jesus' reply is also perhaps an allusion to the destruction of Jerusalem. For the philosopher René Girard, however, it is the sign of 'the scapegoat, the sign of the unfortunate man thrown to the whales by the sailors who hold him responsible for the storm'.[10] In this interpretation, Jesus is referring to his own death, to his destiny as scapegoat who will take on the burden of all the evil in the world.

Our own generation is divided in its opinion of miracles. Some are hungry for them, adoring anything mysterious or miraculous, which they see as confirmation of their faith in the supernatural. For others, the miracles recounted in the gospels hinder rather than encourage faith. These people share the sentiments of Paul Valéry, for whom 'miracles demonstrate God's contempt for humanity';[11] they do not deny Jesus' existence, they are interested – sometimes passionately – in what he said and they are keen to put his teachings into practice, as far as they can. But the miracles!

So let us try to establish, if we can, what is behind them, what really happened and what they mean.

What is a miracle? Dictionaries give two definitions:

  1. An extraordinary phenomenon.

2. Something caused, in the eyes of believers, by divine intervention (distinguishing it from magic, which uses 'occult procedures' or calls on 'some supernatural controlling principle of nature').

Opinions about what is extraordinary change. Something that seemed remarkable to Jesus' contemporaries might seem commonplace to us. Modern psychiatry, for example, can now explain or cause cures that would formerly have seemed miraculous, particularly in relation to deafness, blindness, epilepsy or paralysis, the conditions that Jesus frequently cured in the gospels. But it remains powerless to explain the sudden cure of leprosy or congenital handicap.

The extraordinary still exists. Many people have experienced, either directly or at second-hand from people they know, telepathy, inexplicable cures or strange apparitions, although they do not usually mention these phenomena for fear of being dismissed as gullible or deranged. And rational explanations of such things rely on such an abundance of hypotheses and random coincidences that they begin to seem more fantastic than the original phenomenon itself. Modern scientists admit the existence of 'paranormal' events or of 'other logics' more readily than their counterparts at the beginning of the century. The geometrical laws of the Greek Euclid, for example, which are all verifiable in a limited space, cease to apply over large distances, as the German Riemann (whose work served as a model for the theory of relativity) demonstrated. Scientifically established laws that are valid in the everyday world can lose their validity when the scale of time and space is radically altered, in the infinitesimally small or the infinitely large, in great density or in very high energy. And (why not?) in high spiritual energy.

The objective approach consists of analysing all these gospel accounts of miracles carefully, accurately and without preconceived notions. This means, of course, that they cannot be considered unchallengeable, but equally that everything that seems initially beyond the grasp of the rational mind must not be automatically rejected. 'If something seems strange,' wrote Victor Hugo, 'we conclude that it does not exist. We are quick to say, "That's childish". What is childish, however, is to imagine that by closing one's eyes before the unknown, the unknown disappears.'[12]

Renan was someone who started out with presupposition: the supernatural does not exist, therefore miracles do not exist. 'Miracles,' he wrote,

> never happen; only gullible people believe that they have seen them. Not a single miracle has occurred before witnesses qualified to verify it.... By believing in the supernatural we believe in something that is outside the province of science and whose explanation is therefore beyond reach of the scientist, the astronomer, the physicist, the chemist, the geologist, the physiologist and also the historian. We reject the existence of supernatural occurrences for the same reason that we reject the existence of centaurs and hippogryphs: no one has ever seen them.[13]

Ernest Renan belonged to a century that believed passionately in science. It had already explained so much, it would eventually explain everything. But we now know that the body of scientific knowledge that existed at that time contained, along with incontrovertible and enlightening facts, several serious errors. Jean Rostand, who did not believe in God or the supernatural any more than Renan did, wrote several decades later:

> One thing of which I am certain is that there is nothing that can satisfy our quest for knowledge. We must resign ourselves to living in anxiety and darkness. When, after millions and millions of years, our species is dying out from the earth, man will still be reduced to pondering his ignorance and to bemoaning his lack of understanding. It will be a more elaborate ignorance than ours – but ignorance it will be, all the same.[14]

It is therefore wise to be wary of the preconception that the supernatural does not exist and that every miracle is pure legend.

Another, more recent, perspective (and one that is quite wide-spread among believers) is to say that since miracles are 'unaccept-able to modern man',[15] those that Jesus is supposed to have performed should be mentioned as little as possible or even ig-nored altogether. To which the response is first that if something is true it remains true, even if it is 'unacceptable to modern man'; if something is a question, it remains a question; if it is a mistake, it remains a mistake. The important – indeed, the essential – thing is not to find out what is 'acceptable', but what is true. And one can add that the sweeping stereotype of 'modern man', that photofit picture of some demigod with complete control of both himself and the universe, is very misleading. It was an image that perhaps had some validity just after the Second World War, although it quickly faded. But that is another story.

In any case, anyone who believes in the existence of God can-not maintain that He never, at any time or in any place, intervenes in the affairs of humans or the world, either directly or through an intermediary. The German Protestant theologian Günther Bornkamm, who is highly regarded in Germany and whose work complemented that of the eminent commentator Rudolf Bult-mann, writes: 'Faith [is] very definitely counting on and trusting in God's power, that it is not at an end at the point where human possibilities are exhausted.'[16] In the language of advertising, we can say that God has an 'added extra' – an 'added extra' of infinite proportions.

Miracles, or what we call miracles, were not as strange to the an-cient world as they are to us. People could not master nature, so they attempted to tame it by magic, to tap its resources and to trade with the obscure forces that governed it by offering it sacri-fices in exchange for cures, rain or sunshine. Magicians, sorcerers and idol-worshipping priests expended much energy in trying to control these unknown forces, ward off misfortune and divine the future.

The Jews were of course different from other peoples of the

Mediterranean basin in believing in one God rather than in dozens of idols. Not for them, at least in theory, the reading of chicken's entrails, the throwing of stones into water or indulgence in any other magical practice. The Torah had laid down that such activities were, like all forms of spiritualism or divination, punishable by death. However, it was only in theory; the Old Testament tells, for example, how a desperately unhappy Saul, the first king of Israel, disguises himself and goes to implore a witch to perform divination by calling up a spirit. Unfortunately, it is the recently deceased prophet Samuel who appears, to announce that Saul, his dynasty and the Israelite army will all be destroyed – a prophecy that began to be fulfilled the very next day.

The prophets and priests had therefore long waged a campaign to purge nature of the unknown forces that, according to primitive peoples, inhabited it, and to explain to their people that the one God could not be influenced by magical practices. That campaign was moderately successful – but the primitive mentality was never totally eradicated and tended to re-emerge as soon as things began to go even slightly wrong. The country still teemed with magicians and seers (rohe), with exorcists attempting to get demons to come out of people – almost invariably, in other words, to calm the highly-strung and the insane. In pursuit of a cure, the sick congregated near sources of water or miraculous pools. The famous five-porticoed Bethesda[17] in Jerusalem, the Sheep Pool, which appears in John's gospel, is one example: the first cripple or blind man who plunged into it after 'an angel of the Lord' disturbed the water would be cured.[18] Pools such as this, offering very much the same kind of service, were to be found throughout the Greek-influenced world. An inscription was found at the temple of Asclepius, the god of medicine, in Corinth:

> In thanks for your blessings, O Asclepius, I dedicate this rock that I lifted by my own strength and which will bear witness, to all who see it, to your powers. For before I entrusted myself to you and to the doctors in your temple, I suffered from a terrible illness: I had

an abscess on my lung and my two arms were paralysed. You told me that I could lift this rock. I obeyed and I was cured.[19]

Asclepius' disciples healed in the same way as Jesus – by a laying on of hands, praying or uttering mysterious formulas. This was medicine at the time.

The miracles attributed to Jesus would have surprised his contemporaries less than they surprise us. The men and women whom he addressed would frequently have heard in the synagogue about the parting of the Red Sea, of fire descending from heaven, of the collapse of the walls of Jericho. A deaf man healed, Peter's mother-in-law cured of fever were not, dare I say, quite up to that standard, and were not particularly breathtaking to them. If Jesus had wanted to prove something by such means, he would not have got very far.

The evangelists, however, do not tire of recounting these cures (although one or other of them does not know about some of the most important miracles, such as the resurrection of the widow of Nain's son, which only Luke describes, or that of Lazarus, found only in John). The early Christian communities also attached great significance to them. According to the Acts of the Apostles,[20] Peter, who just a few weeks earlier had been at a very low ebb, declared to the Jews on the day of Pentecost that God had 'commended' Jesus the Nazarene to them 'by the miracles and portents and signs that God worked through him'. Let us pause at this word 'commended'. The men and women to whom Peter was speaking that day would not have considered anyone a prophet unless he were also a worker of miracles. The two activities were linked, even in false prophets. Jesus himself, when he predicted the destruction of the Temple, terrible calamities for Judaea and a sea of troubles for the disciples, declared that 'false prophets will arise and produce signs and portents to deceive the elect, if that were possible.'[21]

The gospels therefore recount Jesus' miraculous deeds so that he can be recognised immediately, 'commended', as a prophet.

And the writers' insistence on them is sometimes heavy: Matthew has him curing every ailment and malady.[22] And then, when they think they have proved their case beyond all reasonable doubt, they go on to present him as a prophet unique among prophets. This didacticism was aimed mainly at the Greeks, who already had a whole crowd of healing, saving gods.

We now need to examine what relationship these accounts have with the truth. And here there is a surprise: none, or almost none, of the scholars questions the authenticity of most of the cures. The Protestant historian and theologian Etienne Trocmé, president of the International Society for the Study of the New Testament, seems to sum up the general position when he writes in his *Histoire des religions*: 'It is impossible to say with the slightest degree of certainty what happened when a sick person went to Jesus. But it is obvious that he had exceptional healing powers and used them selflessly.'[23]

How have scholars arrived at their conclusions? First of all, they try to establish which parts of the gospels are the oldest, having been handed down by word of mouth (the 'oral tradition'). They then ask themselves how much credence to give to that tradition, always keeping the same caveat in mind: those who had passed on Jesus' sayings or deeds, orally or in writing, knew how his time on earth had ended. Now, a story that is still unfolding and one that has reached its conclusion are not described in the same way. When the conclusion is known, the elements are arranged differently, and episodes take on a meaning that had not hitherto been realised.

In making an objective study of the miracles, the four gospels are first compared, so as to eliminate obvious exaggeration or alteration. Then, the most archaic forms of language are studied. When, for example, Jesus raises the daughter of the rabbi Jairus who had been pronounced dead, he says in Aramaic, *'Talitha, kum!'*, which Mark immediately translates for us: 'Little girl, I tell you to get up!'[24] As Charles Perrot, whose methods we are now following, writes, 'such words have a very considerable "realistic feel" to them'.[25] However, he goes on to add that comparable, non-Christian (Greek, for example) texts 'are very fond of putting the quasi-magical words of the healer into a foreign language'.

Other details have a 'realistic feel'. Mark has Jesus asleep in the stern, 'his head on a cushion',[26] before calming the storm that was terrifying his companions. But those who know the evangelist well will advise caution, because he is a storyteller, someone who likes to set the scene for his characters. More convincing, perhaps, are the details that the evangelists might have been tempted to 'forget' because they were somewhat embarrassing, as, for example, when Jesus used his saliva to cure blind men and a deaf mute. Meeting a man blind from birth near the Temple in Jerusalem, Jesus

> spat on the ground, made a paste with the spittle, put this over the eyes of the blind man and said to him, 'Go and wash in the Pool of Siloam.' ... So the blind man went off and washed himself, and came away with his sight restored.[27]

The point is that all healers used saliva in this way. According to Pliny in his *Natural History* and Suetonius in *Vespasian*, people at that time believed saliva was effective in the treatment of eye ailments. To have Jesus using saliva was therefore to relegate him to the ranks of ordinary healers. And then, even more embarrassingly, this practice does not always work immediately. At Bethsaida, when Jesus puts saliva on the eyes of a blind man and lays his hands on him, he asks, 'Can you see anything?' The man is not initially very enthusiastic: 'I can see people; they look like trees to me, but they are walking about.' So Jesus lays his hands on the man's eyes, and the fellow finally 'could see everything plainly and distinctly'.[28]

But the acme is when, according to Mark, Jesus returns to Nazareth and is not very warmly received by his old neighbours. 'He could work no miracle there,' Mark tells us, 'though he cured a few sick people by laying his hands on them.'[29] A fervent propagandist who wanted to prove to his contemporaries that Jesus was all-powerful and divine would have omitted such failures (due, the evangelists mostly explain, to the lack of faith of those who demanded miracles). The insistence on the use of saliva and the inclusion of difficult episodes therefore lend weight to the argument that the miracles really happened.

Scholars use another 'test': originality. Certain episodes are reminiscent of others that have nothing to do with Jesus. In the episode of the tax paid to the Temple, for example, Jesus tells Peter to go and catch a fish: 'There you will find a shekel; take it and give it to them for me and for you.'[30] (A shekel, or *stater*, was a gold coin worth four drachmas; every Jew over the age of twenty had to pay two drachmas to the Temple each year.) Stories containing a fish that had a gold coin or ring in its mouth were widespread right around the Mediterranean at that time. The episode should therefore be viewed with some caution. As should that of the healing of the centurion's servant at Cana, which is recounted by John, Matthew and Luke,[31] although the details vary from one to the other. In John's version, the centurion is a court official whose son is lying ill at Capernaum. The official goes to Jesus and begs him to come and cure the lad. Jesus, as usual reluctant, says, 'So you will not believe unless you see signs and portents!' The man insists, and Jesus then reassures him, 'Go home ... your son will live.' The man believes him and leaves. On the way, his servants come to meet him and confirm the good news: the fever had 'left' his son the previous day, at the seventh hour, the exact time that Jesus had declared that he would live. Now there is a story of the same period in the Talmud[32] that has several similarities. The son of the rabbi Gamaliel falls ill, and he sends two of his disciples to a certain Hanina Ben Dosa who begins to pray as soon as he is given the news. He then tells the disciples, 'Go, the fever has left him.' For some undisclosed reason, before they leave they note the time – and that is how they know, on their return to Gamaliel, that it was at that very moment that the patient had asked for something to drink and the fever had abated.

The similarity is clear. But it is difficult to draw any

conclusions from that. Did one story influence the other? And if so, which? Nobody knows. But the evangelist's meaning is clear: if one trusts Jesus and believes in him, one will live. For John, and doubtless the other evangelists, that symbolic truth was much more important than historical authenticity.

Some people have wondered whether several of the miracle stories were not in fact originally parables that had gradually been transformed, as they were told and retold before being written down as the gospels, into biographical episodes. The story of the fig tree that the hungry Jesus sees as he is walking to Jerusalem with his disciples on the eve of Passover might provide an example. Drawing near to the tree, he sees it is bearing no fruit, although since trees had just begun to blossom, this is hardly surprising. Indeed, Mark states quite plainly that 'it was not the season for figs'. Jesus nonetheless curses the fig tree: 'May no one ever eat fruit from you again.' The next day, when he passes the same spot with the apostles, the tree has withered to the roots.[33] Poor tree! As the writers of *La Bible du peuple de Dieu* (published with the imprimatur)[34] remark, 'Jesus' action would have been uncalled for unless he had meant it as a symbol.' It is Israel who is being condemned because she has not produced the expected fruits. Moreover, the evangelist adds that 'his disciples heard him say this'. It is hard to imagine why Mark should have felt obliged to point this out – since the disciples had obviously not suddenly gone deaf – if he had not wanted to convey that they had *understood* the real meaning of the episode.

Similarly, there is the episode at Gerasa, where Jesus goes after calming the storm. A man possessed by evil spirits ('all night and all day ... he would howl and gash himself with stones') comes out of a cemetery where he lived, reviled by all, and Jesus exorcises the 'legion' of demons that are living in him. These demons ask Jesus, very politely, not to send them 'out of the district' (a district which is not subject to the Law of Moses; this was Jesus' only incursion into pagan territory). There happens to be a large herd of pigs nearby, and the demons negotiate with Jesus: let them be sent into the pigs. To which he compassionately agrees. What happens? The transfer is performed, and 'the herd of about two thousand pigs charged down the cliff into the lake, and there they were drowned.'[35] As these same commentators point out, there are 'aspects of legend' in the story. But above all, it is very funny. A horde of evil spirits cannot think of any other place of refuge than inside pigs, in Jewish eyes the most impure animal (as we noted, the episode took place outside Palestine, where they barely existed). The Jews who heard this story would understand more quickly than we do that Jesus, who certainly had a sense of humour, wanted to ridicule the evil spirits and show that they had lost all power.

It would be impossible, and pedantic, to sift through and analyse here all the miracles that the evangelists describe. We must however look at what are called the 'miracles over nature'. Catholic scholars have stressed that 'a miracle is not in opposition to natural laws (contra naturum); it is in juxtaposition to it (praeter naturum)'.[36] It is illness that goes against natural laws, not the cure. The Jesuit priest Georges Chantraine goes on to write: 'God can do the impossible, but by doing so the Creator does not contradict Himself; He renews His Creation by reconciling it to Him.'[37]

There are four main miracles over nature in the gospels: Jesus calming the storm, walking on water, multiplying food and raising people from the dead. Most of these have something in common with scenes from the Old Testament. The psalmist praises God in Psalm 65: 'You calm the clamour of the ocean, the clamour of its waves.'[38]. In the book of Job, God 'trampled the Sea's tall waves',[39] and in Exodus, He feeds the Hebrews in the desert by sending them manna from heaven. In the First Book of Kings, Elijah raises the son of a widow from the dead, and in the Second Book Elisha does the same for the son of a notable Israelite, the woman of Shunem (the birth of this son was itself a miracle since she, like Elizabeth, had despaired of ever bearing a child, and her husband was moreover very old[40]). Elisha also miraculously filled empty jars with oil[41] and multiplied twenty barley loaves so that there was enough to feed a hundred people: 'For Yahweh says this, "They will eat and have some left over."'

Some commentators have concluded on the basis of these similarities that the evangelists wanted to demonstrate that Jesus acted as the great prophets did and possessed powers which in the Old Testament were attributed to God. This theory cannot be ruled out. But equally we cannot immediately conclude that these accounts are purely legendary, and we must certainly not just put them to one side as being patently absurd.

So let us look more closely at two of the more important miracles. First, at the feeding of the five thousand (or four thousand), which marked a turning point in Jesus' movement, and which is the only episode of his life between the baptism and his last entry into Jerusalem to be recounted by all four evangelists. In fact, Matthew and Mark each recount two such episodes, so that we actually have six accounts of it. Second, at the raising of Lazarus, which only John recounts, but which is very significant.

Jesus began to see his audiences growing in size and his disciples in strength. It is true that he had been given a poor reception in his own village of Nazareth – 'a prophet is only despised in his own country, among his own relations and in his own house',[42] he had declared – where, as we have seen, Mark tells us he could not work any miracles, although adding apologetically that Jesus 'cured a few sick people by laying his hands on them'.[43] But elsewhere the 'multitudes' had flocked to him, and he had healed many people.[44] He had also organised his group by instituting the Twelve,[45] and had sent them out in pairs on missions.[46] According to Luke and Mark the disciples had some success: 'They set out and went from village to village proclaiming the Good News and healing everywhere.'[47]

It is well known that success has a sting in its tail. It creates enemies. And the success of Jesus' movement was such that Herod Antipas, the man who had had John the Baptist beheaded, began to worry. Some people were saying that the man who was inciting the crowds was none other than the decapitated Baptist, returned from the dead, others that it was a reappearance of the prophet Elijah. The tetrarch wants to see him. This does not mean that he had been touched by grace and suddenly wanted to receive the teachings of this new prophet. No; if this were indeed a resurrected John the Baptist, Antipas doubtless had it in mind to cut his head off again.[48]

Jesus, however, decides at that moment that he and the apostles need to go away by themselves. To rest? That is Mark's interpretation,[49] while Matthew implies that it is to escape from Herod's men.[50] Both might be true. In John, Jesus 'went off to the other side of the Sea of Galilee'. It was not so easy to escape from the crowds, however. Word of his whereabouts had got around. John, who as we know likes to fix things in time, specifies that it is shortly before Passover. He also tells us that it was sunny and gives us another detail that fixes the season: in that wilderness, the crowd could sit on green grass. The crowd has caught up with Jesus. We do not know how. That people would have followed him at that time is problematic, as they should have been going to Jerusalem for Passover, not to the region of Bethsaida, as Luke has it,[51] or of Tiberias, according to the most reliable studies of John.[52] This would not have improved Jesus' relationship with the Temple. Of course he had not wanted to attract the crowd, but could the Temple hierarchy, who must have been watching his movements closely, accept that he should in essence say to his companions, 'We won't go to Jerusalem: we have better things to do'? No more than they could accept that instead of sending these people away and reminding them of their Passover obligations, he had concerned himself with feeding them.[53]

It does not matter whether there were four or five thousand of them – and given the total population of the country, that was a sizeable figure. It is a motley crew, composed of tearful families who have brought a sick, handicapped or mentally ill relative in the hope of a cure or an exorcism, strong and devoted volunteers (rather like the stretcher-bearers at Lourdes) carrying feverish or paralytic patients, idle onlookers, agents of all the political or religious powers attempting to control that uncontrollable country, fervent disciples and others who want to hear Jesus' message or who perhaps hope, as we can legitimately suppose from what happens next, to catch him out. And Jesus is worried, for them. What are they going to eat? Four or five thousand people – without counting women and children, adds Matthew, as though they did not really count.[54] John says later that 'as many as five thousand men sat down' to eat.[55] Not the others. That was the way of that world.

When evening came, the disciples, who were perhaps tired, or perhaps frustrated that they have been deprived of time alone with their master, were quite ready to send all these people away to fetch food from the surrounding villages.[56] It was not just a question of getting fed. For the Jews, the evening meal was an important occasion. Jesus asked Philip how they can buy bread – the staple food which even served on occasion as a plate – so that the crowd can eat. Philip, whom John often presents as both practical and reflective, points out that 'Two hundred denarii would only buy enough to give them a small piece each.'[57] Why two hundred denarii? It was clearly not enough, but not a derisory sum either: almost seven times the cost of Judas's betrayal, and six times the monthly wage of an agricultural worker. Mark also tells us that that is what the small band of disciples have at their disposal on that day: 'They answered, "Are we to go and spend two hundred denarii on bread for them to eat?"'[58] This confirms the earlier supposition that Jesus had set up some small financial arrangements. In all this, one gets a sense that Jesus' approach and that of his disciples are completely out of step. They talk of buying, he of giving what they have. When he mentions money elsewhere, it is clear that for him it is something that one gives, advising the rich young man who wants to follow him, for example, to sell all he has and give it to the poor.

To return to the miracle of the loaves, Andrew (the brother of

Simon Peter), who is always close to Philip, notices that a small boy has brought with him five barley loaves and two fishes. The idea of feeding the crowd with that is obviously ridiculous. How had Andrew picked him out of such a teeming mass of people? Perhaps he had been counting on him to provide Jesus and his companions with their evening meal. But why did he not appeal to the crowd to see if any other sensible people had brought something with them, in pouches or bags? These questions are unanswerable. Jesus, at any rate, does not waste time. Taking the five loaves, he 'gave thanks'[59] and distributed them to the dinner guests, like any good Jewish father presiding at the evening meal who thanks the Lord before sharing out the food. Then, when they have had enough to eat, he tells the disciples to collect the many leftovers (enough to fill twelve baskets – one for each apostle, as though by chance). A well-known Jewish rule prohibited the wasting of food, but the evangelists relate this collection of leftovers to underline the sheer abundance of bread and fish.

And then comes the important part of the story, the big misunderstanding. The crowd, which until then had been quite undemonstrative, begins to acclaim Jesus, saying, according to John, 'This really is the prophet who is to come into the world.'[60] *The* prophet, not *a* prophet. This time, he *is* identified as the Messiah. And the Messiah, in the eyes of the people, would be the King of Israel, a political sovereign. Jesus cannot accept this mantle and escapes into the hills, alone.

What meaning can we derive from all this?

Obviously, the various accounts are littered with storyteller's touches and with number symbols. The evangelists like to place Jesus in the wake of the great prophets – if only to demonstrate that he surpassed them – and embroider their texts with biblical quotations, sometimes without acknowledging their sources, as nods to their Jewish listeners or readers. We have seen how the miracle of the loaves is reminiscent of the manna from heaven and Elisha's feeding of a hundred with a few small loaves. The leftovers of that desert meal also evoke the story of Ruth the Moabite, a 'foreigner' who had been assimilated into the Israelite community by marriage; the elderly Boaz, a wealthy and important man, who would eventually become her husband, gives her some roasted grain. 'She ate till her hunger was satisfied,' the Bible tells us, 'and she had some left over.'[61] These leftovers always show the abundant generosity of God. The green grass is reminiscent of Psalm 23:

> Yahweh is my shepherd,
> I lack nothing.
> In meadows of green grass he lets me lie....[62]

Jesus is thus presented as the shepherd of these people. Indeed, Mark had earlier said that as Jesus 'stepped ashore he saw a large crowd; and he took pity on them because they were like sheep without a shepherd'.[63]

The fact that there are five loaves and two fishes is equally meaningful. The loaves represent the five books of the Law and the fish the 'texts' and the 'prophets' that complete the Law. And this is not enough to

> satisfy the hunger of the people of God for knowledge. For the change from the Passover of the Jews to the Easter of the disciples to be possible, Jesus must give people a greater knowledge and a more nourishing manna than those of Moses.[64]

Finally, the division of people into squares of fifty and one hundred, as happens in the gospel accounts, occurs frequently in the Old Testament, both for the organisation of combat and of large meals.

Those, then, are the references to what had happened, or been written, before Jesus Christ. But we must continually keep in mind the fact that the gospels had been transmitted and written after his passage on earth by people who knew the whole story. The miracle of the loaves is clearly also an allusion to the last meal that Jesus would take with the Twelve, the Last Supper. In Mark's version, Jesus 'took the five loaves and the two fish, raised his eyes to heaven and said the blessing; then he broke the loaves and handed them to his disciples to distribute among the people'.[65] And this is Mark's version of the Last Supper: 'And as they were eating he took some bread, and when he had said the blessing he broke it and gave it to them.'[66] With the exception of the fish, the similarity is clear. What happened in the desert was afterwards interpreted as a prefiguring of the Last Supper.

What really happened?

Something significant did, without doubt. All four evangelists mention it, and, as we will see, they did not all have the same sources. Even if they were all drawing, via different routes, on the beliefs of the very first Christian community that had arisen in Jerusalem after the resurrection, it must be admitted that these people would not have pulled the story out of thin air so soon afterwards, however large their appetite for the miraculous. In any case, the evangelists do not really treat the episode as though it were miraculous or phenomenal. On the contrary, they play it down, devoting no more than an average twelve verses to it. They are more interested in what happens afterwards.

Some people have of course tried to find 'rational' explanations for the affair. The principal theory is that in fact not everyone there had set out for the day without provisions; some had come prepared; others, more fervent or less practical, had not. Seeing Jesus and his disciples sharing out their food between them in brotherly fashion, they had followed their example and given food to their neighbours so that all could eat their fill. This miracle of hearts suddenly opening is just as agreeable as the miracle of loaves produced out of thin air, but it is sheer hypothesis and unsubstantiated by a single word or fact.[67] It seems, moreover, to contradict the reactions of the crowd. If the 'miracle' had merely been one of the sharing of provisions, they would hardly have got so excited about it, and they certainly would not have seen it as a sign (as John has it) that Jesus was the awaited Messiah.

Another theory, in similar vein, has been suggested. Like every crowd, this one would have been followed by people selling food, just as today's popular gatherings have their vendors of hot dogs and soft drinks. Suddenly touched by Jesus' words and example, these people decide to give away their stocks, which they had perhaps hidden away with the aim of raising the prices. Again, this sudden conversion of speculators is a nice idea – but equally hypothetical.

The German New Testament scholar Gerd Theissen, professor of New Testament Studies at Heidelberg University, has offered another explanation, in the prudent form of a novel. He focuses on Joanna, the wife of Herod's steward, Chuza, whom Luke[68] includes in the list of women who 'provided for' Jesus and his disciples. It was she, he suggests, who sent the provisions: 'When I or others', she says, 'send him food ... and my people suddenly bring it out, the crowd thinks it's a miracle that there's so much to eat. Those poor people have often never seen so much food all at once.'[69] The people 'lose their fear of hunger. Then they get out the reserve supplies of bread that they've kept hidden so as not to have to share them with others.' However, from caution or conviction, the author then gives his characters the following dialogue:

> 'Do you think that this is an explanation of the story of the miraculous multiplication of the loaves?'
> 'Not directly. You can't say that it happened here or there. The people keep discovering the amazing way in which Jesus finds support without working, begging or organising.'

The word is not explicitly mentioned, but we have returned to the province of the miracle.

Many scholars believe that it is impossible to reconstitute the facts. 'A real incident must surely lie behind the narrative,' writes A.G. Herbert, 'but it has been so transformed that it is impossible for us to say "what happened".'[70] For the great majority of commentators, however, what happened is still important. As H. Clavier puts it,

Whatever form it took, an extraordinary event occurred in which an action by Jesus overwhelmed the minds of the people present, although not in the way that he would have hoped. That is to say, against his will, that action provoked an outburst of political and materialist messianism.[71]

This could have been more simply put, perhaps, but it takes us to the heart of the meaning of the episode. John's version and that of the other three evangelists are different but not contradictory. Let us look first at John, who as usual uses the story to theologise. After Jesus goes off alone, he says, the disciples get into a boat and cross the lake again, this time to Capernaum. After they have set off, a storm blows up; alarmed, they row as hard as they can, but then Jesus appears, walking on the water, and sorts everything out. Of course, several scholars have contested the historical authenticity of this. Others have argued about the translation: it is possible to interpret the Greek to mean that Jesus was walking not on the water but 'on the shore'. This is obviously more down to earth, so to speak, but nonetheless controversial.[72] They do not, on the whole, attach great importance to the debate. The evangelist, they say, wishes principally to show that we have entered into the mystery of Jesus' mission. His walking on the water is a new revelation of his divinity (in the Old Testament, God has mastery over the sea, of which the Jews had always been in awe, believing it to be the domain of evil powers) and also of his promise to the disciples that he would never leave them. The earliest Christian communities, and later the Church, are thus reassured that Jesus would always be with them, including in times of great difficulty. Again, we are dealing with the symbolic rather than the factual.

To return to the story. The following day, says John, the crowd get into boats and cross to Capernaum in pursuit of Jesus. This 'crowd' must have been considerably smaller than that of the previous day, since it is difficult to imagine that there were enough boats on that morning in Tiberias to transport four or five thousand men, plus women and children. When the people find him, Jesus says to them:

> You are not looking for me
> because you have seen the signs
> but because you had all the bread you wanted to eat.
> Do not work for food that cannot last,
> but work for food that endures to eternal life,
> the kind of food the Son of Man is offering you,
> for on him the Father, God Himself, has set His seal.[73]

In other words, Jesus (who is always a little provocative, but never contemptuous – he provokes in order to teach, to raise questions) tells these Galileans that they have not understood anything. Yes, he can produce bread out of thin air, but that is not the essential thing. What matters is that he can give them another kind of bread, life-giving and imperishable, and that God has sent him, the 'Son of Man', for that purpose.

He finds willing ears. 'Lord,' say these good people, 'give us that bread always.'[74] When they had first seen him on the shore they had simply called him 'Rabbi'; now he has become 'Lord'. They seem to have been enlightened, to have understood. Then Jesus launches into a long discourse in which he explains that he has been sent by the Father, that he is the bread of life and that eternal life is guaranteed to those who believe in him.[75] Was this declaration meant as the institution of the Eucharist? In his book, duly sanctioned by all the official seals of approval, Fr Léon-Dufour argues that only a 'naive reader' could believe this to be the case.[76] This is not an exact report of Jesus' words, but a re-interpretation of them, in the light of what the author has seen, heard and understood *afterwards*.

Either way, this time the discourse does not go down well. The Galileans know Jesus, Mary and Joseph, and here he is saying that he has come down from heaven. Some of them must have thought that his success the previous day had unhinged him. According to John, however, Jesus maintains his claim to be of divine origin. In another discourse on the symbolism of bread, he says that it represents his flesh and gives eternal life to those who eat it.[77] His audience begins to mutter. He insists: 'My flesh is real food, and my blood is real drink.'[78]

It is clear to anyone who reads the whole passage that John is not writing history here, but theology. He is not reporting Jesus' words but, using them as a basis, is writing a discourse of his own about the Eucharist. He is, so to speak, writing a catechism for the early Christian communities, explaining to them what the Eucharist means. And whenever he has the Jews muttering, guffawing or getting angry, he is not talking about the Galileans of Jesus' time. The objections that they are putting forward are those voiced by John's own contemporaries. The Christian communities of John's time, who had to endure these taunts and have them flung in their faces first by their opponents and later by their executioners, were still very small in number.

The scene in the gospel echoes this with its conclusion of Jesus' growing unpopularity: 'After this, many of his disciples left him and stopped going with him.'[79] Only the Twelve remain, and Peter professes his faith: 'Lord, who shall we go to? You have the message of eternal life and we believe; we know that you are the Holy One of God.'[80] And John, who does not hesitate to combine different strands of the story, then has Jesus referring to his betrayal by Judas.

John's version of the miracle therefore has two meanings. The first is biographical. The story shows Jesus moving towards apparent failure. The huge crowd of Galileans gradually diminishes until it is reduced to the Twelve, among whom, to cap it all, there is a traitor. The second is symbolic. Having distributed the bread, Jesus offers himself as the bread of life. However, unlike the manna that had fallen miraculously from the sky every morning for forty years to feed the Hebrews in the desert, this bread gives eternal life. Jesus then triumphs over malign waters to accompany his disciples, symbolising his steadfast support of those who place their trust in him.

Matthew, Mark and Luke stress the symbolism of the bread less than John, and their accounts of the miracle are not followed by a long passage on the Eucharist. They therefore allow us to concentrate on another meaning. Let us return to the desert where the crowd has had its fill of bread and fish. Thousands of them are acclaiming Jesus. There can be no doubt this time. D-Day, the moment that their fathers and their fathers' fathers and their fathers' fathers' fathers had awaited, has arrived. They all know the history of the manna. For most Jews, it was the greatest miracle of the Exodus, much greater than the parting of the Red Sea that had enabled the Hebrews to forge a dry passage through two immense, cascading walls of water. Those who could read had recited, ten times, a hundred times, in the synagogues and elsewhere, to those who could not the numerous texts that assured them that when the Messiah came, manna would fall again. And these endlessly multiplied loaves that had appeared not from the sky but in bottomless baskets were the manna for their own time, their own age. There could be no doubt. This was the Messiah.

The disciples must have shared their enthusiasm. For, according to Matthew and Mark, when Jesus leaves to escape the crowd, he 'made his disciples get into the boat'.[81] If he has to make them, it means they are reluctant. For their part, they would willingly have stayed. They would have found sudden elevation to the ranks of the intimate companions of the Messiah an agreeable prospect. They have not yet understood. Mark, who never misses an opportunity to denigrate the disciples, explains that 'their minds were closed'.[82] And to show just how closed they were, he adds another detail. After recounting several new cures – for in Mark's version, unlike John's, Jesus continues to attract the crowds after the miracle of the loaves – he relates another miracle of the loaves,[83] after which the disciples leave with Jesus in a boat. And here are these fools complaining that they are hungry because they have forgotten to bring any food with them. This time, Jesus is annoyed. Will they never understand?

'Are your minds closed? Have you eyes that do not see, ears that do not hear?'[84] The first part of the sentence is Mark's, who does not hesitate to put his own thoughts into Jesus' mouth; the second is a quotation from the Old Testament.[85]

Mark (and Matthew, who also has this second miracle) is far too harsh on the disciples. It was understandable that, witnessing these remarkable events, they should believe that an entirely new and different world was coming into being. Just like the Samaritan woman who had encountered Jesus near a well where she came every day to draw water; a dialogue ensues, during which Jesus likens himself to a spring 'welling up to eternal life'.[86] The woman obviously does not understand him. She exclaims that she will now be spared her daily chore: 'Give me some of that water, so that I ... never have to come here again to draw water.'[87]

To go by the gospel accounts, the disciples and the crowd have pretty well the same attitude. They seem to think that bread will fall from the sky, ready baked, every day. But no. Things continue in the usual way; nothing has changed on that level. Bakers and housewives must go on making bread. Doctors must go on caring for the sick. Fishermen must go on catching fish.

Albert Camus writes about Dr Rieux, one of the main characters in his novel *The Plague*: 'If he believed in an all-powerful God he would cease curing the sick and leave that to Him ... in this respect Rieux believed himself to be on the right road – in fighting against creation as he found it.'[88] He was ignorant of the lesson of the gospels: the miracles that they recount respect humankind's independence, autonomy and freedom, and God moreover proposes to make a 'Covenant' with humanity to perfect his Creation, rather than allowing them to struggle against it. The miracles in the gospels are simply momentary acts of compassion forced out of Jesus.

As we have seen, the incident of the loaves also has another, and crucial, meaning: from now on, the Jews know that they cannot count on Jesus to solve their everyday problems for them or to lead a war of liberation that would establish the society of peace, prosperity and justice of their dreams. They see this so clearly that many abandon him. His movement is now in crisis.

The gospels attribute to Jesus three resurrections from the dead: of a little girl who had just died and whose father, Jairus, was an official of the synagogue; of the son of a widow whom he had encountered at the gate of Nain as the boy's funeral cortège was making its way to the cemetery, accompanied by the sound of the *shofar* (a ram's horn with holes on either side); and of Lazarus – the most spectacular, since it occurred, according to John, four days after his death, when the corpse had begun to rot and smell.

Most Catholic commentators today stress that the word 'resurrection' is incorrect in all three cases. Anne Reboux-Caubel writes about Jairus' daughter:

> We can speak only of 'resuscitation'; she does come back to life, but she does not thereby escape the human destiny of mortality. She will still, all the same, die one day. Whereas resurrection ... involves another kind of life.[89]

A life that never ends.

Only John, that lover of theology, recounts the resurrection of Lazarus. It occurs after a difficult moment in Jesus' life. The Judaeans, or some of them at least, are about to stone him. What he does might suit some of them, but what he says is deeply disturbing. They tell him, quite bluntly: 'We are not stoning you for doing a good work, but for blasphemy; you are only a man and you claim to be God.'[90] To which he replies: 'Even if you refuse to believe in me, at least believe in the work I do; then you will know for sure that the Father is in me and I am in the Father.'[91]

He manages to escape them, and withdraws to the other side of the Jordan, near to where his cousin John baptised.

The Judaeans will indeed soon see some of Jesus' work. For a message is sent to him: his friend Lazarus is lying seriously ill at Bethany, a stone's throw from Jerusalem. This Lazarus, John tells us at the beginning of a very long passage,[92] is the brother of

Mary, a woman who had poured ointment on Jesus' feet and wiped them with her hair, to the horror of several of the disciples. Jesus immediately declares the outcome of Lazarus' illness: a miracle. 'This sickness will end not in death but in God's glory, and through it the Son of God will be glorified.' But he does not move.

He waits two days and then finally decides to go. The disciples attempt to dissuade him. To return to Judaea when the Judaeans want to kill him would be madness. Naturally, he does not listen to their arguments. 'Lazarus is dead,' he says 'and for your sake I am glad I was not there because now you will believe.' His meaning is clear: I am going to perform a miracle – or as John would say, I am going to give you another sign – so that your eyes will be opened. This time, they courageously follow him, even if with trepidation. 'Let us go too, and die with him,' says Thomas the Twin. The dramatic scene is set. We might be reading Shakespeare or listening to certain operatic choruses.

So we come to Bethany. Jesus is not mistaken. Lazarus has died and been buried for four days now. Martha, the other sister, runs to meet Jesus and says to him, in essence, 'If you had been here this would not have happened, but now you have come, anything is still possible.' Then follows a crucial dialogue. She begins by speaking of the 'resurrection on the last day', at the end of time, something in which almost all Jews believed. But he replies:

'I am the resurrection. If anyone believes in me, even though he dies he will live, and whoever lives and believes in me will never die. Do you believe this?'

To which Martha responds: 'Yes, Lord ... I believe that you are the Christ, the Son of God, the one who was to come into this world.'

It is tempting to comment that this says it all and that what happens next is nothing more than anecdote, even if it is anecdote that has impressed many people. But let us go on with the story. Martha goes to find her sister, who is weeping with the visitors who have come, as was customary, to comfort the family. Mary's tears cause Jesus 'great distress', and he speaks to her 'with a sigh that came straight from the heart', as though the confidence that he had demonstrated earlier when speaking to his disciples had deserted him. In fact, many scholars believe that this is a reference to Psalm 42 and to Jesus' emotions at his own death.[93]

Jesus goes to the tomb and orders the stone that blocks the entrance to be removed. Martha objects: 'Lord, by now he will smell; this is the fourth day.' He reassures her, reminding her of his promise: 'If you believe you will see the glory of God.' As soon as the stone has been rolled away, he thanks God for answering his prayer, although we do not yet know that it has been answered. He calls Lazarus' name. His friend emerges from the tomb, still wrapped in linen bandages, a cloth around his head, an obvious allusion to the linen bandages and cloth that would be found in the tomb in the accounts of Jesus' resurrection. But Jesus would remove his own grave clothes. It was not the same kind of resurrection. The scene ends with Jesus' order: 'Unbind him, let him go free.' Lazarus has not said a word.

Does this story have any historical reality?

Several details give it, as scholars say, a 'realistic feel': the mention of four days (the required time for the observance of a death), the stone in front of the tomb, the entourage of mourners at the home of Martha and Mary, and so on. One could add the bandages and cloth if they did not mirror what would be found in Jesus' tomb. In addition, although the episode is found only in John, the other gospels at least confirm the details. Mark has Jesus going through Bethany near the end of his life,[94] and Luke has him eating a meal at the home of Martha and Mary, although no Lazarus is mentioned. This is the famous episode in which the active Martha complains that she has had to deal with all the serving by herself while the contemplative Mary 'sat down at the Lord's feet and listened to him speaking'.[95]

However, these corroborations and clues are obviously not enough to establish that the resurrection of Lazarus actually happened. Renan, in the first edition of his *Life of Jesus*, suggested that Lazarus had been victim of a temporary syncope, a theory that was recently taken up again in a more scientific analysis by Gérald Messadié, who speaks of catalepsy or cataplexy.⁹⁶ In the third edition of his best-seller, Renan presented a rather different hypothesis: 'We are occasionally led to surmise that the Bethany family [Lazarus' two sisters] ... suffered from a certain excess of fervour.'⁹⁷ To help Jesus in his mission, they therefore invent this publicity stunt. 'A resurrection must have seemed to them the most convincing ploy. We can imagine them opening their hearts to Jesus about it.'⁹⁸ This suggestion involves a lot of surmising, making the book's success with people who considered themselves rational and scientific somewhat surprising. Modern scholars, Catholics included, do not surmise. They declare quite openly, like Fr Léon-Dufour, that 'the historian of today is at a loss, and yet he must offer some kind of solution.'⁹⁹

Some commentators have compared this scene in John with a story told by Jesus in Luke,¹⁰⁰ in which a poor man named Lazarus, covered with sores, which even dogs come to lick, lives at the gate of an unnamed rich man. Lazarus dies and is taken by the angels to Abraham, where he is restored to happiness. The rich man, who had been indifferent to Lazarus' suffering, also dies and finds himself in hell, where, looking up, he sees the poor wretch whom he had despised in life. He beseeches Abraham to relieve his agony in the flames, but it is too late. So he asks for Lazarus to be sent to his five living brothers so that they can avoid 'this place of torment' after their own deaths. Abraham replies that they have only to listen to Moses and the prophets. The rich man, however, has no illusions about his brothers' faith: 'but if someone comes to them from the dead, they will repent'. Abraham replies, 'If they will not listen either to Moses or to the prophets, they will not be convinced even if someone should rise from the dead.' John, according to these scholars, transformed this parable into a biographical episode, but only the name Lazarus and the conclusion of the story back up this unprovable theory. According to others, the parable in Luke and the episode in John were based on the same incident of healing, which got transformed in the telling into a story of resurrection.[101]

Most contemporary scholars, including Catholics, believe that the story of the resurrection of Lazarus was loosely based on 'a Jewish tradition of a return to life'[102] which John would have combined with some unknown deed of Jesus, probably a spectacular healing, to advance his various theological aims. The prefiguring of Jesus' resurrection and victory over death is obvious. As early as AD 202, St Irenaeus had commented: 'The dead man emerged, his feet and hands wrapped in bands, symbolising man wrapped in sin.'[103] And Jesus has him untied, liberates him. The essence of the story, of course, is in the dialogue between Jesus and Martha when Jesus says: 'I am the resurrection. If anyone believes in me, even though he dies he will live.' Martha replies, 'Yes, Lord.... I believe that you are the Christ, the Son of God.'

9

The Message

THEY nearly always called him 'Rabbi', that is, 'Master.' The title was in no way an official one but was conferred on people who taught and who gathered a group of disciples around them.

This particular rabbi led an energetic campaign, ceaselessly teaching, explaining, proclaiming. He had spent his first thirty years in a small village, and his examples and references were taken from everyday country life, never from the lives of city-dwellers. He expressed himself in the language of the people, in a style that was sometimes poetic but always concrete. To explain that charity should not be ostentatious, he said: 'When you give alms, do not have it trumpeted before you.'[1]

As a man from the Middle East, he was not frightened of exaggeration, speaking of a 'plank' in the eye, of faith that moves mountains, of a camel trying to squeeze through the eye of a needle, and so on. And he did not hesitate to poke gentle fun at people. Speaking to Nicodemus, a leading Pharisee, and a sympathiser, he jibed: 'You, a teacher in Israel, and you do not know these things!... We speak only about what we know.'[2] When the Samaritan woman told him that she had no husband, he replied, 'You are right to say, "I have no husband," for although you have had five, the one you have now is not your husband.'[3]

This style had some success, according to Mark. 'And his teaching made a great impression on them because, unlike the scribes, he taught them with authority.'[4] The scribes apparently vied with one another in delivering great doctrinal monologues that went completely over the heads of most Galileans and Judaeans.

He often spoke in parables. The gospels contain around fifty or so,[5] John being the exception, as usual, in having only five, all different from those of the other evangelists. In Greek, 'parable' meant 'comparison'. A parable is a short story full of imagery and imagination, which usually calls on the listeners' experience of daily life, and which enables a great truth to be more easily understood, in the way that a small torch can help us find a precious object in the dark. Rabbis frequently used parables (called *mashal*), and the young Jesus would undoubtedly have often heard them at the synagogue, remembering some that would later inspire him.[6]

Although their meaning is often crystal clear, the parables pose two kinds of interpretative problem. The story of the dishonest steward who had wasted his master's property[7] provides an example. The man is denounced, and the master orders him to draw up his accounts before leaving the master's employment. With a knife at his throat, therefore, this wheeler-dealer calls on each of his master's debtors, asking them to falsify their bonds, reducing the amount they owe. A good method, he thinks to himself, of winning friends and influencing people for when he is jobless. Such behaviour obviously has little to recommend it, yet Jesus concludes:

> The master praised the dishonest steward for his astuteness. For the children of this world are more astute in dealing with their own kind than are the children of light. And so I tell you this: use money, tainted as it is, to win you friends, and thus make sure that when it fails you, they will welcome you into the tents of eternity.

Here we have a parable that has caused difficulties for many a preacher and which many readers of the gospel prefer to ignore. What is going on? Jesus does not utter a word of reproach to this thief who, having been found out, steals yet more! Even the author of the gospel, it seems, had doubts about it, gathering several sayings of Jesus together and adding them to the parable – 'You cannot be the slave both of God and of money,'[8] for example – so as to make sure that his audience does not draw the wrong conclusions.

Now what Jesus means is that we must, like the steward, confront and prepare for the difficulties that arise in life, including, of course, death: make your peace with the material things of the world so that you will be fulfilled in the hereafter. It is the forethought and the cleverness of the thief he admires, not the theft. In other words, not all the characters in the parables are examples to follow, and not all the details in them have a hidden meaning. Often they are just for decoration, to make the story more interesting and more realistic. Obviously, this is not always the case. Sometimes the details are important. But to interpret a parable properly, one must always look for the 'point', the essential meaning. Luckily, this is usually the most obvious one. A parable is meant to enlighten, not to obscure.

A passage in Mark, however, does not follow this rule. And this is the second difficulty. Jesus has just told the famous parable of the sower[9] whose seed falls onto the path where the birds soon peck it up, onto stony ground where it cannot take root properly, onto thorns where it is choked, and finally onto good soil where it produces a crop. Then, when he is alone with the disciples, he interprets the parable to them. The seed represents the word of God, the birds Satan, the rocky ground unstable, superficial people who change their mind at the least opposition, and the thorns the cares and the attractions of the world and its riches.[10] So much is clear.

But the disciples, like us, are puzzled: why talk in parables only to have to decode them afterwards? Jesus' reply (according to the translators of the *Jerusalem Bible*) is this:

> The secret of the Kingdom of God is given to you, but to those who are outside everything comes in parables so that they may see and see again, but not perceive; may hear and hear again, but not understand; otherwise they might be converted and be forgiven.[11]

And that is not clear at all. If there is one passage of the gospel that has given the commentators, preachers and exegetes headaches, this is it. Would Jesus have worn himself out speaking in parables in the express aim of not being understood, or understood by only a few people.? Such an aim would seem to reveal very strange logic and would contradict the words of this same evangelist: 'Using many parables like these, he spoke the word to them, so far as they were capable of understanding it.'[12]

How do we unravel these contradictions? Three explanations have been given:

1. Matthew gives a quite different interpretation of Jesus' words. When the disciples ask him why he speaks in parables, he replies, 'Because ... the mysteries of the Kingdom of Heaven are revealed to you, but they are not revealed to them.... The reason I talk to them in parables is that they look without seeing and listen without hearing or understanding.' In other words, the parable is designed to help them hear and understand, which is reassuring.

2. Jesus is here quoting a passage from Isaiah, who, seven centuries earlier, had complained that he was preaching in a wilderness, that none of his contemporaries heard what he was saying. Exasperated, the prophet derides his audience and tries to provoke them into a healthier attitude by having God say to him, in effect: 'Go and speak to them so that they do not understand you and will not convert.' Jesus, who also feels that he is not properly heard, takes up Isaiah's words and uses them to people who know their meaning and context. It is as though he is giving them a knowing and provocative wink, in order to be better heard and understood.[13]

3. The parables are accessible only to those who want to understand them, who are open to the Word and who do not close their eyes or their ears. To be understood, parables assume a certain involvement on the part of the listener. What seems like a pleasant little story can, if the listener is inclined to interpret it, actually turn into a teaching on God and His Kingdom.

Let us now move on to the essential aspect of the parables. What did Jesus say through them or through his sermons, such as the Sermon on the Mount (the Beatitudes)? Essentially, he was proclaiming a new society. Or, even more than that, a new world.

* * *

A new world was exactly what his audience was waiting for. This small nation of people divided into sects and parties, rich and poor, resistance fighters and collaborators, racked with bitterness and regrets, all repeated to themselves the glorious declarations of the prophets and awaited the dawning of those sunlit days when all the promises would be fulfilled and the King of Israel, who would reign over all nations, would be enthroned. As the prophet Zechariah had exulted:

> Shout with gladness, daughter of Jerusalem!
> See now, your king comes to you;
> he is victorious, he is triumphant,
> humble and riding on a donkey,
> ... the bow of war will be banished.
> He will proclaim peace for the nations.
> His empire shall stretch from sea to sea,
> from the River to the ends of the earth.[14]

They also knew the portrait of the Messiah painted by Psalm 72:

> ... all kings will do him homage,
>   all nations become his servants.
>
> He will free the poor man who calls to him,
>   and those who need help,
> he will have pity on the poor and feeble,
>   and save the lives of those in need;
>
> he will redeem their lives from exploitation and outrage ...[15]

Waiting for the fulfilment of these prophecies, the people of Israel were getting a little angry, a little impatient. God had already manifested Himself as their King, delivering His people from the Egyptian bondage by granting them a series of miracles enabling them to escape Pharaoh's cavalry and then starvation in the desert – and yet He was now allowing His own people to be humiliated, oppressed and maltreated. Things could not go on like this. And here was Jesus saying, 'The time has come ... and the Kingdom of God is close at hand. Repent and believe the Good News'.[16] Generations of preachers have, incidentally, used this phrase to induce guilt in their flocks, without realising that the true meaning of the Greek word translated in the gospels as 're- pent' was not 'to pour ashes on one's head' but to change one's mind, one's ideas, so that a new way of life could be adopted.[17] And Jesus was going much further than that; he was claiming that the reign of God had already begun.

What did he mean – already begun? Injustice still held sway, the poor were still oppressed, the powerless still had no voice and Roman feet were still marching through the streets of Jerusalem and of Judaea. It is not hard to understand why Jesus' listeners were confused, perplexed, disappointed. For them – as for most of us – a kingdom was a territory or a state governed by a king and, in this case, no ordinary king, but God Himself. But according to Jesus, 'The coming of the kingdom of God does not admit of ob- servation.... the Kingdom of God is among you.'[18] And, 'Anyone who does not welcome the Kingdom of God like a little child will never enter it.'[19] Such words could obviously not be applied to a territory or a state and did not involve politics or power. They had nothing to do with a king of Israel whose sovereignty would stretch 'from sea to sea' and to whom every other king would do homage.

So what did Jesus mean? First, and fundamentally, that the Kingdom of God had arrived because Jesus had come. 'Since John the Baptist came, up to this present time, the Kingdom of Heaven has been subjected to violence and the violent are taking it by storm,' Jesus said in Matthew.[20] This allusion to 'violence' has given rise to various interpretations and translations, but the pas- sage indicates, at least, the presence of the Kingdom. Secondly, he meant that the Kingdom of God, the new society, existed but had not been completed. It was a story that was still being told. 'The Kingdom of Heaven is like the yeast a woman took and mixed in with three measures of flour till it was leavened all through,'[21] and it is also 'like a mustard seed which a man took and threw into his garden; it grew and became a tree, and the birds of the air sheltered in its branches'.[22] The new society would begin among humankind and would develop amongst them. That is why, when his disciples ask him to teach them how to pray and he teaches them (in Matthew and Luke, though in slightly different versions[23]) 'Our Father', he tells them to ask God, the Father, that 'Your Kingdom come'. He has begun the work and instituted the age of salvation, but people must undertake, with him, the construction of the Kingdom. It is for this that Jesus recruited the Twelve and the other disciples, that he launched his campaign, and that he demanded 'repentance' – which did not mean that people should flagellate themselves, beat their breasts or believe that they were invariably at fault. It meant that they should change their way of life.

How was this to be done? Through the heart, always. One had to lose one's heart to this new society and do everything for love – and everything really meant everything, without exception. What is more, compliance with this rule was not some great feat of piety. It was no more than the bare minimum. 'When you have done all you have been told to do, say, "We are merely servants; we have done no more than our duty."'[24] Perhaps even more startling, this love was not to be shown only to fellow members of the new society but to everyone, including those who were ignorant of, indifferent to, or even hostile to it. Sigmund Freud believed that groups of people in which a real harmony and mutual love existed had to direct towards external groups the aggression that could not be expressed internally: 'It is always possible to unite considerable numbers of men in love towards one another, so long as there are still some remaining as objects for aggressive manifestations.'[25] Yet the law of the new society goes beyond that. One must love everybody. The Judaean must love the Samaritan, his traditional and inveterate enemy. And the Samaritan must love the Judaean. But to love was not just to experience good or pleasant feelings towards someone: 'Love your enemies, do good to those who hate you, bless those who curse you, pray for those who treat you badly.'[26]

This was something of a tall order. Prophets before Jesus had said that people should love one another, and the rabbis repeated their message. Indeed, he himself, when interrogated by the Pharisees (those lovers of precision) who want to know what commandment he thinks is the most important, had first quoted Deuteronomy: 'You will love the Lord your God with all your heart, with all your soul, with all your strength.'[27] And then another biblical text, Leviticus: 'You must love your neighbour as yourself.'[28] But no one had gone as far as Jesus did. David Flusser of the Hebrew University of Jerusalem writes:

> The commandment to love one's enemies is so much [Jesus'] definitive characteristic that his are the only lips from which we hear the commandment in the whole of the New Testament.[29]

And:

> Although not really a Pharisee himself, he was closest to the Pharisees of the school of Hillel who preached love, but he pointed the way further to unconditional love – even of one's enemies and of sinners. As we shall see, this was no sentimental love.[30]

Indeed not. It was a love that would in fact lead Jesus to attack religious rules, money and power. Jesus did not despise religious rules. He followed them. But for him they were secondary to the essence of things. Talking of the religious tax, the tithe, he cried,

> Alas for you, scribes and Pharisees, you hypocrites! You who pay your tithe of mint and dill and cummin and have neglected the weightier matters of the Law – justice, mercy, good faith! These you should have practised, without neglecting the others. You blind guides! Straining out gnats and swallowing camels![31]

Similarly, it is well known that Jesus respected the rules of the sabbath, attending worship at the synagogue. But for him, 'the

sabbath was made for man, not man for the sabbath'.[32] Other rabbis had said as much. Simon Menasha, for example, who had said
(commenting on the passage in the book of Exodus where the
Eternal speaks to Moses about the sabbath), 'The sabbath has been
"delivered" to you, but you have not been "delivered" to the sabbath.' Admittedly, those who spoke like this did not go on to draw
any conclusions about religious formalism. Jesus acted on his
teaching, healing people on the sabbath who were not at death's
door and who could doubtless have been cured the following day
– although that would of course have meant that they would
suffer until the following day.

As always happens, over the centuries the Law of Moses had
been encrusted with a multitude of traditions that, once upon a
time, had had some reason and justification. It is true that the rabbis had also occasionally softened the proscriptions to make it easier to respect the Law. But Jesus went much further. He placed
individual conscience above the traditions and rules, and he did
not construct an elaborate system of precepts himself. This is not
to say that he was permissive or lax. 'Love your enemies, do good
to those who hate you, bless those who curse you, pray for those
who treat you badly' – that was a tough demand, for to love the
whole world requires great selflessness. But Jesus placed this
commandment above all other commandments, even the religious
ones.

Selflessness also raises the question of money. The story of the
rich young man is well known. Kneeling before Jesus, he asks
him, 'Good master, what must I do to inherit eternal life?' He is
told that he must obey the commandments. The young man assures Jesus that he has 'kept all these from my earliest days'. This
young man was therefore a good young man, and Jesus, says
Mark,[33] loves him. There is just one problem. 'There is one thing
you lack. Go and sell everything you own and give the money to
the poor ... then come, follow me.' The young man, crestfallen,
turns away and leaves, 'for he was a man of great wealth'. Jesus,
contrary to what is often written, did not condemn him. He

simply, and sadly, observed: 'How hard it is for those who have riches to enter the Kingdom of God!' There then follows the celebrated image of the rich man and the eye of a needle. The disciples, however, who doubtless had not themselves lost all interest in money, wondered, 'In that case ... who can be saved?' Jesus replies that 'everything is possible for God'. Even threading a camel through the eye of a needle.

Money had always had a bad reputation among the prophets. Renan remarks that they had established 'a close relationship between the words "rich", "impious", "violent" and "wicked"' on the one hand and between "poor", "gentle", "humble" and "pious" on the other.'[34] Psalm 69 – among many others – cries, 'Yahweh will always hear those who are in need.'[35] Jesus was in complete agreement with this teaching. As we know, he stressed that no one could serve both God and money, and he continually demonstrated his preference for the poor and the despised. However, unlike the Essenes, for example, he does not reject the rich simply because they *are* rich. He welcomes them, listens to them and counts them among his friends. Renunciation of wealth is not an absolute condition of entry into the new society, even if it can sometimes be so. Money and possessions are tools. What matters is how they are used. As the conclusion of the story of the dishonest steward puts it, 'use money, tainted as it is, to win you friends'. In other words, money is a serious obstacle, but you should be prudent and careful with it and sensible enough to invest it wisely, so that you will one day reap the rewards in the form of eternal life – and I, Jesus, wish you luck because it will not be easy. Money, Mammon, will always try to get you in its grip and onto its side, and it has the trump card because you cannot live without it. It is dressed beautifully, in many lovely colours; but look instead at the birds of the air, which are not exactly ugly either and yet do not sow crops or amass wealth.

The other temptress that prevents people from joining the new society is the taste for power. And so James and John, the sons of Zebedee, get what we would call swollen egos at Jesus' success (although the episode occurs, according to Mark, at the time of the entry into Jerusalem, when things had begun to go badly wrong). James and John foolishly go and ask Jesus if they can sit in the seats of honour, 'one at your right hand and the other at your left'. Jesus uses this to give a teaching to the whole of his small band:

> You know that among the pagans their so-called rulers lord it over them.... This is not to happen among you. No; anyone who wants to become great among you must be your servant, and anyone who wants to be first among you must be slave to all.[36]

These are words that Luke attributes to Jesus during the Last Supper (with the addition that the greatest is the one who serves at table, not he who is waited on[37]), while John, also during the Last Supper, has Jesus washing his disciples' feet[38].

He who wants to be the greatest must be everyone's slave! It is difficult to find anything so revolutionary in the texts of the prophets or in the psalms. Did Jesus mean that the love of power was worse than the love of money, even though the two are so often linked? In any event, the teaching is clear: in the new society, each must be the servant of all the others. It is a teaching that perhaps deserves more attention than the famous debate about the tax payable to Caesar.

The story is well known and has inspired much commentary. Jesus is concerned with the Kingdom of God, concentrates on the highest matter, and they come to talk to him about something trivial and ephemeral (although, as he knows very well, it is certainly important to the Jews, who cannot easily accept the occupation of their country by a foreign power). 'Is it permissible to pay taxes to Caesar or not?'[39] They all know that the question is a trap. To reply that the tax must be paid was to pass for a docile subject of the occupier, or even an active collaborator, while to say that the tax should not be paid was to put oneself in the ranks of the followers of the rebel Judas the Galilean, who had incited people to withhold its payment. Jesus, however, extricates himself by showing them a coin: 'Whose head is this?' he asks. 'Caesar's.' 'Very well, give back to Caesar what belongs to Caesar – and to God what belongs to God.'

Was Jesus just cleverly side-stepping the issue? Partly. These people do not agonise over the question when it comes to spending money, so why are they suddenly so scrupulous? Why does their faith forbid them to use Caesar's effigy when they are paying the tax, but not when they buy, sell, borrow or lend? Jesus' answer puts them firmly in their place. But there is also a teaching behind his reply. The words do not imply a clear separation between affairs of state and those of God so that the state has absolute autonomy. This interpretation of Jesus' words certainly has the happy consequence of preventing too close a relationship between politics and religion, and of demonstrating that God respects, in this area as in others, human freedom. But this was not Jesus' real point, because he would not have placed dues to Caesar and dues to God on the same level. What is due to God – that is everything. In fact, Jesus was re-establishing the true hierarchy. Caesar made himself revered and venerated as a god, but Jesus was affirming that God was greater than all the Caesars, all the powers and all the states. Among the principal victims of Jesus' reply, therefore, is the totalitarian state, which claims absolute power.

But we must be careful. God is not greater than all the Caesars and all the kings because He out-Caesars the Caesars, because He has the same powers but simply more of them. That vision of a divine Top Dog who owes his position to the magical powers that he possesses was the very vision that Jesus wanted to overturn. But it blossomed, nonetheless, and has continued to blossom over the centuries. Many people have had and have such a vision of God, including those claiming to be Jesus' disciples. But the true God proclaimed by Jesus was the Father of the parable of the prodigal son.[40] One of His sons leaves home, taking advantage of his freedom. If, as certain of His traditional interpreters and their modern counterparts have claimed, God demanded obedience to hundreds of rules and regulations, along with hundreds of commentaries and additions, such a bid for independence would be commendable. To be a human being is to escape from such a father. And even when the son returns, he has not understood who God the Father really is. He still thinks that he has to appease His anger by being treated as one of His servants. The other, dutiful, son is equally deluded; he thinks that his Father should reward him and punish the prodigal. Yet God hugs the first and comforts the second. We must celebrate, He tells him, because your brother has come back.

The God of this parable has no relation to the one presented by a certain kind of Christianity, who can be summed up as follows. In the beginning, He placed His trust in humankind, but the first of them abused that trust, and that was the original sin. Furious, God punishes them, and their descendants with them, and then, to reconcile humanity to Him, He demands a sacrifice. As He is truly good, He decides to sacrifice His own son – that is, Himself in another guise. Jesus therefore came to 'wipe out original sin' and to appease his Father's wrath by the sacrifice of his death. So goes the formula, variously expressed, in many religious books and sermons.

Jesus' teaching is in complete contrast to this. He never spoke of original sin; everything he said ran counter to the notion of a collective guilt that would fall on generation after generation. He never talked of the expiation of sins being the condition of entry into the new society, into the Kingdom. On the contrary, one's very entry into the Kingdom means that one's sins have been washed away – which does not mean that this Kingdom is one where anything goes, for as we have seen the rules of the new society are truly demanding. Jesus never presented God as an accountant noting everyone's faults in a large audit book or in the memory of a huge computer, and marking them up as debts to Him. All the parables show that what was important in God's eyes was that people *are* what they made of themselves. Jesus never claimed that he had to die to 'atone for' humanity's sins. This would mean that a God who demanded, through His son, that one should forgive 'seventy-seven times seven' – that is, always – would Himself be unable to do as much. It would also mean that the father of the prodigal son would desire the death of an inno-cent son or resign himself to it in the name of I-don't-know-what rule or inevitability. And that would be completely nonsensical.

In fact, Jesus called people to joy and to a renewal of the Covenant between God and men. There are many calls to joy in the gospels: 'The Kingdom of Heaven may be compared to a king who gave a feast for his son's wedding;'[41] 'You will eat and drink at my table in my kingdom;'[42] 'Rejoice with me.... I have found my sheep that was lost;'[43] 'The Kingdom of Heaven is like treasure hidden in a field which someone has found; he hides it again, goes off happy, sells everything he owns and buys the field'[44] – and so on.

It is also true, of course, that in Matthew Jesus says, 'If anyone wants to be a follower of mine, let him renounce himself and take up his cross and follow me.' But this comes in a passage in which Jesus announces his Passion and begins 'to make it clear to his dis-ciples' that he must go to Jerusalem, suffer much there, be killed and 'be raised up on the third day'.[45] A number of scholars be-lieve that such a precise prediction must be an addition. The allu-sion to the third day, like the mention of the cross, would have been put in Jesus' mouth after the events by someone who knew his story. It is moreover difficult to imagine that Jesus, who would feel the cross on his shoulders only at the time of his death, would have asked his future disciples voluntarily to take up such a bur-den before their trials had begun. Earlier in the gospel, Jesus had said that his disciples must 'shoulder my yoke', but he immed-iately adds, 'my yoke is easy and my burden light'.[46] The historian Jean-Paul Roux tells us that the yoke 'became a symbol of servi-tude (the "Roman yoke"), but originally it symbolised only re-integration into society'.[47]

The yoke was therefore another sign of the renewed Covenant, the Covenant that Jesus would re-evoke at the Last Supper: 'This cup is the new covenant in my blood,'[48] the Covenant between God and man that would fulfil Creation. For the world had not been created fully formed and complete. Genesis relates the story of the Creation as a series of divine interventions to reduce the initial chaos and make a world fit for human habitation.[49] And then God stopped creating. It was the 'seventh day'. Since the 'previous day', He had had a partner, humankind. With them, He would pursue the goal of fighting evil. That was the first Covenant between the Creator and the whole of humanity. According to the gospels, Jesus had come to renew that partnership with God after people had – from stupidity, love of money or power, and selfishness – rejected it. In the eyes of believers, this is still the seventh day.[50]

IO

The Opposition Mounts

THE more he preaches, the greater the threats against him. On one occasion, he dines at a Pharisee's house, and a row erupts because Jesus does not begin with the ritual ablutions. His host expresses surprise, as do the lawyers (that is, those appointed to interpret the Law). Jesus replies, addressing the Pharisees as a whole: 'You clean the outside of cup and plate, while inside yourselves you are filled with extortion and wickedness.' And then to the lawyers: 'You load on men burdens that are unendurable, burdens that you yourselves do not move a finger to lift.' The meal evidently ends badly. Jesus leaves, and the others, according to Luke, 'began a furious attack on him' and plot 'to catch him out in something he might say', trying, that is, to force him to say something contradictory or blasphemous.[1] A little later, according to the same evangelist, some Pharisees go to Jesus as he is making his way to Jerusalem and warn him. '"Go away", they said. "Leave this place, because Herod means to kill you.'"[2] It is perhaps meant sincerely – or it might have been a threat. Whatever the case, there is clearly growing conflict.

Why should there be such a threat against a man who goes from village to village proclaiming, in every possible way, a message of total love? There are several answers to that question. The first concerns Jesus' attitude to the law of Moses, the Torah. This attitude is apparently contradictory. On the one hand, Jesus says, 'Do not imagine that I have come to abolish the Law or the Prophets. I have come not to abolish but to complete them.'[3] And, as we have noted, he often behaves like a good Jew: he quotes the Scriptures, he observes most Jewish customs, even if he takes certain liberties with the sabbath, he almost always practises the ritual purificatory ablutions – if he did not, the rigorous Pharisees would never, ever, have invited him to dine with them – he wears tassels on his shawl. It is true that he occasionally bends these rules, particularly those that had been laid down by the scribes or the lawyers, but he was far from being the only one to do so. Certain Jews at the time thought that it was 'intolerable' that they should wear tassels, for example. And there were other such debates. This was a nation divided on many issues, including the observation of religious rules.

On the other hand, Jesus proclaimed, in the famous Sermon on the Mount: 'You have learnt how it was said to our ancestors ... You must love your neighbour and hate your enemy,' and five times he repeats the formula, 'But I say this to you,...'[4] thereby placing his own authority in opposition to that of the Law and the prophets. Now Moses had not claimed to be the author of the Law, since it had been given to him by God on Mount Sinai, any more than the prophets had claimed to be the authors of their words or imprecations; when they laid down rules or denounced infringements, they always added, 'thus spoke Yahweh' or 'the oracle of Yahweh'. Jesus, however, spoke in his own name. And he forgave sins. The prophets would never have presumed to do that, for in their eyes that was the sole prerogative of God. They simply advised the faithful to repent so that God could forgive them. Whereas Jesus had proclaimed, for example, that the sins of the woman who had wiped his feet with her hair during a meal with a horrified Simon the Pharisee were forgiven. And he had not even demanded any form of penance from her: 'Her sins, her many sins, have been forgiven her, or she would not have shown such great love.' Then he addresses the woman: 'Your faith has saved you; go in peace.' It is therefore faith, not repentance or sacrifice, that saves. But the guests at the meal say to themselves, 'Who is this man, that he even forgives sins?'[5] Who was this man who attributed God's powers to himself?

Jesus also said that he brought a new revelation, a new message from God to men: 'My teaching is not from myself: it comes from one who sent me.'[6] He could, just, get away with that; the prophets had spoken in this way. But he adds later, 'The Father and I are one'. John, never slow to see an opportunity for some theologising, explains, 'Not content with breaking the sabbath, he spoke of God as his own Father and so made himself God's equal.'[7]

In fact, however, this apparent contradiction means little. If Jesus said that he had come to 'complete the Law', that meant that it had not reached its definitive stage, that it was only a rough outline, a sketch, a mustard seed – to use a gospel expression – that was meant to be developed. As Gérard Israël writes, 'Even if Christianity was, from its inception, the completion of Judaism and did not intend to break with it, the Jewish religion was no less outgrown or obsolete.'[8] The Sermon on the Mount with its 'You have learnt ...', and its five-times repeated 'But I say this to you ...' demonstrates a more absolute opposition. But the end result is the same. Whether the Law was superseded or directly opposed, it no longer had authority and the Torah had outlived its usefulness. And if the Torah had outlived its usefulness, a new image of God had come into being and – less significantly, of course, except for Jesus' Jewish contemporaries – the politico-religious power of the Temple was threatened. Eventually, although Jesus' audiences did not realise it straightaway, this transcending of the Law would also call Israel's national identity into question.

The image of God that was prevalent then, and which is still largely prevalent today, was that of a judging, legislative Being who rewarded each according to his merits. In this vision, God was like a powerful merchant who traded benefits for prayers, or even one of those vending machines that deliver a coffee or a can of drink if money is put into the right slot: in exchange for a sacrifice or a lamentation, He would automatically grant a request for a healing, the success of some venture or a reconciliation. The parable of the eleventh-hour labourers who were just as well paid as the first shows clearly that the God whom Jesus proclaimed did not keep an precise tally of merit marks and could not be reduced to a mechanical, predictable Being who would automatically reward good actions and punish bad. As Eduard Schweizer, a Protestant New Testament scholar at Zurich University, writes, 'When a person thinks he has some claim to a reward, he does away with God,'[9] because he limits His freedom. It is impossible to take out a comprehensive insurance policy with God or bargain with Him in a tit-for-tat exchange.

The real image of Jesus' God is one of a Father, as has already been emphasised apropos the parable of the prodigal son. When Jesus teaches his disciples to pray, it is with the 'Our Father'. This prayer, whose authenticity is rarely doubted, and which most scholars believe was originally in Aramaic,[10] is in some ways like the *kiddush*, one of the few Jewish prayers in Aramaic. It was a prayer of the Jewish Jesus.[11] Certain biblical texts spoke of God as Father, as did the Dead Sea Scrolls. But, writes the Dominican Fr Refoulé, 'The fatherhood of God is not a dominant theme in the Old Testament or in first century Judaism.'[12]

The word 'Father' evokes many different images. Now the best specialists think that Jesus would actually have used the Aramaic word *Abba*, which means something like 'Daddy'. The 'Father' of Luke's gospel is simply the Greek translation of *Abba*. When, in Mark's version of the night in the Garden of Gethsemane, Jesus is overwhelmed with a sense of failure and with terror at his impending death, he uses the word *Abba* followed by the Greek translation.[13] *Abba* was a child's word. 'It is undoubtedly', writes Joachim Jeremias,

> a way of speaking that is absolutely peculiar to Jesus and which expresses his omniscience and his consciousness that he was sent by the Father.[14]... In passing his prayer on to men, Jesus was elevating them to his own level, one on which God was addressed as 'Daddy'.[15]

To get close to this God, then, one had to become like a child.

Mark recounts a scene that encapsulates this aspect of Jesus' teaching. Jesus is, as usual, preaching, when small children are brought to him so that he can touch them, lay hands on them. The mothers crowd round Jesus, their offspring – perhaps yelling or crying – in their arms. And his disciples try to stop them. This makes Jesus angry. He is truly furious. 'Let the little children come to me; do not stop them; for it is to such as these that the Kingdom of God belongs. I tell you solemnly, anyone who does not welcome the Kingdom of God like a little child will never enter it.' And so saying, he kisses the children, and blesses them by laying his hands on them.[16]

We must understand the disciples. At that time and throughout that society, children were not little kings and queens, enjoying the lavish attention that they do today. A child had more duties than rights: 'A wise son is his father's joy, a foolish son his mother's grief,'[17] and, 'The stick and the reprimand bestow wisdom; a child left to himself brings shame on his mother,'[18] says the Bible. Such sayings were plentiful. In addition, children had only a tiny place in religious affairs, because they were too young to obey the Law. And it was to these second-class citizens that Jesus was giving pride of place, whom he was ushering into his new society of the Kingdom of God. Accompanying them in this privileged access were the blind, the lame, the paralysed, lepers, prostitutes, and all those who were in varying degrees on the fringes of, even excluded from, society. As long as they had the soul of a child and were able to accept the gift of God, the love of their Daddy, they were welcomed into His Kingdom like princes.

The Father of the prodigal son did not want his son to repent, to become his servant, to kneel at his feet or beg his forgiveness. He did not launch into recriminations along the lines of 'You would insist on having your own way.... I warned you ...'. No, he weeps with joy and hugs his child who has returned home. The only thing that he expects is that his child rejoice in the love of his Father – and that the celebrations should begin.

Jesus, then, is someone who stresses the demanding nature of

God – difficult demands of love and self-giving, with all that that entails – but who does away with the notion of a judging, legalistic God that is so useful for maintaining order in this world. 'Before Abraham was, I am,' he said, and, as John stresses, he dared to claim that he was 'God's equal'; he also dared to demand that he be honoured in the same way as the Father.[19] The amazing thing, according to the German commentator Rudolf Augstein, who finds evidence in this of the gospels' implausibility, was that when he said such things he was not immediately 'lynched by outraged Jews and stoned, without further ado'.[20] But a careful reading of the gospels makes it clear that Jesus narrowly escaped just such a fate on several occasions.

Such an image of God and Jesus' claim to have an intimate relationship with Him not only seemed blasphemous to some of his audience, but it also had very practical consequences for the Temple hierarchy. Such a God had no need of sacrifices – and indeed, much later, the prohibition of human sacrifice was one of the main charges that the philosopher Nietzsche laid at the door of Christianity.[21] The biblical tradition had already turned away from such sacrifice, as is shown by the scene in which God holds back Abraham's arm as he was about to sacrifice his son Isaac to Him. But John the Baptist, as we have seen, took the idea a stage further: even the sacrifice of animals was unnecessary. Jesus had largely confirmed this. In his eyes, sacrifices were idolatrous. In writings of the Ebionites, a Judaeo-Christian sect[22] that denied Jesus' divinity, Jesus even declares: 'I have come to abolish sacrifices, and if you do not turn away from sacrifices, anger will not turn away from you.' Many scholars believe that this must be put in the context of a polemic between the Jews and the first Christian communities, but the fact that such a polemic existed shows how important this question of sacrifice was. In attacking it, John the Baptist and Jesus were not being totally original. The prophet Hosea had said before them: 'What I want is love, not sacrifice.'[23] And the Essenes (this is one point, at least, on which Jesus' teaching was similar to theirs) also believed that sacrifices were unnecessary – or at least that the ritual sacrifices carried out at the Temple were, for among themselves they still performed them.

Jesus' condemnation of sacrifice was radical. It threatened the finances and the religious practices of the Temple,[24] and therefore its authority. It roused the hostility of all those who depended on the Temple for their living, from the High Priest to the Levites, from the sellers of doves to the inhabitants of Jerusalem. That was a lot of people. And then there were the Romans, who also found it convenient to support the Temple. And when Jesus put his words into action and chased the traders from the Temple, an incident that as we shall see was limited but significant, and when he announced the destruction of the Temple, he provoked an absolute hatred.

Other Jews, who were less tied to the Temple and even critical of it themselves, were nonetheless quick to line up against him. They believed that his teachings, which overturned the religion of Israel, endangered the very existence of that small country, occupied by the Romans and isolated in a Mediterranean world dominated by Greek culture. These people had, in spite of everything, stubbornly clung to their belief in the one God. They had refused to bow down to the idols that were so firmly established in culture and worship elsewhere, including among their conquerors. Their ability thus to hold firm was due partly to their complex structure of beliefs, rites and observances. They believed that if those observances were no longer followed or were considered relatively unimportant, the whole structure was in danger of collapsing.

In the eyes of these people, therefore, everything hung together. That is why they insisted that pagans entering Jewish communities, particularly those who had been dispersed throughout Egypt or Syria, followed all the observances laid down by the Law, without exception. Contrary to popular belief, Israel did not see its God as its exclusive property. Had He not promised Abraham to bless in him 'all the families of the earth'? And everyone knows the story of Jonah, who was punished because he refused to go and proclaim the one God to the pagans of Nineveh. But not all Jews had learnt the lessons of these stories; some preferred to take as their guide a passage from Sirach, which had become one of Judaism's favourite texts:

> If you do a good turn, know for whom you are doing it,
>> and your good deeds will not go to waste.
> Do good to a devout man, and you will receive a reward,
>> if not from him, then certainly from the Most High....
> For the Most High himself detests sinners
>> and will repay the wicked with a vengeance.
> Give to the good man,
>> and do not go to the help of a sinner.[25]

This is just the opposite of Jesus' teaching. Such rigidity may, however, be explained by the Jews' consciousness that they had been entrusted with the absolute truth and were safeguarding values whose quality and importance far outweighed even the existence of the twelve tribes of Israel. These people had been chosen for that task, and that was why they, and they alone, had made covenant after covenant with God. And here was Jesus threatening to jeopardise everything by taking the people off into the unknown. One could, certainly, agree with some of what he said, admire some of his actions – but he was an idealist, a utopian, who was unaware of the risks and dangers run by the nation that had held a sacred trust. If he was allowed to continue, he would end up carrying the people along with him, the illiterate and uncultured peasants and country people, the *am-ha-rez*, who were already too inclined to stray from the Law and its rules.

This was how the Pharisees, in particular, thought. They felt that they had been given a twofold mission: to purify Judaism of all the contaminants and deviations introduced by the corrupt and collaborating priestly caste, the Sadducees, and also to preserve the integrity of their faith. The Pharisees were minor worthies recruited mainly from the ranks of traders and artisans, and occasionally from those priests who were, so to speak, at the forefront of their profession. There were only about six thousand of them, according to Josephus. But they ran the synagogues, and because they railed against the dissolute behaviour of the Sadducees, many who were oppressed and frustrated by or envious of those fat cats were won over to the Pharisees' cause. The Pharisees also campaigned for greater lay participation in the rites of the Temple – the access of non-priests, for example, to the inner areas of the building where new popular gatherings were proposed. And they had managed to impose several of their policies on the priests. As Josephus wrote,

> the Sadducees ... do not observe anything other than what the Law enjoins them to ... but their views carry little weight, for when they are elevated to influential positions they are obliged to conform to the ways of the Pharisees, because the people would not countenance anything else.[26]

That this power had given the Pharisees a certain arrogance is beyond doubt. They claimed to be the rightful heirs of the prophets, charged with passing on the divine revelation, and they sought to exclude everyone else, even priests, from that role.[27]

Obsessed with the need to safeguard the revelation that God had given His people, they believed that every Jew was duty-bound to study the Law and its many commentaries as it had been passed down from generation to generation. This was the highest occupation, greater even than the building of the Temple. And as they also believed that the whole universe was sacred and that every gesture and every word touched on the sacred in one way or another, they never ceased adding new rules to the mass that already existed – to the point where they often became objects of ridicule. Not to everyone, however, since the Pharisees did occasionally try to adapt the rules and regulations to changes in society. The Essenes – who were even more intransigent in their religious practices – believed that they sought to 'lighten' the Law. But most Essenes stayed in their own little patch of Qumran (although, as we have seen, a few lived in towns and even went to

Jerusalem), while Jesus, going from synagogue to synagogue, came into direct contact with the Pharisees. He was clearly attracted by their religious fervour. They, like him, believed in the resurrection of the dead, stressed the role of divine providence and attacked the Temple hierarchy. Their views were often close. Yet a superficial reading of the gospels makes the Pharisees seem like Jesus' greatest enemies.

Because every movement or organisation is particularly sensitive to competition from the movements or organisations closest to it, it needs to accentuate the differences – a phenomenon that can be observed during electoral campaigns, for example. It is therefore likely that the first Christian communities, whose beliefs and views had inevitably had an influence on the transmission of Jesus' words and deeds and on the writing of the gospels, had intensified his opposition to the Pharisees. It is also possible that certain translations had altered Jesus' words. Claude Tresmontant,[28] who believes that the gospels were originally written in Hebrew, considers that Jesus' famous declaration that the Pharisees were hypocrites (although this seems to us redundant since the two terms have now become identical in meaning) was due to translators who had not exactly worn themselves out by rendering the Greek *hypokrites* as 'hypocrites'. He argues that, by referring to the original Hebrew, this should actually be rendered as 'unfaithful'. In other words, the Pharisees were unfaithful to their own injunctions and were past masters of the 'do as I say and not as I do' school. However, whether it is translated as 'hypocrites' or as 'unfaithful', Jesus demonstrates a rare harshness towards the Pharisees: 'You appear to people from the outside like good honest men, but inside you are full of hypocrisy and lawlessness.'[29]

Did Jesus therefore condemn *all* Pharisees? The Essenes certainly lumped them all together: 'They follow false prophets and they stagger around like the insane because their works are nothing but lies.'[30] But this was not Jesus' view. He accused only those who did not practise what they preached. He numbered Pharisees among his friends, and they invited him to dine;[31] one of the most powerful of these, Nicodemus, whose post was roughly equivalent to that of a modern deputy mayor, even pledges his allegiance to Jesus in these terms: 'You are a teacher who comes from God; for no one could perform the signs that you do unless God were with him.'[32] But Nicodemus goes to Jesus at night, for one can never be too careful, and this gives us some idea of the risks run by the Galilean and those who followed him.

In short, the Pharisees were not united in their view of Jesus. There was, John tells us, 'disagreement' about him after the incident in which he cures the man born blind – an incident that shows just how serious things were getting. Having debated this miraculous event without coming to any conclusion, they decide to hold an inquiry to settle the matter. They interrogate the man's parents. These good people, wary, evade the issue: ask our son, they say, he is old enough to speak for himself. So they send for the man again, who can only repeat his story. He could not see, and now he can. Yes, but how? 'Well,' he says, 'it is unheard of for anyone to open the eyes of a man who was born blind; if this man were not from God, he could not do such a thing.' At which, furious, they throw him out.[33]

This is a crucial scene, since it highlights what is really the Pharisees' sore point. It is not that Jesus attacks their bigotry and their ultra-rigorous adherence to the pettiest of rules – he was not the first to do so. It is not that he accused some of them of having hearts of stone and swollen heads while claiming to praise God humbly and to follow the commandment to love – they have to admit that there was some justification in that, because everyone knew it. But that he claimed 'to come from God' and that even a wretch such as this man born blind (and if he was born that way, then it was to atone for the sins of his parents, who were therefore undesirables) should repeat it – that was unacceptable. And they make just one thing clear to the cur, who until he was healed had spent his days begging beside the Temple: they are the disciples of Moses, and it was to Moses that God had spoken. Whereas Jesus claimed to take his power directly from God, thereby going above

Moses's head. He also claimed to forgive sins, something only God could do. He insulted God by pretending to take His place. That was intolerable.

The Pharisees were undoubtedly some of the most fervent and visible believers in Israel, but they could not believe Jesus' claim. And, immediately after this incident, it is with this that Jesus reproaches them. Jesus asks the man whom he cured of blindness, who had just been driven out by the Pharisees, whether he believed in him. The man declares that he does and Jesus says that he has come so that the blind may see. And then some other Pharisees who are present ask Jesus (whether provocatively or sincerely it is difficult to decipher), 'We are not blind, surely?' And Jesus replies: 'Blind? If you were, you would not be guilty, but since you say, "We see," your guilt remains.'[34] In other words, you think you know, but you are so hemmed in by your certainty and your fervent belief in the God of Moses that you cannot accept the new message or, above all, the new messenger whom He has sent you and who is none other than Himself. And that, Jesus concludes, is your sin. Their conclusion, on the other hand, is that if Jesus says he is God, he is blaspheming.

Judaism did not allow God to be represented in images or statues in case this would constitute idol worship. People were also enjoined not to speak His name, from respect for His majesty. And now Pharisees were being asked to acknowledge a man as God. As Charles Guignebert, a materialist commentator who was influential at the turn of this century, observed, 'Simply to enunciate such a monstrous claim constituted a blasphemy such that [the Jews] had inevitably to begin collecting avenging stones.'[35] There was no greater blasphemy.

For this reason the Pharisees would eventually join forces with the hated Sadducees and Herodians, and with the Temple hierarchy, who for their part opposed Jesus for the political reason that he threatened their power. They would join forces with them or, perhaps, simply allow them to proceed. And this would lead Jesus to his death.

II

Jerusalem

THE town hates him, and he knows it.

Even though it depends so heavily on religious tourism, Jerusalem is an enclosed, unwelcoming place, a city shut in on itself. The big trade routes are along the coast or east of Jordan. Judaea as a whole is rather poor. Big business and 'the traffic involved in it', as Josephus put it, are not therefore part of the region, and contact with the outside world is limited. Professions linked to trade are despised, and certain imports (luxury goods from pagan territories and various agricultural products) are, for religious reasons, banned or limited.[1] In addition, most of the administrative services, centralised under the Roman occupation, have been moved to Caesarea.

But the Temple remains, and has great, not to say enormous, influence. It is the biggest employer in the town. The craftsmen in the lower part of the town – potters, fullers, weavers and stone-cutters – work for the important people and the priests, who all live in the upper town. They envy their illustrious clients. Not for them the sumptuous sarcophagi that they fashion and decorate out of a single block of stone; all they can look forward to themselves is burial in the ground where the worms will eat their flesh. However, if these rich people did not exist, the craftsmen and their families could not even look forward to their next meal. If the Temple did not exist, the small traders and artisans who sell souvenirs to pilgrims or those who swindle them would be equally hard hit. If the Temple did not exist, all its employees, caretakers and Levites would be out of a job. They would have no choice but to join the beggars, cripples and blind men who loiter around the precincts of Herod's superb construction, or to leave in a massive caravan to try to find a living elsewhere.

Deep social tensions divide Jerusalem. But the residents close ranks around the Temple, because the Temple is the sole reason for living for the most religious and the sole means of living for everyone. Anyone who takes on the Temple and tries to reduce its influence is therefore the enemy of Jerusalem and of all who live there. And so the Essenes rarely come to the capital, and avowed opponents of the Roman occupier, with the exception of a few undercover agents, prefer to stay outside it. As does Jesus ...

The four evangelists differ in their accounts of Jesus' journeys across Galilee and Judaea – but his itinerary is, in any case, apparently of little interest to them. What matters is what Jesus said and what he did. The main discrepancy is over his trips to Jerusalem. Matthew, Mark and Luke give the impression that he went there only once, to die. John, however, recounts five journeys there. Most scholars tend to give him preference on this. Matthew and Luke in fact imply that Jesus had spent some time in the capital: 'Jerusalem, Jerusalem, you that kill the prophets and stone those who are sent to you! How often have I longed to gather your children....'[2] In addition, Luke repeats several times, as though it were the refrain of a song, that Jesus was 'making his way' to Jerusalem, without ever having him arrive until the episode known as Palm Sunday.

Some scholars have suggested that John interwove different scenes from a single trip to Jerusalem throughout his gospel. But he gives dates and precise details about these different trips; one particularly interesting incident, for example, coincided with the Feast of Tabernacles, or 'Sukkot', celebrated in the week beginning 15 Tichri (September–October). Sukkot was one of the three feasts of pilgrimage for which Jews went to Jerusalem. They built shelters or put up tents to commemorate the wandering of the Hebrews in the desert before they had returned to the Promised Land from Egypt. And as the festival came just after the harvest, it was – unless the harvest had been very bad – a huge, joyous celebration. On this occasion, however, it was rather troubled.

Jesus, explains John,[3] did not want to go to Judaea where the people 'were out to kill him'. His brothers, who must have known that, nonetheless encouraged him to go to Jerusalem. Jesus' relations with his family were decidedly not straightforward; Mary does not appear in this scene. 'If a man wants to be known he does not do things in secret,' say the brothers, as though they suspected Jesus of cowardice, or wanted to push him into making a mistake or, in the kindest interpretation, hoped that he would finally demonstrate his power. But Jesus makes the classic reply: the time is not right. Jesus always took this attitude when he was challenged, when a sign was demanded from him. He exercises his freedom. But after they have gone, he does in fact go to Jerusalem, in secret. Again, this seems to confirm the theory that he had a network of support in the city.

The moment he arrives, he learns that people are very interested in his whereabouts. The many Galileans who are in the capital for the festival are talkative; the Judaeans, who have had less opportunity to see and hear him, question them. What does he say? Who is he really? Is he coming? All this in undertones, for 'no one spoke about him openly, for fear of the Jews' (since we are in Jerusalem, we should doubtless take 'the Jews' to mean 'the Jewish authorities' or even 'enemies').

And then he shows himself. He doesn't really have a choice. His movement is in crisis, as we saw a little earlier, when Jesus had preached in the synagogue at Capernaum (which was, incidentally, set amid basalt houses, as we know from an inscription authorised by Herod Antipas[4] and the episode of the centurion from the Roman garrison there[5]). Ordinarily, Jesus was fairly well received in the town, but on that occasion he had caused a scandal with such pronouncements as, 'I am the living bread which has come down from heaven. Anyone who eats this bread will live for ever.'[6] Pronouncements that were, as we have seen, unacceptable to most of his audience, and which had caused many of his disciples to leave him. The crisis was acute – so acute that Jesus had asked his intimate circle, the Twelve, whether they also wanted to leave. To which Peter had replied, 'Lord, who shall we go to? You have the message of eternal life.'[7]

And so only a few of the faithful are left. As Jesus outlines who he is and the meaning of his mission, his audience dwindles. So he has to speak again, and again, in the face of all the dangers, to explain and convince. That is why he goes to the Temple – into the lion's den, one might say. But this was where the pilgrims congregated. This was where the heart of Israel beat.

He goes to the Temple and he teaches, tirelessly. At first, he impresses his listeners: how can this Nazarene, when it was known that Galileans were comfortably off but essentially yokels, be so knowledgeable? And, as far as one knew, he had not been the disciple of any rabbi. Where had he learnt all this? His answer: it is God who makes me say it. Such a pronouncement was tolerable: the prophets had also spoken in the name of God. As long as he does not claim to be the Son of God, there is no scandal. All the same, the crowd is perplexed, disorientated. He claims to speak in the name of God, but he had abused the sabbath … a strange prophet. Is it not rather a demon that inspires him? Some believe him to be the *Mashiah*, a word that was translated into Greek as *Christos*, literally meaning 'Anointed' or 'Consecrated' (and, figuratively, 'Messiah' or 'Saviour'). But that this man should be the *Mashiah* is impossible for most of them because he comes from Nazareth. 'When the Christ appears no one will know where he comes from,'[8] they say.

And so the debate rages. The audience marvels at the extraordinary fact that the 'bosses' are letting him preach. Perhaps *they* have recognised him as the Christ? In fact, informed by their sources of this debate, which is a little too near the knuckle and which seems to be holding the people's attention, the bosses had immediately decided to put a stop to it. They send their policemen to the scene. These policemen do not, however, rush to intervene. With someone like this, you never know … and their work was apt to take a nasty turn. What if the crowd were to take his side?

And so they sensibly decide simply to listen to this Galilean about whom so many rumours are flying around, hoping, perhaps, to catch him in some scandalous pronouncement that will justify their intervention in the eyes of the crowd. And, listening, they are impressed by what they hear.

It is the last day of the festival, and the commotion around Jesus continues. He cries: 'If any man is thirsty, let him come to me! Let the man come and drink who believes in me!' His audience knows what it is to be thirsty. They also know what water symbolises: the rabbis at the synagogue have told them, sabbath after sabbath, that it symbolises the Spirit that will come at the end of time.

But Jesus' words cannot have met with universal acclaim. Far from it. The policemen could have seized their opportunity, grabbed hold of this troublemaker, explaining that they were only acting for the good of everyone, to prevent the Romans — always, as was well known, nervous and wary during festivals — from intervening. But they prefer to retreat — and are severely reprimanded by their superiors for their hesitation: you band of ignoramuses, if you knew the Law, you would not have let yourselves be spellbound, and nor would the crowd. 'This rabble knows nothing about the Law — they are damned.' And there we have it, the eternal contrast: those who know — or think they know — and are complacent because they have read the books and heard the experts, contrasted with those who lack their culture and their knowledge but whose ears and eyes are open. And the former despise or even, as here, curse, the latter.

There is a righteous man at this meeting of the powers that be: Nicodemus, whom we have already met; he speaks up. Since they are talking of the Law, he reminds them that those who pride themselves on their obedience to the Law must be the first to obey it, and that the Law states that a man should not be judged before being heard. But Nicodemus is suspect in their eyes. They even liken him — this important figure, one of the wealthiest men in Jerusalem — to a Galilean. They tell him that he would do well to study the Scriptures, and then he would know that a prophet could not come out of Galilee. These men prefer texts and ideas to facts. And, as usual, their ideas prevent them from seeing the truth.

This time, however, they take no action. They disperse. Doubtless they decide that the police have been seduced, as has the crowd, and that an arrest would cause too much of a stir. They bide their time. It would not be long in coming.

Three months later, according to John's gospel, Jesus is again in Jerusalem, for the Feast of the Dedication, which commemorated the reconsecration of the sanctuary altar in 164 BC, after its defilement three years earlier. It is winter. Jesus is walking to and fro in the Portico of Solomon, a passage on the east side of the Temple, which is protected from the wind by a wall. Later, the apostles would often come here. But right now Jesus is being questioned by his enemies. They crowd round in a menacing circle: let's have done with these mysteries. 'If you are the Christ, tell us plainly.'[9] Jesus replies: 'I have told you, but you do not believe.... The Father and I are one.' And that is the blasphemy. He has gone too far. They begin collecting rocks, to stone him. Hesitating a moment, they give Jesus time enough to allude to a Psalm,[10] in which God upbraids judges ('No more mockery of justice! No more favouring the wicked!') but which adds,

> I once said, 'You too are gods [the phrase Jesus quotes]
> sons of the Most High, all of you,'
> but all the same, you shall die like other men;...

In other words, if these judges whom God has appointed – and who are not exactly wonderful – can be considered gods, why is 'someone the Father has consecrated and sent into the world' accused of blasphemy when he claims to be the Son of God? Jesus is certainly quick-witted in his replies. The argument carries weight, at least for several seconds, allowing him to escape from these violent men.

175

He goes to a region that he knows and likes: the far side of the Jordan, 'where John had once been baptising'. It was here that Jesus had begun what is known as his 'public life'. His movement is still strong here and his audiences large. People crowd round, listening. It is a last respite, but a brief one, since he is sent for by Martha and Mary to go and cure Lazarus, who is said to be dying at Bethany, a few miles from Jerusalem in Judaea. And what happens there will contribute to the fury of Jesus' enemies.

And so they hold another meeting to decide what to do about him. The supreme authority of the Temple, the Sanhedrin – a kind of upper chamber and high court combined, a self-assured group, part of the Establishment – is presided over by the High Priest but closely watched by the Romans. The High Priest at that time, Joseph ben Caiaphas, was the son-in-law of his predecessor Annas, but he also owed his appointment to the occupier. On this occasion, it seems, Caiaphas called together only a section of the Sanhedrin, which comprised seventy-one members.

This Caiaphas was a shrewd politician and certainly what we would call a high achiever. He kept his office for nineteen years (eleven according only to Renan) – which was quite a feat, for since the Romans' invasion, the office of High Priest had ceased to be a tenured one. He also knew how to handle Annas, the elderly head of the tribe, who had seen much and knew all the traditional ways – as well as all human foibles and schemes, which he himself had not been above deploying when need be – and whose influence remained great, even though he no longer held any official post. Caiaphas had accumulated great wealth. He lived in the upper part of town, in a superb edifice of white marble, precious wood and stucco, where fountains cascaded in stone pools and birds sang in the trees of huge courtyards. It was perhaps here that he held this assembly of his confederates.

Caiaphas' argument is simple. The Feast of Passover was approaching, with its attendant crowds of pilgrims who made the Romans so jittery. One might have hoped that this agitator Jesus, lucky to have escaped by the skin of his teeth on the Feast of the

Dedication, would have stayed in his Galilee on the banks of the
Jordan. But the Lazarus business had brought him back into the
vicinity. Everything is at stake, now: the authority of the Temple
and the national interest. The matter therefore had to be dealt
with, before Passover if possible, so as to avoid a popular disturbance which would lead to Roman reprisals.

This Caiaphas does not mince his words. 'You don't seem to
have grasped the situation at all; you fail to see that it is better for
one man to die for the people, than for the whole nation to be destroyed.' There is general assent. Particularly since, as High Priest,
he is believed to have a certain gift of prophecy.[11] It is true that according to the Law, the accused should be heard before being
judged. But when it is a question of the national interest ... The
interests of the state have always taken precedence over the law
and justice. The interests of the Church too, on occasion.

And so the Temple decides to have Jesus killed. And Lazarus
too, John tells us, for he is attracting people to Jesus' cause. Jesus,
forewarned (he too has his informants), leaves again. He is not
looking for death. He will do what he has to do, take all the necessary risks, but he is not looking for death. According to John (the
other three evangelists do not mention this episode, any more than
they recount the meeting that perhaps took place at Caiaphas'
beautiful house), he goes with his disciples to Ephraim, a little
backwater north-east of Jerusalem, near the desert and Samaria.

His disciples were perhaps invigorated by the events at
Bethany, but these men must have been weary. For months now
they had been roaming Galilee, and occasionally Judaea, going
from one little township to the next, meeting with a reception that
was sometimes courteous, sometimes brutal, surrounded by enthusiastic, marvelling crowds or harassed by hostile groups and
constantly spied on by the authority's men.

How long and hard the road was! In their native Galilee, it was
just about tolerable. Even Judas, the only one not from the region,
appreciated the leafy shade of the walnut trees bordering the
route, the mosaics of meadows and flowers, hedged with fig trees

and bushes, the serenity of the small valleys where goats and sheep grazed peacefully. Of course there was always a cousin or a brother somewhere or other, a wife somewhere else, to tell them that a child was sick, a father was showing signs of age and in fact was not very well at all, or that their presence was sorely missed at home – and for how long was this going to go on? For how long, and to where, would they follow this rabbi Jesus? And was he really worth leaving home for? Were not some people in the village saying that he was nothing but a fraud, a spinner of tales, a madman who took himself for a prophet? And these Andrews, Peters, Philips would have to explain themselves, justify themselves, make promises – yes, yes, I will come back for the harvest; and if father gets any worse, let me know and I will come straight back, at least for a few days. Galilee was therefore not without its drawbacks, but at least they were in their own country and, when all was said and done, well treated.

Samaria, on the other hand ... Don't even talk about it! A region of dust, thistles and sun, which one had to cross at a rate of knots. This was the country of ancient enemies, who had dared erect on their Mount Gerizim a temple to rival the one in Jerusalem – though the Jews had fortunately long since destroyed this blasphemous edifice. The Samaritans had a heartfelt hatred for their compatriots – and the feeling was mutual. Each side believed the other to be degenerate betrayers of the Torah, and occasionally added stones to their insults. Most Jews avoided Samaria, and when the Galileans went on pilgrimage to Jerusalem, they made a long detour so as not to have to go through it. But Jesus, for reasons known only to himself, had taken it into his head to journey through this pagan territory. He had even dared ask for a drink from a peasant woman who had come to draw water from an old well, when the rabbis had declared that the Samaritans' water was more impure than pig's blood. Everyone, Samaritans and Jews alike, knew that.

It was not a promising beginning. The woman was stupefied by his request. And then Jesus had explained to her, as he had to others, that he was himself living water. Since she reminded him of everything that separated them – 'Our fathers worshipped on this mountain [the rounded, grassy Mount Gerizim], while you say that Jerusalem is the place where one ought to worship' – he took up her theme to announce the new age:

> Believe me, woman, the hour is coming
> when you will worship the Father
> neither on this mountain nor in Jerusalem ...
> When true worshippers will worship the Father
>   in spirit and truth.[12]

And so he had revealed his universal mission to this stranger at the well.

In the end, the conversation had finished well. The woman was won over, persuaded far more easily than others would be. As a sinner who had had five husbands and was now living with a lover, her testimony bore little weight (not that any woman's bore much), but she was not timid, this good lady, not afraid of speaking up for herself, and she succeeded in getting the people of her village to believe in him. They went to listen, brought him gifts of food, lovingly prepared. It was the usual scene, the one they had had in Galilee, in Judaea, the same questions and the same discussions: Who are you? What is it like, this Kingdom of yours? Where is it?

And so that was Samaria; they had one good memory of it, but only one. For the rest, it was nothing but forced marches in the burning sun, parched throats and the insults of shepherds, of donkey-drivers leading their overloaded charges, and even of children.

At last, they had reached Judaea, which was no better. It might even have been worse. Here, they had to face the bandits in their foxholes along the road to Jerusalem and the locals' contempt for Galileans in general, which for many would soon turn into hatred for Jesus and his companions in particular. In Jerusalem, the Temple surrounds are thick with spies. Everywhere there are closed faces, people spoiling for a fight, dangerous men waiting to twist the least word to make trouble. The disciples had to be always on their guard and to watch out for Jesus' safety. In the midst of a hostile crowd, it would be easy to attack him. Even he, normally so patient, would speak of this mob as a 'faithless and perverse generation'.[13] He is exhausted, and they are at the end of their tether when the supreme test begins.

It is almost, but not quite, Passover, the Feast of Passage, which is also the Feast of Unleavened Bread (for the Jews had been in such a hurry to leave the land of Pharaoh that they had not had time to wait for the dough to rise) and of spring, as it also marks the beginning of the barley harvest. It is not yet Passover, then, but Jerusalem is already beginning to swell with people, with Jews from every part of Palestine and also from Alexandria and Syria. The 'God-fearers' are here – Gentiles, that is, who have not been circumcised but who have accepted the one God. And then, just as Fatima, Lourdes or Rome would later attract them, Jerusalem has its tourists. Curious onlookers mix with the crowds and attend the ceremonies. There are also quite a few Greeks among the hordes, some of whom have heard of Jesus and want to meet him – and ask his disciple Philip because he has a Greek name and lives at Bethsaida, a trading border town where their language is spoken. And then, of course, there are the Galileans and Judaeans.

These country people wonder if Jesus is coming. Crowds sometimes have such an instinct, a sort of nose for something important, that can smell thunder in the air. And he is indeed coming. He can no longer avoid a confrontation that will decide things one way or the other, and does not want to.

At the same time, he does not want to draw attention to himself. According to Matthew, Mark and Luke, he first sends out two emissaries: go to the village opposite, and there you will find a young donkey that no one has ever ridden, untie it and bring it to me.[14] There are two possible interpretations of this. The first is that this is the behaviour of a man who can rely on a network of aid, like a resistance fighter or a fugitive who knows that a car has been left for him on the edge of town. The second involves the donkey. This unfortunate animal now has the reputation of being stubborn and stupid because it knows what it does and does not want. But in the ancient world, in India, China and Mesopotamia, the donkey was the mount of the gods.[15] One of the oldest texts in the Bible, the Song of Deborah,[16] addresses the 'rulers of Israel' thus: 'You who ride on white she-asses, you with caparisons beneath you ...' The horse had become man's greatest conquest long before the Christian era, but the donkey kept its good image for some time to come. In Jesus' time it was still praised for its good sense and its powers of endurance. Matthew, always anxious to convince the Jews that what happened was in accordance with the Scriptures, immediately adds, 'This took place to fulfil the prophecy:

> Say to the daughter of Zion:
> Look, your king comes to you;
> he is humble, he rides on a donkey
> and on a colt, the foal of a beast of burden.'[17]

John gives a shorter version of the same quotation, but in his version we get the impression that Jesus found the donkey by chance and took it to ride after the people had already begun to crowd around him and acclaim him.[18]

These people were doubtless less numerous than we would suppose. Jerusalem had only 20,000 or 25,000 inhabitants, and a few hundred people grouped together in one of its narrow alleys would give the impression of a large crowd. Josephus tells us that 250,000 sheep were burnt each year at Passover, but like today's organisers of demonstrations, he must have over-estimated. If we accepted his figures, it would mean that around two million pilgrims assembled in the town and its surroundings for the festival, which is hardly credible. And in any case, if Jesus' supporters had been so abundant that day, the Roman garrison, specially manned for the occasion and primed for action, would have intervened immediately. These officers knew from experience that such demonstrations had to be nipped in the bud. Moreover, while Matthew may speak about 'crowds' and Luke about the 'whole group of disciples', Matthew and Mark add that these were 'the crowds who went in front of him and those who followed'. It was not, therefore, a huge throng. But they were noticed.

These were the real militants of Jesus' movement, mostly Galileans, certainly not inhabitants of Jerusalem; John emphasises that they were people 'who had come up for the festival', which explains an apparent contradiction in the accounts. Many people wonder how this adoring crowd could demand a few days later that Pilate should have Jesus killed. The obvious answer is that they were probably not the same people. The Galileans (and also, according to John, friends of Lazarus from Bethany) play the principal roles in the events known as Palm Sunday, roles that would fall to the inhabitants of Jerusalem (and the Romans) in Jesus' condemnation and crucifixion.

The palms (which only John specifically mentions) also pose a problem. Jerusalem had no palm trees at that time, and they had to be imported for the Feast of Tabernacles, when their use was ordained.[19] The other gospels say that Jesus' admirers spread their cloaks on the ground for him, which was a common practice to honour a great man. Matthew then has them simply cutting down branches from trees, without saying what they did with them, while in Mark they spread 'greenery which they had cut in the fields' along the roads. The use of palms would confirm that a network or group existed in Jerusalem who would have procured them in advance. If this were so, the demonstration would have had nothing spontaneous about it. Palms had a political meaning for the Jews; when the High Priest Simon, 'military commissioner and leader of the Jews', had liberated the citadel of Jerusalem two centuries earlier, he had entered 'with acclamations and carrying palms, to the sound of harps, cymbals and zithers, chanting hymns and canticles, since a great enemy had been crushed and thrown out of Israel.'[20] Palms were therefore considered, like the donkey, as messianic signs: they heralded the liberator who would drive out the occupier and establish his kingdom.

The four gospels recount that the crowd were shouting 'Hosanna', a chant that always accompanied a pilgrim making for the Temple, followed by a customary, 'Blessed is he who comes in the name of the Lord,' a verse from a psalm that was used as a processional hymn for the Feast of Tabernacles.[21] If one accepts these versions, one can go along with the view of Jean-François Six[22] that

> Jesus had simply been integrated into a pilgrimage procession, of which he became the focus; this had arrived at the Temple where a priest blessed the whole group in the person of its leader .... The procession had been a short one and the diminishing crowd would not have worried the Roman garrison.

But John, once again, goes further. According to him, the enthusiastic crowd milling around Jesus was shouting 'Hosanna! Blessings on the *King of Israel*, who comes in the name of the Lord'[23] [author's italics]. This confirms Luke's account, and would seem logical if they were carrying palms. But one is immediately reminded of the episode after the miracle of the loaves when, according to John, though not the three others, a 'large crowd' had acclaimed Jesus as king. John's account of Jesus' entry into Jerusalem clearly alludes to the other great miracle, the raising of Lazarus, and implies that the crowd saw in it the same sign and had drawn the same conclusions. John, the theologian, insists on the political meaning of what is to follow, since there would be much talk of the Kingdom in the days to come. The ambiguity of the title of king would dominate the discussions between Jesus, his followers and his enemies; Pilate would ask Jesus if he were the king of the Jews and nail this title to his cross.

On the day of the procession into Jerusalem, several Pharisees – the chief priests (principally the family of Annas) according to Luke, and the scribes according to Matthew – content themselves with asking Jesus to calm the crowd. This he gently but firmly

refuses to do: 'If these keep silence the very stones will cry out.'
They conclude that they can expect absolutely nothing from him
('You see,' they say in John's version, 'there is nothing you can
do'[24]) and also, doubtless, that Caiaphas had been quite right to
propose that he be killed for the good of the whole nation. For the
Romans, who had not yet made a move, could very well swoop if
Jesus continued stirring up the crowds.

There would be many such incidents in the next few days.
Jesus would confront the Temple head on and affirm his identity
more clearly than ever.

12

In the Shadow of the Temple

THE same motley crowd congregates in the Courtyard of the Gentiles, the gigantic esplanade at the entrance to the Temple. There are the same swirling tides of people in coloured veils, red turbans and ritual white shawls, the same hubbub, in which imprecations, prayers, squabbles, songs and the cries of animals being brought for sacrifice mingle into one powerful cacophony. The strident voices of the money-changers offer the Temple currency, which the pilgrims will use, 'for the purchase of their soul', to pay the tax of the priestly caste; all other money, Greek or Roman, is impure and would defile the sacred precincts. A little further away, the Levites are selling salt, bread, incense and oil to be used as offerings. Queues are forming behind the stalls at which the 'seals' are bought and exchanged for lambs, rams and kids.

The chink of coins is heard as they pass from hand to hand; most of them will eventually fall into the priests' moneybags. The priests have almost exclusive financial control of the commercial transactions at the Temple, when they do not carry them out themselves. One priestly family has the monopoly of the sale of perfume, another of the shewbread (loaves, offered a dozen at a time, twelve being the number of the tribes of Israel, and laid out in lines of equal length on a marble table; the priests would subsequently eat them). The family of Annas and Caiaphas, the chief priests, take the lion's share of the Temple business, as befitted their rank. Most pilgrims know this, and Jesus is equally well aware of it. That noisy market-place had been familiar to him since Mary and Joseph had brought him to the Temple as a boy when he had been undoubtedly amazed, perhaps amused, by it. Now, however, he is enraged.

If there was a place where one could find God, this, for every Jew, was it. Here, Yahweh is both present and absent. No image is to be found within the Temple or its surrounds, which surprises the pagans, used as they are to worshipping gods in the form of humans or animals. Yahweh is so overwhelming and so transcendent that He can not be represented in any way or enclosed in any place, not even in the Holy of Holies, in the heart of the Temple. But if God can be anywhere, He will be here. And so if there is a place where it is vital to distinguish between the sacred and the profane, the pure and the impure, this is it.

This time, Jesus does not hesitate. Go on, out! An end to this soiling of the Temple, an end to this commerce and this profiting from the piety of a people who want to make offerings but feel they are being duped! He wants to rid the place of these merchants, and it is of little consequence – none, in fact – whether they are priests or Levites.

John, transforming himself from theologian into journalist for the occasion, finishes the story, recounting that having made a whip of cords, Jesus marched into the courtyard and

> drove them all out of the Temple, cattle and sheep as well, scattered the money-changers' coins, knocked their tables over and said to the pigeon-sellers, 'Take all this out of here and stop turning my Father's house into a market.'[1]

* * *

Almost all scholars believe that this episode, which is also recounted by the other three evangelists, did actually happen. But it poses several problems. First, its precise date. John places his 'report' in the early chapters of his gospel, just after the miracle at Cana, whereas the other three place it after Jesus' spectacular entry into Jerusalem on Palm Sunday. Most historians prefer the later date. If Jesus had attacked the Temple so directly at the beginning of his ministry, it is doubtful whether he would have been allowed to continue and even less likely that he would have been able to return to Jerusalem several times without running into serious problems.[2]

John placed the episode at the beginning of his gospel because it constituted a kind of summary of Jesus' story: Jesus did not want just to purify the Temple of Israel, where God had chosen to live in the middle of His people, he also wanted to announce that he himself was the real home of the Father, the real Temple. This is what the sequel to the episode effectively signifies. The Jews – which we should understand as 'Judaeans' or, more narrowly, as 'the Pharisees and the Temple hierarchy' – ask Jesus what permits him to act in such a way. His reply: 'Destroy this sanctuary, and in three days I will raise it up.' Which 'the Jews' counter with, 'It has taken forty-six years to build this sanctuary: are you going to raise it up in three days?' We should note in passing that Herod the Great had begun the building of the Temple in 20–19 BC, which would place the scene in AD 27–8; if we presume that he was born in 6 BC, Jesus would then have been thirty-three or thirty-four years old.

But to return to the astonishment of 'the Jews'. It is not difficult to understand: rebuild the Temple, reconstruct its Greek columns, put those enormous blocks of stone back in their places – in three days? Even for a world that took wonders in its stride, that was hard to swallow. They would have concluded that Jesus really was mad, a deranged and disturbing braggart. 'But', John adds, 'he was speaking of the sanctuary that was his body, and when Jesus rose from the dead, his disciples remembered that he had said this, and they believed the Scripture and the words he had said.'[3] Clearly, this is yet another example of something written after the event by someone who knew how the story ended, and who wanted to interpret it. John, who is decidedly fond of prefaces, added a third one after his celebrated prologue ('In the beginning was the Word …') and the episode at Cana. Indeed, it could be argued that the whole of his text is nothing more than a long preface to the story of the Passion and the Resurrection. But

this scene, unlike that of Cana, is confirmed by the other evangelists and seems to have a stronger historical base. This raises other
questions.

What is its true significance ? If one takes the gospel accounts
literally, Jesus took on the traders and their animals single-
handedly. We know that the disciples are there because we are
told that they hear his subsequent discussion with 'the Jews', but
they are present only as passive and frightened witnesses of the
scene. Nor are we told anything about the reactions of the crowd.
The reader is also forced to wonder why neither the Temple police
nor the Romans, who watched over the area from the heights of
the nearby Antonia Tower, had thought it necessary to intervene
– which they could have done without committing sacrilege since
the commotion was taking place in the Courtyard of the Gentiles.

The British scholar S. G. F. Brandon, who believes there were
connections between Jesus' movement and that of the Zealots,[4] is
not wrong to observe that the gospel account

> can scarcely approximate to the truth. Surely no man, no matter
> how dynamic his personality, could have succeeded unaided in dri-
> ving from their place of legitimate business a company of traders
> when engaged with their customers.

From which he derives this hypothesis:

> It is improbable that his action in the Temple was unsupported;
> indeed, far to the contrary, it is likely that it was achieved by the
> aid of an excited crowd of his supporters and was attended by
> violence and pillage.

It is indeed easy to picture the pilgrims rushing to collect the
coins that had fallen from the money-changers' stalls or the tables
of the sellers of seals. But such a shambles would necessarily have
brought in the police. The author has thought of that and argues
that when Mark, a little later,[5] and also Luke[6] have Pilate asking
the crowd to choose between Jesus and Barabbas, they say that the
latter had been 'in prison with the rioters who had committed

murder during the uprising', from which Brandon concludes that we can legitimately 'wonder whether this attack by Jesus on the Temple ... was a far more serious affair than the gospels show.'[7]

In Brandon's view, Jesus was closely allied to the Zealots, but the evangelists erase that aspect of his movement from their records in order to stress the religious, rather than political, reasons for Jesus' execution. His explanation of what happened at the Temple is consistent with that theory, but there is nothing to corroborate it, especially since the Zealots apparently did not really figure until later. And one wonders why, if the theory were true, Jesus was not arrested after this uprising like Barabbas and the other 'rioters'. Brandon's response to this is that 'it could ... indicate that the action of Jesus was so powerfully supported by his followers that the Temple police either dared not intervene or were swept aside.'[8] In other words, this 'powerful support' would have forced the police to turn tail, thus saving Jesus – but not Barabbas and the others. This is difficult to believe, and it is legitimate to wonder why none of the texts mention it.

In conclusion, it seems likely that the incident was a limited one which went unnoticed by most people, except by the priests' informants, who shadowed Jesus relentlessly. Their bosses must have decided that this was the thin edge of the wedge, that they had to put a stop to this unrest before it developed and that they were right to determine to have him killed. There was no time to lose.

Another question concerns the place where the incident occurred: the Courtyard of the Gentiles, to which the pagans had access, was sited inside the Temple but was outside the frontier that separated pure and impure. We cannot therefore interpret Jesus' gesture as an attack on the defilement of purity because the sanctuary itself was not affected by the trading; after all, there had to be some place where impure and pure could be separated, the impure coins of the Romans and the Greeks replaced by Temple money and animals that were guaranteed 'unblemished' sold.[9] The Courtyard of the Gentiles performed this function, rather like the decompression chamber of a submarine. Another English commentator, E. P. Sanders,[10] argues that if Jesus nevertheless took on the people who were legitimately trading there, it was because he wanted not to 'purify' the practices but rather launch a direct attack on the Temple and its sacrificial rites. This theory fits in with the logic of Jesus' teaching. On the other hand, there was already a body of people who wanted to purify the Courtyard of the Gentiles, and such a desire would not therefore seem totally new and strange. Indeed, several years later, measures would be taken to move the sale of offerings outside the Temple precincts.[11]

The debate is important. If one concludes, with most people, that Jesus simply wanted to purify the Temple, that would mean that he was not questioning the Temple itself. If on the other hand one accepts the theory of a direct attack, it is easier to understand the extreme tension of the following days. Now several of the gospels attribute to Jesus prophecies of the destruction of the Temple. For example: 'You see these great buildings? Not a single stone will be left on another; everything will be destroyed.'[12] Most historians believe that something which Jesus really said about the destruction of the Temple[13] lies behind the evangelists' additions and alterations to the scene. That is what he means by overturning the tables – it is not a question of purification but of replacement. Jesus wants to demonstrate to everyone that God was no longer to be found in the Temple but in himself, and for the Jewish authorities this would be the official, religious reason for his execution. But the gesture also meant that Jesus was taking on the political and financial power of the priestly aristocracy. That would be the unacknowledged reason for his execution. It is also why the Jewish population, particularly the residents of Jerusalem, who were so attached to the Temple and its rites, would abandon him.

The theory of a direct attack appears all the more probable in the light of what the evangelists – with the exception of John – describe next. Everything that Jesus then says and does tends towards the direction of a complete rupture with the Temple: the miracle of the withered fig tree, the parables of the murderous husbandmen and of the wedding feast, the cursing of scribes and Pharisees, the proclaiming of catastrophes for Jerusalem, and finally the cry: 'The hour has come. Now the Son of Man is to be betrayed.'[14]

On each of the succeeding days, pilgrims flood into Jerusalem. And each morning Jesus appears in the Temple. Groups of people amass there. Priests, Pharisees and Temple officials slip in and out of the crowds, talking, quibbling, trying to catch him out. Jesus is no longer careful in what he says. He admonishes them violently: 'John came to you, a pattern of true righteousness, but you did not believe him, and yet the tax collectors and prostitutes did.'[15] Or he tells them the story of the landowner who plants a vineyard, fences it off and builds a tower to watch over it; he then leases it to tenants and goes abroad. When the grapes are due to be picked, he sends his servants to collect his share, but the tenants beat one, kill another and stone a third. He sends a larger group of servants; the same thing happens. Finally, he sends his son, presuming that he, at least, will be respected. But he, too, is killed. The owner of the vine declares that henceforth he will lease it to tenants who will deliver his produce to him on time. And Jesus quotes the Scriptures:

> It was the stone rejected by the builders
> that became the keystone.
> This was the Lord's doing
> and it is wonderful to see.[16]

And then, according to Matthew, he explains: 'The Kingdom of God will be taken from you and given to a people who will produce its fruit.'[17] He could not have been clearer. Israel was to have its mandate, and its mission, taken away.

His audience, particularly the Temple people, understand him very well. They know the 'song of the vineyard' in Isaiah, in which a tower and a vine that produces only bad grapes also figure; the text ends:

> The vineyard of Yahweh Sabaoth
> is the House of Israel ...
> He expected justice, but found bloodshed,
> integrity, but only a cry of distress.[18]

But Jesus (who also seems to be alluding to the trouble that would later break out among the peasants) goes much further than Isaiah. He presents himself as the Son of God, and announces to the Temple authorities that it is all over. They are no longer the keystone.

Continuing in the same vein, he tells the story of the wedding feast organised by a king, to which the invited guests refuse to come. The monarch does not, however, abandon the affair. The feast will still go ahead. He sends his servants to invite those that they meet on the roads, 'bad and good alike': the door would be wide open for everyone. But when all the guests have had time to make themselves at home, the king, patient thus far, throws out a man who has flouted the rules by not wearing the traditional wedding garment....[19] Some writers have detected a problem in this: how would the other vagabonds and tramps have procured such a garment? One could plausibly suggest that the king had, in his goodness, furnished them all with the necessary clothes. In any case, the meaning of the parable is clear. The Kingdom is no longer open solely to Israel, who refused to enter, but to all those who accept its commandments. And the tension continues to mount.

Jesus will raise it a notch higher. The scribes, he says, say that the Christ is the son of David. That was not possible, however, because David himself calls the Christ 'Lord'. 'If David can call him Lord, then how can he be his son?'[20] In other words, the Christ is certainly close to David, but he surpasses him because he possesses the authority of God. This, of course, horrifies the Pharisees and the Temple hierarchy, but disappoints those who still hoped to find in Jesus a political leader, since the Messiah who would drive out the occupiers and establish his kingdom must be the son of David.... At that moment, Jesus loses another section of his potential support.

He had refused the title, fearing political confusion and knowing very well that his audience was awaiting a nationalist and military Messiah. But they might have thought that he was simply being careful, concealing his hand until the decisive moment. Now the people sensed, or knew, that that moment was approaching, and Jesus was still refusing the title. They did not understand him any more.

He, for his part, had gone beyond such things. He prepares his disciples, warning them that they will be persecuted because of him. Finally, he declares: 'Now the hour has come for the Son of Man to be glorified.'[21]

This expression 'Son of Man', which the evangelists use ninety-two times and put ninety times into the mouth of Jesus, has given scholars quite a few problems.[22] For practically all of them, not every use of 'Son of Man' in the gospels is authentic. Scholars mostly belief that Jesus would have used the term only when speaking of his future, his glorification and his elevation to the right hand of God.

The Jews – or at least the most learned of them – who heard Jesus would have known the term. It is used in the Bible in two ways:

1. It designates humankind as distinct from God. For example, God addresses Ezekiel and Daniel by the title 'Son of man'.[23]

2. In other texts, the expression has a very different meaning. The book of Daniel[24] speaks of a 'son of man' who was served by 'men of all peoples, nations and languages', whose 'sovereignty is an eternal sovereignty which shall never pass away'. This was not, however, an incarnation of Yahweh; such a concept does not really exist in the Old Testament. The awaited Messiah was no more than a sort of envoy of God.

What conclusions can be drawn from this? The title 'Son of Man' seems to convey two things. On the one hand, it shows that

Jesus had power; on the other, that he was rejected and would be tortured and crucified. He shares in the human condition but is also divine. The Protestant theologian Günther Bornkamm believes, as do others, that:

> The historical Jesus ... did not give himself the title Son of Man.... We may thus assume with even greater certainty that it was in the first instance primitive tradition which, through faith in the risen Lord who will come to judge the world, added the name of majesty even to those sayings of the Lord in which it did not originally occur.[25]

Had Jesus used the term only twice, for example, they still would have had him saying it ninety times. But there is hardly a consensus about this.

During those last days, Jesus and his disciples lived at fever pitch. They spent the night in Bethany or on the Mount of Olives; in the daytime, the tireless Jesus returned to the Temple to proclaim the Word and to tell his opponents a few home truths.

The disciples do not always understand. Clearly, they trust him, but they perhaps question his strategy, are doubtless somewhat shocked by his aggression towards the Temple – like most Jews, they resent the priestly aristocracy but have been brought up to respect the Law, and they realise that by taking on the Temple, Jesus was also casting doubt on the sacred precepts of which it was the guardian. Certainly he acted in the name of Yahweh. But what if he were wrong? Many others had begun to think that he was and had left him. They had stayed; it is possible – even probable – however, that some of them had also begun to doubt him and had been tempted to leave. It might have broken their hearts to do so – but they were tempted. To finish with this life of wandering, secrecy and fear and return home to wives, children, brothers and sisters.

But they had stayed, perhaps filled with foreboding. He was disconcerting as well as attractive. There was that evening during this period, for example, when, seizing a moment of rest and respite that occasionally interrupted their restless wandering, they had taken refuge at a sympathetic house. Lazarus and his sisters were also present. 'A woman', according to Matthew and Mark, Mary according to John, comes and pours onto Jesus' head or feet (and then wipes with her hair, although there the accounts also differ) a jar of nard, a precious perfumed oil derived from a Himalayan plant.[26] This was a surprising gesture, especially since modesty forbade a woman to let down her hair in public.[27] One of the Twelve protests. Several of them were unhappy about this waste, according to Mark, but only one of them challenges Jesus directly: Judas, the disciple who manages their funds. This was an utter waste of money, he objects – the oil would have cost three hundred denarii, perhaps more – roughly the average annual wage of an agricultural worker. Why had the ointment not been sold and the money given to the poor? John adds, 'He said this, not because he cared about the poor, but because he was a thief; he was in charge of the common fund and used to help himself to the contributions.' But if he had been putting his hand in the till – a till that could not always have been very full – it is curious that the others had never noticed. We rather have the feeling that John (the only evangelist to make the accusation) had wanted to lay yet another charge at Judas's door and perhaps give a motive for his betrayal: greed. A little earlier, after the sermon at Capernaum that had had such terrible consequences for Jesus' movement, John had already labelled Judas a 'devil'[28] and would say a little later, apparently unaware of the inconsistency, that 'Satan entered him' at the Last Supper.[29]

Jesus, less severe than John, saw that Judas was not the only one to grumble. He says to them, using the plural form of 'you', 'You have the poor with you always, you will not always have me.' This does not mean that this notorious defender of the poor had suddenly resigned himself to the fact that they could never be helped, but that he would soon have to leave them, and his disciples must continue to carry the load. Judas, according to Matthew,

Mark and Luke, was not convinced. At the end of their accounts of the anointing at Bethany, the treasurer goes to the people of the Temple to deliver Jesus up to them.

Was it really necessary to tell them of Jesus' whereabouts in that way, when he was appearing every day in and near the Temple? There is only one possible answer: a public arrest might have sparked off some public disturbance. Whenever Jesus finished speaking, he would disappear into the sea of pilgrims, some of whom, with his network of sympathisers in Jerusalem, would probably have helped him escape the Temple staff. He therefore had to be taken quietly.

It is not difficult to picture Jesus and his circle threading their way through crowds of people, running down alleyways to escape someone in hot pursuit, breathlessly crossing courtyards, jumping onto terraces, spreading out so as not to attract attention, fixing a time to meet in the evening, in a friendly house or under a tent on the Mount of Olives – where Jesus would spend the night, as every night, in hiding. Indeed, John specifies that 'the chief priests and the Pharisees had by now given their orders: anyone who knew where he was must inform them so that they could arrest him.'[30] Judas, of course, would know Jesus' movements from day to day.

Judas is someone whose personality and motives are so mysterious that they have inspired many questions and theories – and a whole library of literature. Before looking at him more closely we must of course rid ourselves of any ideas about predestination, of the suggestion that is sometimes put about that there had to be a traitor so that the divine plan could be accomplished and that God had assigned the role to Judas. These have little meaning for the historian and not much more for the theologian: they hardly tally with the teaching of Jesus and of the Old Testament on the freedom that God gives to each individual.

It has also been suggested that Judas was in the employ of the Temple, a kind of spy sent to infiltrate (as we say today of the secret police) Jesus' group after he had begun to be known. This is an attractive theory. There is nothing, however, to corroborate it. And it does not help us understand why, when he had done no more than his job and had doubtless received congratulations, as well as a fee, from his superiors, he would then hang himself. Unless Jesus' execution at the hands of the Romans had shocked and disturbed him. But again all that is purely hypothetical.

It is also argued that he acted from greed: thirty shekels (not thirty denarii) was not exactly a negligible amount. It was equivalent to a hundred and twenty denarii, the usual price of a slave. But as we have just seen, this was only four times an agricultural worker's monthly salary, and not a payment that would justify the betrayal of a figure as important as Jesus. If Judas were filching from the group, as John claims, he would surely have had the opportunity to get his hands on more than that. In fact, the thirty shekels is a reference to a prophecy of Zechariah, whom we have already encountered and of whom, because he was rich, the gospels often made use in allusions to the awaited Messiah. In a rather complicated passage, some 'dealers' who are interested in buying some sheep pay a shepherd thirty silver shekels for them; the Lord says to the shepherd, with bitter irony, 'Throw it into the treasury, this princely sum at which they have valued me.'[31] In short, it is hard to believe that it was desire for personal gain that motivated Judas.

Another explanation has received greater support. It is based on the fact that the gospels give him the surname 'Iscariot' which could correspond, it is said, to *sicarii*, a term that the Romans used, without any differentiation, for bandits and resistance fighters. Two hypotheses have been derived from this. First, that Judas is a resistance fighter who is disappointed that Jesus is clearly not going to lead the revolutionary uprising that he had hoped for. By doing what he does, he hopes to force Jesus into action, into crossing the Rubicon, thinking that the threat of an imminent arrest will push their leader into ordering the taking up of arms. The second theory is that Judas, again a resistance fighter, realises that the non-violent Jesus is taking the people to a fruitless destination and thinks it is better to derail him, even if that means betrayal.[32] This is all very ingenious, but the links between Judas and the resistance movement and his feelings on the subject have hardly been proved. And then, according to Josephus, the *sicarii* did not really manifest themselves until after AD 50. And John twice tells us that Judas was the son of a certain Simon Iscariot,[33] who would therefore have had the name long before any *sicarii* had appeared on the scene. Iscariot could simply mean 'man of Kerioth', a little village situated above Hebron.

So what should we make of it all? Perhaps Renan gives part of the explanation: 'It is tempting ... to believe in some manifestation of jealousy or some internal strife. The particular hatred of Judas demonstrated by the Gospel according to John confirms that hypothesis.'[34] He is alluding, of course, to the accusation of theft. Other commentators have suggested that not all was sweetness and light within the community of the apostles. And Judas was the only Judaean of the group.

Daniel-Rops might also be getting warm when he speculates:

> Perhaps Judas was even motivated by love, not the pure disinterested love which Peter and the other ten had for their Master, but one of those devouring exclusive passions which can thrust a man into the worst excesses of jealousy, a love so near to hate that in certain circumstances it indeed becomes hate, only to recover itself, when the worst has been committed, in the extremity of pain and despair.[35]

One can add that Judas, like his companions, believed implicitly in the coming of the earthly kingdom of Jesus. The Acts of the Apostles even has them sharing a meal with Jesus after his death and resurrection and asking, 'Lord, has the time come? Are you going to restore the kingdom to Israel?' And so, writes Fr Léon-Dufour,

> Judas, like the other disciples, could have thought that the Kingdom would be established by some cataclysmic event. When

Jesus persists in his refusal to take drastic action, Judas, with a fanatical logic, takes matters into his own hands and speeds things up: if he hands his Master over to the authorities of the Temple, would that not put him into the very heart of his opponents' base of power, like Samson in the temple of the Philistines? The all-powerful Yahweh would then produce a thunderbolt to liberate and enthrone the Messiah. But the strategy failed. Nothing of the sort happened and Jesus was condemned to death.[36]

And finally there is the basic, unfathomable explanation of the darkness that lives in men's hearts.

Jesus, who knows what is in Judas's heart, does not curse him. Rather, he pities him: 'Alas for that man by whom the Son of Man is betrayed!'[37]

13

The Last Supper

THEY are at another celebration meal. The last. They all know that, or sense it. There have been so many close calls, and there could be another at any moment. They have raced down pathways and alleys, continually looking over their shoulder for someone following them or spying on them, having to stop to catch their breath; when they meet, they check that no one is missing, especially, of course, the Rabbi, the Master, for whom they have abandoned all and risked all and who is now in danger.... When you live like that, any opportunity for relaxation, joy, self-esteem, affection or friendship begins to seem like a wonderful bouquet of happiness, whose scent is savoured all the more because it is so fleeting.

Jews liked eating, and they liked celebrations. Meals were an occasion for relationship, for friends and family to gather together in the communion of Yahweh, the source of all life.[1] Numerous passages in the Old Testament begin or end with meals — as do numerous incidents in the gospels. Jesus, 'a glutton and a drunkard' as some called him, did not spurn good food or good wine. This particular meal is also lit with the radiance of the greatest festival of all, Passover. The Passover meal, the Seder (which Christians would later call the Last Supper), was the central feature of the celebration.[2]

But they feel as though they are being watched. They know that danger is ever present and that the Temple hierarchy could descend at any moment. They must have come under cover to that large room or that terrace,[3] to which they have never been before and which a member of the support team had found for them.

Jesus had sent Peter and John as an advance guard, doubtless from the Mount of Olives: 'As you go into the city you will meet a man carrying a pitcher of water. Follow him into the house he enters.'[4] The support network worked well: they were expected, the meal prepared. The table had been laid with a white cloth and the ritual dishes.

The Passover meal usually comprised unleavened bread, horse-radish, bitter herbs, parsley that was dipped in vinegar or salt water and which represented the bitterness of the days spent in exile, far from the Promised Land, hard-boiled egg, a mixture of chopped fruits and nuts, a leg of lamb with more or less meat on it, and, of course, wine. But no gospel makes any mention of the Passover lamb at this meal, which has given rise to interminable debates. Was this last meal that Jesus shared with his companions really the Seder? We will return to that question.

The guests would have been reclining on benches. This easy posture was demanded by ritual and symbolised the freedom of the chosen people after their return from Egypt. They were alone – there is no mention of servants, of the householder or of their usual companions at that time, Lazarus and his sisters – but if they were respecting the custom of the Passover meal, a place would have been left free and laid for the prophet Elijah who had announced the Messiah. In this way the past and present were intermingled. One could almost say that there is no past, no present and no future, or rather that they have all merged. As Robert Aron comments, 'The Messiah is present at every moment, in every gesture by which life is made into history. Life is fleeting and history is incomplete, but the Messiah's place is always ready beside us, even if he never comes to occupy it.'[5]

John (and only John) places a scene in the middle of the meal that flabbergasts the disciples, when Jesus gets up, leaves his place at the head of the table, undresses, and then wraps a towel around him like a loincloth; this was the dress of the Jews when they had been in bondage, enslaved, in Egypt. And he begins to wash his disciples' feet.

The purification of feet was not an exceptional ritual. The priests habitually performed it because they had to tread the sacred parts of the Temple barefoot (often to the detriment of their health in winter). The ritualistic demands placed on them were so exacting that they would also have a basin outside the door of their home for washing their feet before entering.[6] This ritual was not exclusive to the Jews. It was practised throughout the Middle East as a way of honouring a guest – but with one difference: it was the task of an inferior. To wash someone's feet was to acknowledge subservience: a servant washed his master's feet, a woman her husband's, children their father's.

Let us envisage the ensuing scene. It is hardly surprising that Peter, never at a loss for words and often presented as the spokesman of the group, begins to protest: 'Lord, are you going to wash my feet?' Jesus replies: 'Later you will understand.' This reply does not convince the apostle: 'Never. You shall never wash my feet.'[7] Jesus then gives two replies, two explanations. First, to Peter: 'If I do not wash you, you can have nothing in common with me.' In other words, we will be separated. Peter, in the exhilaration of the occasion, replies feverishly to this that if that is how it is, then he wants his hands and his head washed as well. Jesus calms him: if someone has taken a bath, they do not need to wash. That is not the point.

He gives his second reply, addressed to all of them, when he has finished and is sitting at table again: 'You call me Master and Lord, and rightly; so I am. If I, then, the Lord and Master, have washed your feet, you should wash each other's feet.'

Most scholars feel that these two replies do not have the same origin. But they are not contradictory. Jesus, who can no longer have any doubts about his destiny, is establishing the rules for the little community that he will leave behind: each member of it must be the servant of all the others, without pride or vainglory because, he repeats, 'No servant is greater than his master, no messenger is greater than the man who sent him.' This has two potential meanings: do not become puffed up with arrogance, or do not have any illusions – what is going to happen to me will happen to you also.[8]

So the party resumes talking, eating – laughing, perhaps, over the story of how they had fooled some Temple policeman who had thought he had recognised them and escaped from another who had given chase. Several, doubtless, are still wondering about this extraordinary gesture of washing their feet – but then they are used to such things! He has often caught them unawares, and they have grown accustomed to waiting for the meaning of what he says and does to become apparent.

Soon, however, the laughter stops, and conversation dies away. The drama of Judas's break with them approaches. Jesus has already declared, when he was washing their feet, that they were not all 'clean'. And then, suddenly, back in his place and clothed again, he delivers the blow: 'One of you will betray me.'[9]

They seem neither stunned nor horrified by this pronouncement. But what deep distress and self-doubt lies behind their nervous laughter? For most of them dare to ask him, 'Is it me?' They also begin to wonder, 'Is it him?' They remember gestures, words, even facial expressions, that now seem suspicious. That chap who now appeared so distraught – had he not shown signs of discouragement or weariness, the desire to have done with it all? They turn to Jesus, who has said too much or too little for their liking. But he, says John, is 'troubled in spirit', a phrase that the evangelist has twice used earlier. Jesus had been 'troubled in spirit' when he saw Mary weeping for her brother Lazarus, and also when he had been questioned by some Greeks after the procession into Jerusalem and had alluded to his approaching death, adding, 'Father, save me from this hour.'[10] On both occasions, what troubles and terrifies him is the brush with death – the death of a friend, or his death. His sees his own death in the same terms as he would that of one of his faithful, one who had loved him with a particular love and been loyal to him despite insults and mockery, doubts and blows.

The tension is almost palpable. It is too much for Peter. He gestures to one of their company, 'the disciple Jesus loved', according to John, who introduces this apostle here for the first time, without naming him.[11] This disciple is the best placed to question Jesus: he is sitting on his right, on one of those long benches that run the length of the table, and has only to lean back and rest his head against Jesus' chest to ask him in a low voice, 'Who is it?' And Jesus tells him: 'It is the one … to whom I shall give the piece of bread that I shall dip in the dish.' To offer someone a piece of bread or a morsel is to honour him. By this gesture, Jesus – who has overcome the terror that, just a moment before, had gripped him – shows his acceptance of what was to come. Or was it a gesture of friendship and respect for Judas, in a last attempt to save him? Did Judas instinctively recoil when the bread was offered him? Had Jesus decided to have done? Jesus says brusquely, 'What you are going to do, do quickly.'

The others hear and see all this, without understanding any of it. John feels that he has to come to their defence and explain that they think Jesus' command relates to the purchase of food or a gift of alms that should be taken urgently to a poor person – a rather strained explanation. Normally, it is Mark who denigrates the disciples, but here it is John who is treating them like simpletons. How can men inured to danger and plots, who have learnt to be habitually careful, allow someone who has just been denounced as a traitor to leave without some kind of explanation? Are they perhaps past caring? Or do they not hear Jesus' reply to his neighbour, and so rest assured that if Jesus has sent Judas out, he knows what he is doing? But 'the disciple Jesus loved' knows very well what has happened; if he does nothing, it must be in imitation of his Master, to accept as he accepted, whatever the cost. These are all possible interpretations. They are, in any case, more plausible than John's clumsy explanation.

And so Judas goes out, leaving – the first in a long line to do so – the community whose rules Jesus has just laid down. 'Night had fallen,' says John. Darkness.

'… a light that shines in the dark, a light that darkness could not overpower,' John wrote in the very first lines of his gospel.[12] Light is life, and the absence of light is death. In the Old Testament, 'darkness' and 'nothingness' are synonymous. At the beginning of John's gospel, creation is described as the gradual victory of light over darkness. But there are people who prefer the darkness to the light.

The third act of this unusual meal begins: the sharing of bread and wine, which Christians call the institution of the Eucharist. Strangely, John makes no mention of it whatever – which has provoked many unsatisfactory hypotheses.[13] It is important to note the similarity between the 'Do this in memory of me', that, according to the apostle Paul, Jesus said twice as he shared out the bread and wine, and his 'I have given you an example so that you may copy what I have done', said after the washing of the disciples' feet. It is also reminiscent of the long discourse that Jesus delivers to the Jews at Capernaum after the miracle of the loaves, a discourse that would baffle most of them and cause them to leave him:

> I am the living bread which has come down from heaven.
> Anyone who eats this bread will live for ever;
> and the bread that I shall give
> is my flesh, for the life of the world....
> He who eats my flesh and drinks my blood
> lives in me
> and I live in him.[14]

These words, almost more explicit than those spoken by Jesus at the Last Supper, are given only by John.

After Judas has left (or not; according to Luke, he is still there), and as the meal is drawing to a close, Jesus takes some bread, prays, blesses it, breaks it and gives it to his companions.[15] 'Eat,' he says. 'This is my body given up for you.' And then he does the same with the cup of wine; this is the cup of my blood, 'the blood of the new Covenant which will be shed for you'. Only Matthew, always something of a moraliser, adds that the blood would be shed 'for the forgiveness of sins'. Jesus then announces that he will not drink wine again until the day that 'the Kingdom of my Father' has come.

It is important to stress the brevity of this episode, from which the Catholic Church would derive the central sacrament. There are just a few lines, without commentary, in Matthew, Mark and Luke. Paul was more detailed and more voluble. In his first letter to the Corinthians, he gives them a piece of his mind because their community meals are not all that they should be: 'One person goes hungry while another is getting drunk,' and then he reminds them of the Last Supper, giving a version of it that corresponds to Matthew and Luke, but with the addition of 'Do this as a memorial of me' and 'Every time you eat this bread and drink this cup, you are proclaiming his death, and so anyone who eats the bread or drinks the cup of the Lord unworthily will be behaving unworthily towards the body and blood of the Lord.'[16]

Did Paul therefore play a major part in the institution of the Eucharist? The brevity of the evangelists' treatment of it makes us suspect that he did. It is possible that the disciples had not been deeply impressed by Jesus' words at the time, preoccupied as they were with the solemnity of the occasion, and anxious about their safety and the prospect of a betrayal. Jesus' gesture was, moreover, not totally new to them. It was based on a Jewish tradition well known among the rabbis: the covenant meal. The Talmud prescribed that bread be broken (and divided, symbolising each person's independence) and the pieces shared among the guests (who thereby receive a token both of their independence and of their unity). This ritual is followed by

> a blessing giving thanks to God and to the sages of Israel who continue and consolidate the link of the Torah between the generations and the link between he who gives the bread and they who receive it and between Master and disciples.[17]

To eat is to affirm both independence and the link that exists

206

between eater and those who first fed him, who enabled him to become independent. As we have seen, this meal was also the ritual
linking of past to present. Jesus' gesture would not have surprised the disciples in the sense that it followed on from that tradition, but it is also possible that it had reminded them of his
words at Capernaum.

It is likely that the rituals adopted by the first Christian communities after Jesus' death had some influence on the writing of
the gospels. In the Acts of the Apostles, the breaking of bread is
mentioned very early on, immediately after the account of
Pentecost, when the apostles began speaking in tongues to people
of many different nationalities (some of whom were sceptical,
scoffing that Jesus' followers must 'have been drinking too much
new wine', although three thousand of whom were baptised on
the spot). Luke says of these new disciples: 'These remained faithful to the teaching of the apostles, to the brotherhood, to the
breaking of bread and to the prayers.'[18] This rite of breaking
bread, which had been so quickly adopted, seems to have been
performed in various different ways.

As for Christ's exact words, after lengthy dissections of the
translation from Aramaic into Greek, most scholars think that he
would actually have said 'This is my flesh' rather than 'This is my
body'.[19] Jesus had already spoken at Capernaum about his 'flesh'
and his 'blood', which would serve as the seals of the renewed
Covenant[20] between God and humanity – an eventful and continually renewed love of which the Bible is the story.

One last point has inspired numerous debates: the date of this
meal. John says that it took place 'before Passover', and when
Judas leaves them they think it is perhaps to buy some item needed for the celebration. For the other three evangelists, however,
the meal is itself the Passover meal, and therefore takes place the
night before Passover.

Several elements seem to confirm this latter date. The dipping
of food into sauce, for example; the Passover Haggadah says, in

essence, 'On other nights we do not do this ... even once, but on this night we do it twice.' On the other hand, it is very unlikely that the trial and the execution of Jesus would have occurred during the Passover, since all forms of work, including meetings of the Sanhedrin, were forbidden during the festival, and none of the texts mentions lamb or unleavened bread, the two main elements of the Passover meal.

It has been suggested, in an attempt to solve the contradiction, that Jesus was following not the official lunar calendar but the Essene solar calendar, according to which Passover occurred on the Tuesday evening. He would thus have celebrated the Essene Passover on the Tuesday evening and been crucified on the eve of the official Passover. This is an ingenious theory,[21] but it assumes close links between Jesus and the Essenes that did not exist. It would also mean that Jesus was arrested two days before his crucifixion, which contradicts all four gospel accounts.

Practically all historians are inclined to think that the Last Supper was not the Passover meal, but took place shortly before it. Matthew, Mark and Luke would have altered the calendar slightly and taken certain liberties with the dates in order to emphasise that Jesus was the new Passover lamb, offered to everyone through the Eucharist. John, who ignores the Eucharist in his account of the Last Supper, places Jesus' death – correctly, according to most historians – on the day before Passover, when lambs were slaughtered for the festival that would begin that evening as soon as the first star appeared.

If one agrees with most scholars and with John, therefore, Jesus died on the 'Day of Preparation': that is, 14 Nisan (March–April). The Jewish tradition[22] seems to confirm this. Now, according to Mark and John,[23] Jesus died on a Friday. During Pilate's term of office, 14 Nisan falls on a Friday in AD 30 and 33. Jesus would therefore have died on 3 April 33, when he would have been nearing forty, or on 7 April 30, when he would have been around thirty-six. Most scholars opt for the latter date.

* * *

In all probability, therefore, the Last Supper takes place on 6 April 30. The meal over, Jesus announces his death: 'My little children, I shall not be with you much longer.' He repeats the basic rule of their little group: 'love one another; just as I have loved you...'.

Peter protests – 'Lord, where are you going? ... Why can't I follow you now? I will lay down my life for you' – provoking the reply that has become so famous: 'I tell you most solemnly, before the cock crows you will have disowned me three times.'[24] The crowing of this cock, incidentally, has been presented as miraculous, but in fact it serves to mark the time: cocks, of course, crow at dawn. Jesus realises that his arrest is imminent and, knowing his companions as he does and having witnessed their swings between terror and bumptiousness, that they will soon desert him. Has not Judas already left? – and he a Judaean, who had run every risk to follow Jesus and who had inspired such confidence that they had entrusted their funds to him ...

Jesus continues his farewell talk. He has no illusions about them, but he trusts them. They should also trust him: he has to go on ahead, mark out the territory, but he would come back to fetch them, he would set aside places for them in his Father's house. He knows his death is very near, but shows total confidence in God. He and his Father are one.

Philip, expressing a desire that so many men and women would echo during the centuries to come, says, 'Let us see the Father, and then we shall be satisfied.' And Jesus' reply will form the basis of Christianity: 'To have seen me is to have seen the Father.' In other words, God is that man who had wandered the streets with them, who has been acclaimed, worshipped, mocked, despised, hissed at, humiliated and nearly stoned. God is this man who is going to suffer and be put to death.

Jesus insists: 'I am in the Father and the Father is in me.' And then: 'I will not leave you orphans.... Peace I bequeath to you.... Do not let your hearts be troubled or afraid.' And finally, 'Come now, let us go.'[25]

He, to die. They, at first, to sleep.

14

The Trials

HAVING sung the Hallel, the thanksgiving at the end of the meal, they leave. It is time for the great trial – perhaps the greatest, Gethsemane, and Jesus' agony.

They cross the lower districts of Jerusalem to the Kidron, a dried-up stream for most of the year until brown, muddy flood waters gush through it for a few days each April. It is after dusk, but it is not completely dark; in the west, a few last fingers of red linger in the sky, and in the east the moon gives off a pale glow. Soon, it will light up the night, since it is full moon, 14 Nisan. Jesus has not tried to hide from them the fact that they are leaving for some sort of fight. Before, he says to them, even though I sent you out without money or provisions, you never wanted for anything. But now that is finished with, and you must take precautions. Indeed, if anyone does not have a sword, he should sell his cloak to buy one. They reply that they have two swords between them. 'That is enough!', he says.[1]

This business of swords has, like so many things, given rise to lengthy debates. It seems to contradict the theory that Jesus had decided to offer himself as a sacrifice that would erase the sins of the world, although some people have understood 'swords' to be a figure of speech, rather than something that signified direct action. Fr M.-E. Boismard, for example: 'The reference to the buying of swords should probably be understood in a metaphorical sense: the courage to engage in battle with the forces of evil.'[2] But a little later Peter would actually draw his sword and use it, and the group charged with Jesus' arrest would also be equipped with weapons. This, according to S. G. F. Brandon (who continually stresses the links between Jesus and the Zealots), 'suggests that Judas had given warning [to the High Priest] that the disciples were well armed and that armed resistance was to be expected.'[3]

On the other hand, when Peter tries to prevent Jesus' arrest by force, Jesus stopped him with a 'That will do'[4], corresponding to the earlier 'That is enough'. We can legitimately suppose that Jesus was tempted to defend himself with weapons: he would experience other temptations in Gethsemane. *Gethsemani*, *gethsamanei* or *gethsemanei* meant in Aramaic[5] 'oil mill' or 'oil press'. It was a little area filled with olive trees and enclosed by a wall of dry stones, situated on the road to Bethany and to Bethphage, another of Jesus' haunts.

Let us go back to the scene:

They are weary, somewhat disorientated, above all moved by the scene that they have just witnessed. They are also suffering from the effects of the testing days that they have lived through. Jesus leaves some of them to rest – 'Stay here' – in a cave (according to certain traditions), and sets off again with Peter, James and John. Again he stops. 'My soul is sorrowful to the point of death. Wait here, and keep awake.' But they are exhausted; sleep will overcome them. Jesus goes off to a secluded spot nearby and throws himself on the ground to pray. Thus begins the moment of his severest trial and a night of suffering and inner struggle.[6]

Stories of initiation trials in which the hero must confront pain, or sometimes simply fight against sleep as a sign of spiritual strength, were fairly widespread in primitive folklore and in contemporary texts. Once again, numbers play an important role in the gospel accounts. The principal actors have separated into three, Jesus is accompanied at first by three companions, he will say three prayers, go three times to shake his sleeping disciples, Peter will deny him three times, he will go before three sets of judges, three crosses are erected on Calvary, and finally he is resurrected on the third day. There are echoes in all this of numerous mythological tales in which heroes are subjected to three trials before being recognised and glorified.[7] One may see in it also an allusion to the Trinity.

The account clearly corresponds to the literary genre that scholars have called 'the trial', which includes, for example, the famous struggle between Jacob and the angel. The divine emissary 'wrestled with him until daybreak', striking him so brutally that Jacob's hip is dislocated, and finally conceding his opponent's strength, saying, 'Your name shall no longer be Jacob, but Israel [which probably meant "How strong God is!"], because you have been strong against God, you shall prevail against men.'[8]

Similarly, when a desperate Elijah had escaped into the desert, he had cried to God, 'The sons of Israel have deserted you, broken down your altars and put your prophets to the sword. I am the only one left, and they want to kill me.' Elijah had, like Jesus, sought solitude, and had left his servant behind on the way. Unlike him, however, he had wanted to die – and when an angel arrives, it is not to fight but to offer comfort.[9] But the pattern is the same: the protagonist survives the trial and moves towards his mission and his destiny.

The similarities to the general literary genre and the fact that Jesus' prayers can have had no witnesses – his three companions were some distance away and, in any case, asleep – have caused doubts about the authenticity of this episode. But before leaving Peter, James and John, Jesus, usually so confident, had not hidden his fear and anxiety from them. He had quoted a passage from Psalm 42: 'My soul is sorrowful to the point of death.' This Psalm is the long wailing of one who is convinced he has been abandoned:

> 'Why do you forget me?
> Why must I walk
>   so mournfully, oppressed by the enemy?'
>
> Nearly breaking my bones
>   my oppressors insult me ...[10]

But the psalmist is eventually reassured of God's presence. Jesus had woken his disciples three times – which allows us to wonder whether he had not also revealed to them the horrors he was undergoing and the prayers he had addressed to God: 'Abba!... Everything is possible for you. Take this cup away from me,' and his final acceptance: 'But let it be as you, not I, would have it.'

In several biblical texts, the chalice or cup symbolises the destiny that man receives at the hands of God. The two phrases, one of refusal ('Take this cup away from me'), the other of acceptance, therefore express a confrontation, a meeting of two wills that are not inevitably the same. This is another temptation scene, but one in which the Devil does not figure. Until now, Jesus has always been in total agreement with God, speaking in His name, describing himself as His Son and proclaiming that whoever saw him saw the Father. But this separation from Him is not opposition, because there is still total confidence – 'Everything is possible for you', 'Let it be as you, not I, would have it.' Rather, it is a questioning, a debate, an inner struggle. 'Agony' means 'combat'. All of which, again, moves away from the image of Jesus going willingly to his death to atone for the sins of others – an image that was familiar to Judaism at that time and which the Catholic Church would soon take up and develop. He did not seek this death. For a long time, he did not know on what day or at what hour it would be.

The battle that he would wage that night – a truly painful one that shows that the evangelists are more than just apologists for Jesus – was waged alone. His companions, those good chaps, are asleep. Indeed, from the human point of view, his mission has failed. The crowds left him when he proclaimed the essence of his teaching; they had not understood, wanting from him only miracles, magic, demonstrations of power or the fulfilment of political hopes. His only choice now is between flight and death. Above all he feels, or knows, that they are going to try to condemn him officially on the basis that he is a political agitator and an impostor laying claim to the kingdom. They will try to draw a veil over the religious reasons. That is why, according to the gospels (although this was possibly a later addition), he would struggle throughout the various interrogations to which the Jews and Romans subjected him to preserve the real meaning of his death, and to ensure that they do not take his identity from him along with the life that Mary had given him. He would repeat forcefully: 'Mine is not a kingdom of this world;'[11] 'From this time onward you will see the Son of Man seated at the right hand of the Power and coming on the clouds of heaven;'[12] and '"So you are the Son of God then?" He answered, "It is you who say I am."'[13] As he is shunted from one authority to another, imprisoned and tortured, he does not try to save himself, but rather to complete his mission, expose the rigged trial, and win recognition. Death was a violence inflicted upon him, but he transforms his Passion into action.

That night, however, in that garden filled with twisted olive trees, he is not certain that he can manage it, can explain and affirm who he is. Perhaps he fears an anonymous death, summary execution without fair trial and without the chance to speak. Now, as Fr Jacques Guillet writes

> In this state, if he says he is God's son, it must be that between him and God there exists an imperishable and invulnerable bond that no disappointment can ever break, an intimacy that none can violate, an indestructible bond of loyalty. To be God's Son does not mean, as Satan supposed or as men imagine, to be able to count on miracles, to be sheltered from harm, to force men's hearts; it means to expect strength from the Father's will alone; it means, when everything seems to show that God is abandoning him, to be able to entrust his soul into the Father's hands like a child.[14]

That is what the few lines devoted to the agony in Gethsemane by Mark, Matthew and Luke suggest. Historians have of course raised many questions on the subject. A rationalist such as Guignebert, for example, wondered: 'Who could have seen or heard Jesus to be able to relate the scene afterwards, when its only witnesses were asleep?'[15] But he adds that it was hardly in the evangelists' interests – at least not from his point of view – to describe such a painful scene, and that they would not have done so 'if the disciples had not remembered Jesus' troubled and anxious state of mind.'

His mind was so troubled that, according to Luke, 'his sweat fell to the ground like great drops of blood'. This phenomenon is known as hematidrosis and is caused by haemoglobin, the coloured agent in blood, passing into sweat.[16] The extraordinary, 'marvellous' nature of this has impressed many people, but it does not pose particular problems for historians. It is a rare sign of extreme anxiety.

Jesus has overcome this anxiety when he wakes his companions for the third time: 'Get up!... My betrayer is already close at hand.' A group of people – a 'crowd' according to the evangelists, who like Josephus often exaggerate the size of gatherings in this little nation – then enters the small area of Gethsemane.

And here a critical problem arises. Who was it that came to arrest Jesus? The evangelists, with the exception of Luke, emphasise that it is the emissaries of the chief priests (with, in John, the Pharisees, the elders and the scribes in the others). In short, it was the agents of the Temple hierarchy, the priestly caste. This would fit in with the logic of events. And the Romans held the priests, scribes and elders responsible for the maintenance of order, in the town as well as in the Temple. And so the Temple sent its policemen, who were mostly Levites.[17]

John's gospel also talks about a 'cohort', in other words a large troop of Roman soldiers: six hundred men, commanded by a high-ranking officer, a tribune. What a battalion to arrest someone who had the support of a dozen or so men! Its presence there is as doubtful as that of the Pharisees, especially since John does not say why or how Pilate had sanctioned the use of these legionaries for Jewish business.

It is true that the Romans would have known about the troubles, even if they were limited, that had occurred in Jerusalem since Jesus' entry into the city. They were generally well informed, as we can see from Acts. There Paul has been seized by the Jews (principally because, we are told, he had taken Greeks into the Temple), and a cohort led by its tribune had immediately intervened – although the informants, who were people from the East, rather given to exaggeration, had told the tribune that 'there was rioting all over Jerusalem', which explained the size of the troop.[18]

As we have seen, it is also true that the Romans must have been on their guard at that time, as they always were during Passover – and there had just been some trouble, during which Barabbas had been arrested 'with the prisoners who had committed a murder during the uprising'.[19] It is not therefore impossible that the Romans were involved in the arrest. It is even possible that the legionaries on watch had seen the men from the Temple bearing lanterns and torches, as John tells us, and had gone to find out what was happening – but not a cohort of them.

This is not an irrelevant debate on a tiny point of history. It opens, in fact, the great debate to which we will return and of which the repercussions have been many and serious: who was responsible for the condemnation and death of Jesus? The Jews? Or the Romans, and through them all nations?

There they are, then, in the garden. Judas goes up to Jesus and bends to kiss him. It was customary for a disciple to kiss the hand of his master, and the kiss of peace on meeting was also commonplace in the East. But the evangelists tell us that Judas kissed Jesus as a way of identifying him to those he was with: 'The one I kiss ... is the man.' This confirms that Jesus was still not widely known in Jerusalem, and that the events of the preceding days had not mobilised the crowds or seriously disturbed public order.

Jesus' companions begin by putting up a show of resistance. According to John, Peter even cuts off the ear of a servant of the High Priest called Malchus, a common name at the time. However, Jesus soon brings these half-hearted attempts at violence to an end. There is no question of starting a riot, not because they are few in number but because he obviously does not want to assert himself through violence. His companions then desert him, not only because they are frightened, because they see their movement dissolving, crumbling away, but also doubtless because the misunderstanding has persisted even until then. They had expected some divine intervention on Jesus' behalf, and they had expected that he would take direct action. And in the event – nothing. If this misunderstanding really did exist, and subsequent events make it a tenable theory, then Peter and the others – if one dare say it – were not so different from Judas.

Among those who ran away was, according to Mark, an anonymous figure who has been the focus of much debate: 'A young man who followed him had nothing on but a linen cloth. They caught hold of him, but he left the cloth in their hands and ran away naked.'[20] Some people believe that this was Lazarus, even suggesting that he had been one of the Twelve under another name.[21] Nothing confirms that. In all likelihood, Jesus' arrest had other witnesses than the forces of so-called order. Above all, we can see in Mark's insistence on this detail a symbol. On several occasions, the evangelists tell us that the sick, the woman with haemorrhages, for example, had been cured simply by touching Jesus' cloak. Clothes were signs of strength, and nudity of absolute poverty and powerlessness. On the morning of the Resurrection when three women went to the tomb to embalm Jesus' body, Mark has another anonymous 'young man', wearing a white robe, who tells them of the miracle that has occurred.[22] Luke has two men and the others have angels at the tomb, but they are all wearing this garment that is 'white as snow', 'brilliant' or simply 'white'.[23]

And so Jesus is delivered into the hands of the priests. One might almost say 'of the mob', because he is first taken not to the titular High Priest, Caiaphas, but (according to John, who is little contested here) to Annas, who at another time and in another place would perhaps have been nicknamed 'The Godfather'. This Annas had rather a doubtful reputation, to say the least. His image was not as snow-white as the fine linen tunic he wore or as golden as the threads that ran through the turban on his head.

He was no longer a high priest who entered the Holy of Holies, but he had kept the title. Many important people of the priestly caste bore it, even if they performed no specific function in the Temple.[24] Annas was more entitled to it than many others; he had been High Priest for many years, had put up with the old Herod and the Romans, eluding their webs, spinning his own, and managing to transfer his office to his sons or his son-in-law Caiaphas when the Romans finally got rid of him.

There was no legal reason why Jesus should have been taken to Annas. Was the old man being honoured by having the Galilean brought to him before being taken to the Sanhedrin? Had he expressed a desire to meet this man who had been portrayed as such a dangerous character? John, who is quite well-informed about the ensuing events, does not give us any clues. Whatever the case, the appearance before Annas shows that the men who had been plotting Jesus' death for some days were not overly concerned about following the letter of the law.

Jesus himself does not fail to point this out. He asks Annas why the old man was questioning him. If it were a matter of finding out what Jesus' teaching was, those who had heard him preach could have been asked. 'I have spoken openly for all the world to hear; I have always taught in the synagogue and in the Temple where all the Jews meet together; I have said nothing in secret.'[25] In short, Jesus challenges Annas's authority and is slapped by an outraged Temple policeman for his audacity. This was another infringement of the rules, for it was strictly forbidden to strike an accused. But that would not prevent Jesus' guards doing what they liked with their prisoner afterwards.[26] In their eyes, Jesus had already been found guilty.

And that is what Peter, the last disciple to remain with Jesus, also thought. He had accompanied Jesus as far as Annas's house – near Caiaphas's impressive mansion – where he had managed to gain access to the courtyard, thanks to 'another disciple ... who was known to the High Priest'. This, according to some scholars, was Nicodemus; it would have been his duty, as a member of the Sanhedrin, to interview every witness in a forthcoming trial, and he would therefore have been able to have anyone he liked brought into Annas's house.[27] In any case, it seems certain that Jesus had sympathisers, or at least an informant, within the Sanhedrin. And so that is where Peter spent part of the night, among the policemen and minor officials, before being recognised, denying Jesus three times, and then running off, weeping.

The cock had crowed. Dawn had broken. Jesus was brought before Caiaphas; it was the moment of judgement. But who was going to judge Jesus? Once again, it seems that the procedures were not followed. Luke, Matthew and Mark state that Jesus was taken to the Sanhedrin, the high court, which was composed of seventy-one members. They had had many powers before the Roman occupation, but now they had only the right – significant, admittedly, to the Jews – to try religious cases. John makes no mention of the Sanhedrin.

Many scholars have questioned this appearance before the Sanhedrin, for various reasons. It is doubtful that it would have held a regular, plenary session at that time; the trial would in any case have taken place not at the home of the High Priest, but within the precincts of the Temple, in the 'Chamber of Hewn Stone'; there had to be a gap of at least twenty-four hours before a death sentence ordered by the Sanhedrin was carried out, which did not occur; the right to a defence should have been respected, but was not; Jesus was not buried in one of the two places set aside by the Sanhedrin for condemned prisoners. Moreover, if Pharisees, some of whom were members of the Sanhedrin, had attended the meeting called some time earlier by Caiaphas, those sticklers for the rules would have insisted that they be followed in dealing with Jesus. Later, in AD 62, when the Sadducee High Priest Ananias, without telling the Pharisees, called an assembly of the Sanhedrin at which Jesus' brother James and several other

Christians were condemned to death, they argued that the assembly was illegal because they had been excluded from it, and got the High Priest suspended from his office.[28] We might wonder, then, why, if they had not been present at Caiaphas's meeting, they had not similarly protested at being left out of it. In any event, in the trial accounts of Mark, Matthew and Luke, the Pharisees are never mentioned.

It is difficult to draw any conclusions, but one point remains clear: the people who were in charge of events, and who had sent Jesus to Pilate by declaring him guilty, were the same as those who had already decided to have him killed. They were what we would call the political majority, the Sadducees, with the possible complicity of some – and the certain passivity of most – of the Pharisees. Fr François Refoulé explains: 'The gospels tend to place all the responsibility for Jesus' death on the Pharisees – doubtless because at the time they were written, after AD 70, the Sadducees had disappeared and the Pharisees were hostile to Jesus' disciples. In fact, it must have been the Sadducees who were Jesus' real enemies. Moreover, they constituted the majority in the Sanhedrin.'[29] Twenty-three judges (out of a total of seventy-one) could provide a sufficient majority to sentence someone.

Jesus was therefore brought before those who had already sworn that he had to die. For form's sake, they question him and call witnesses. The rules stipulated that there had to be at least two witnesses with corroborating evidence;[30] eventually they dig up two men to say that Jesus had declared he would destroy the Temple. Jesus is silent, but he replies, and affirmatively, when Caiaphas solemnly asks him whether he is the Son of God, the Christ, the Son of the 'Blessed One' (the gospels use all three expressions). Jesus replies: 'You will see the Son of Man seated at the right hand of the Power and coming on the clouds of heaven.' This has a precise meaning for those who hear him. God will one day give Israel the right to judge all nations, and it is Jesus himself who will come at that time. He is therefore proclaiming that he is above all the chosen people.

That was a double blasphemy. But it was preferable to take a political crime to Pilate. In a world in which religion and politics were so closely linked, were sometimes the two sides of the same coin, it was easy to extract from Jesus' answer a claim to be the Messiah. And that concerned the Romans – directly.[31]

Why did the Sadducees want the Romans to condemn Jesus? The most common answer is that the Jews no longer had the *ius gladii*, the right to sentence someone to death since, according to Josephus, it had been taken from them in AD 6, which is confirmed, among other texts, by a *baraita* (a judicial formulation) in the Talmud.[32]

It was in any case an astute political gesture to hand Jesus over to the Roman procurator, who was in Jerusalem for Passover, as a token of good will towards the occupiers. As Caiaphas had said, 'It is better for one man to die for the people, than for the whole nation to be destroyed.' Caiaphas was behaving like certain collaborating heads of state during the Nazi occupation of Europe. He is prepared to concede, even though it may be dishonourable, to the rulers. What matters to him is that the body of the nation be saved, even if it has to lose its soul in the process. He would certainly not be ignorant of the fact that some of his compatriots would disapprove of handing a Jew over to the Romans – but this Jesus was a Galilean, his movement had experienced successive failures, the demonstration of support that had accompanied his entry into Jerusalem had died away, the traders and money-changers were installed as usual in the Temple, order had been restored, and the damage limited.

Pilate. We all know the image that Christian tradition, inspired by the evangelists, has given him: a rather weak, indecisive and hesitant man who wants to save Jesus but hardly dares oppose the Jews who are calling for his death. That image, however, is false. The procurator, ex-cavalry officer Pontius, surnamed Pilate (according to some because he had been decorated with a *pilum*, a javelin of honour), was in reality a hard, uncompromising and stubborn anti-Semite. The Jewish philosopher Philo of Alexandria quotes a letter from the Jewish King Agrippa I to the Roman Emperor Caligula (who ruled from AD 37 to 41), a letter that Philo had probably written himself in the Emperor's name, accusing Pilate of fraud, violence, theft, torture, crimes, summary executions and 'endless, insufferable cruelty'.[33] This might have been an exaggeration, but it is unlikely that the smoke was not based on some fire.

Since 63 BC, when Palestine had become part of the Roman Empire, the occupiers had applied various policies to it, vacillating between centralisation and decentralisation, direct and indirect administration. In Jesus' time a procurator had been placed in charge of local administration and legions. His powers were fairly limited – even if, as sometimes occurred, he also occupied the post of prefect[34] – and was dependent on the legate in Syria, particularly for military reinforcements in the case of insurrection. The Jewish authorities also had the right to go over the head of the procurator and appeal directly to the Roman emperor – and the emperor had occasionally granted in their favour, against the procurator. Pilate would in fact later be dismissed from his post by the governor of Syria after an armed insurrection by the Samaritans.

The Romans usually respected the religious customs of the peoples they subjugated, and at the beginning of the occupation, the Jews were able to practise their religion freely. But, as Robert Aron comments, Romans 'used tactics, far more subtle and insidious, of assimilation. They treated the native gods as protectively as they did the native population. By contributing sacrifices to their altars, they made them into "satellites".'[35] The occupiers might have exploited the country, notably through the taxation system (most uprisings were sparked off by a refusal to pay these taxes), but they respected the Jews' religious sensibilities. When legionaries committed some act of profanity or in some way caused offence to Judaism, they were transferred, sometimes even executed. Roman legions on manoeuvre avoided Judaea so that their standards, which bore the portrait of the deified emperors, would not cause offence.

This deference did not imply respect. The Romans and most of the peoples of their empire despised the Jews. In a passage that is, sadly, famous, the Roman historian Tacitus would later describe the people of Israel as an 'abominable race' and 'haters of the gods'.[36] In the eyes of the Romans, and of the Greeks and their neighbours, who all worshipped dozens of gods, the Jews were effectively atheists. With their sabbath and their purification rituals, they were too different from other ancient peoples. And an accusation that would reappear in various forms over the centuries was beginning to surface: the Jewish conspiracy. An Alexandrian worthy named Sidorros, director of a gymnasium (an important post in that ancient Hellenised city), brought a case against the Jewish King Agrippa I to the Roman Emperor Claudius because, he said, the Jews 'were trying to plunge the whole world into a state of rebellion' and were conspiring against the Roman peace. Agrippa I had had much trouble defending himself against the charge.[37]

Pilate more or less shared these feelings. He had been appointed to Palestine by Sejanus, the Emperor Tiberias' right-hand man and a notorious anti-Semite. Pilate would prove a zealot. His predecessors had refrained from sending troops to Jerusalem bearing ensigns with ornate designs of symbols that the Jews considered sacred or objects of worship. Pilate had no time for such delicate scruples and allowed these ensigns into the capital – although he tried to be cunning by having the troops enter at night. The Jews, of course, were not slow to notice. They walked to Caesarea, where they stayed for six days, demonstrating peacefully by holding a kind of sit-in in front of Pilate's palace until he gave in. There were other problems. Anxious about the enormous demands that the pilgrims placed on Jerusalem, Pilate decided to build an aqueduct and took money directly from the Temple coffers to finance it. This provoked serious trouble.[38] Luke alludes to the death of Galilean pilgrims, 'whose blood Pilate had mingled with that of their sacrifices',[39] these victims being sacrificed animals.

This was the man, then, to whom Jesus, who cannot have been in a good state after a night of interrogation, beatings and torture, is brought. The Temple police and the emissaries of the High Priest take him to the praetorium, the place where Pilate, as praetor (a magistrate; under the Empire, a post filled by the governor of the province), heard cases and made judgements. It was often also his home. The Jews do not want to go inside, for fear of defiling themselves. His 'pagan' residence was impure in their eyes, and the Passover was near. And so it is he who comes out to them, doubtless very annoyed at having been disturbed, wearing a short leather garment that left his legs bare, and a cape pinned to his shoulder. He listens to them. As planned, they accuse Jesus of claiming to be king of the Jews, adding, for good measure, that he was preaching rebellion and preventing good citizens from paying their taxes.[40]

According to John, the most detailed and the best informed about the affair – and always ready of course to add a few details in the cause of theology – Pilate calls Jesus into the praetorium. This would hardly have bothered his accusers. It was of little consequence if a man who was already condemned were defiled.

Pilate asks: 'Are you the king of the Jews?'

Jesus: 'Do you ask this of your own accord, or have others spoken to you about me?'

Pilate: 'Am I a Jew?'

It was not his affair, and, so close to Passover when a torrent of pilgrims (in other words, potential rioters) were gathering in the city, it does not amuse him. But he asks: 'It is your own people and the chief priests who have handed you over to me; what have you done?'[41]

Once again, Jesus seizes the opportunity to explain who he really is and to avoid any distortion of the meaning of his death, if death there has to be. 'Mine is not a kingdom of this world; if my kingdom were of this world, my men would have fought to prevent my being surrendered to the Jews.' In other words – and it is important that this is clear – he was refuting the political ambition he had been charged with. A little later he says, 'I came into the world for this: to bear witness to the truth; and all who are on the side of truth listen to my voice.' That is the purpose of his mission. He had not come to offer himself as a sacrifice but to proclaim who God really is.

Pilate's reply, 'Truth? What is that?' are the words of a sceptic perhaps, but they are also those of a Roman, for whom truth is only what is real and concrete and who knows enough about the Greeks to be sick and tired of their endless theoretical discussions on the subject – which amounts to saying that for him truth does not exist. And this business is of decidedly little interest to him; he would wash his hands of it as soon as he could.

It so happens that Herod Antipas, of whom Jesus the Galilean is a subject, has also come to Jerusalem for Passover. Pilate does not like him, perhaps (for according to a minority view, it happened after Jesus' death) because of the incident of the shields, when the procurator had hung shields bearing the name of the deified emperor on walls in the city, which had upset the Jews. Herod had sided with them and Pilate had had to capitulate. To send Jesus to Herod might therefore both rid Pilate of an irritating business and also to set a trap for the other man.

And so Jesus is taken to Herod. He is being passed from pillar to post, the plaything of every cruelty, conscious or unconscious, the victim of every hatred, scheme and stupidity. Herod Antipas, still haunted by the memory of John the Baptist's execution, has long wanted to meet Jesus and question him, and he does not disguise his eagerness. But Jesus, exhausted or contemptuous, does not reply to his questions. The priests' envoys, on the other hand, are vociferous in their accusations. And so the little king of Galilee, who is not lacking in political sense, pays Pilate the courtesy of sending Jesus back to him, thereby killing two birds with one stone. He is apparently showing respect for the procurator's authority, whilst also giving satisfaction to Jesus' accusers. It did not cost him much: this Jesus seems inoffensive, isolated, even a little ridiculous. Indeed, so that he would look even more ridiculous, the guards have dressed him in a purple (or scarlet) cloak, making him into a carnival king.

The sad pass-the-parcel continues, and Jesus appears once more before Pilate, who already has at least three prisoners chained up in the Antonia fort, including Barabbas, the rebel who has just been arrested during a violent riot. A custom (at least according to the evangelists, because its existence is not really certain) allows that every year at Passover the Roman procurator bestows his favour on a Jewish prisoner and frees him.[42] Groups of Jews have therefore come to ask Pilate for the release of Barabbas, whom they perhaps think of as a sort of hero, or as an innocent victim of Roman repression. Mark's gospel suggests that they have come for that purpose, and not for Jesus' trial:

> At festival time Pilate used to release a prisoner for them, anyone they asked for. Now a man called Barabbas was then in prison with the rioters who had committed murder during the uprising ... the crowd went up and began to ask Pilate the customary favour.[43]

The crowd therefore seem unaware that they will have to choose between Jesus and Barabbas. They go and ask Pilate to release Barabbas, or one of his companions. Pilate, who probably wants them crucified, but is in no hurry to see it done, preferring to wait until the festival is over and the pilgrims have left, has in Jesus an excellent way of appeasing the crowd. He can free a Jew, while keeping those whom he judges far more dangerous safely chained up in the Antonia fort.

According to Matthew, he therefore gives the people pressing around him the choice between Jesus and Barabbas. But Mark and Luke (John makes no mention of this episode) have Pilate simply proposing to release the one he mockingly calls 'King of the Jews'. At which the people, egged on by the chief priests, the Sadducees and the Annas–Caiaphas clique, call (as pre-arranged, according to Mark) for the release of Barabbas instead. The Sadducees are playing their hand cleverly, because by pushing for Barabbas they are, for once, pleasing a crowd that hates them, whilst also preventing Pilate from getting rid of Jesus. They are forcing him to make a judgement.

This brutal man does not hesitate. When 'the chief priests and the guards' (alone, according to John, or with, according to the other three texts, the crowd that they had whipped up) demand the crucifixion of Jesus, Pilate abandons him to them. The life of this Jew is of little import to him, especially since the Annas clique is among those who have accused him. According to John, they invoke the Law. 'We have a Law ... and according to that Law he ought to die, because he has claimed to be the Son of God.' And then they resort to blackmail: 'If you set him free you are no friend of Caesar's; anyone who makes himself king is defying Caesar.' This is a political argument to which Pilate is sensitive. The Jews are some of the most rebellious people in the Empire, but they never hesitate to complain to Rome about the prefects or procurators who govern them. He is wary; these people are more than capable of causing him trouble. So be it. This Jesus shall die if that is what they want. He will catch up with Barabbas later. He need only have him followed by an informant after his release.

(We should say in parentheses that there is another possible interpretation of the episode, given that the existence of this custom obliging the procurator to release a prisoner at Passover is uncertain. Mark says that Barabbas has been arrested with rioters who have committed a murder, which allows us to suppose that he had not been directly involved, and he would have been released around the time that Jesus was condemned and executed. And the evangelists would simply bring these two events together. Jesus, who is completely innocent, is condemned, while Barabbas, who is perhaps innocent but probably guilty, is released. And that encapsulated the injustice of Jesus' fate.)

The screaming crowd has, according to the gospels, demanded a crucifixion. This is a Roman sentence, for the Jews' normal method of execution was stoning. The procurator, who has had enough of the whole business, therefore leaves Jesus in the hands of his legionaries.

Mark and Matthew now recount the physical abuse of Jesus which Luke and John had placed at the time of the appearance before Herod. It was so habitual that, although it is impossible to know when it happened, that it did happen is certain.

Other peoples were very ready to mock the Jews' longing for their Messiah. The philosopher Philo of Alexandria tells how during a visit of the Jewish King Agrippa I to his city, the inhabitants got hold of a simpleton called Karabas and crowned him with roses, dressed him in straw, and gave him an escort of young people carrying sticks for spears and hailing him with cries of 'Marin!', an Aramaic form of *Maran,* which meant 'Lord'.[44] Other such episodes occurred elsewhere.

And Jesus, according to the evangelists, is crowned with thorns, dressed in a purple cloak and a reed put into his hand in the guise of a sceptre. The soldiers play at kneeling in front of him with cries of 'Hail, King of the Jews!' Jesus is at the end of his reserves, already dying, for Pilate has had him whipped, a terrifying ordeal inflicted with *flagra,* iron chains with bone and lead balls at the end, which not only tear the skin but rip off the flesh as well. People died from such scourgings.[45]

It is thus a man who is half a corpse who will be pushed, dragged, to the place of execution.

Who was essentially responsible for the condemnation? The priests, certainly. But not solely. The gospels, or at least the texts that we have, were written at a time when the first Christian communities had to face the onslaught of the Jews' opposition, who considered them heretics. These communities also sought to convert others, and if they wanted their faith to take root in other colonial countries, they had to avoid confrontations with the imperial power. For those reasons, the texts tend to place the bulk of the responsibility on the Jews and to excuse the Romans. The portrait that the gospels paint of a weak and vacillating Pontius

Pilate is, as we have seen, contradicted by other, non-Christian texts.

The notion would also grow up among these communities that the people of Israel's rejection of the Messiah was the will of God,[46] and that Jerusalem was destroyed in AD 70 to punish the people who had been responsible for Jesus' death and who had refused to listen to his message. This anti-Jewish tendency was, admittedly, sometimes tempered; in Acts, for example, Peter says to the Jews of Jerusalem: 'Now I know, brothers, that neither you nor your leaders had any idea what you were really doing.'[47] And at the scene of the trial before Pilate, Luke and John draw a distinction between the leaders and the people.

Most scholars today stress Pilate's responsibility. Their view can be summed up by Fr Léon-Dufour.

> There can be no doubt that Pilate was legally the one responsible for the death sentence, and for the subsequent crucifixion of Jesus. The trial by Pilate was manifestly a gross miscarriage of justice, and Jesus was manifestly innocent. Pilate, therefore, was morally guilty for yielding to pressure by the high priests, whether through negligence or cowardice. Caiaphas and his clique, however, were even more to blame, for they initiated the proceedings and spared no pains to force the governor's hand....[48]

To sum up, in answer to the question of who was responsible for Jesus' condemnation, we can say that it was all the actors in this drama, and principally the Annas clan and Pilate.

15

Death and Resurrection

H<small>E</small> drags himself along narrow alleyways that edged with stalls and bustling with pilgrims and locals busy with last-minute preparations for the festival. The word has spread – they are going to crucify the Galilean – and the curious, the fanatical, the sympathetic and the broken-hearted faithful have come running.

He makes his way through that little crowd, sagging beneath the beam he is carrying, dazzled by the sun, which dries and burns the blood of his wounds. Soldiers walk in front – 'Make way, make way!' – using their batons to force the crowd out of the way.[1] He falls. So the centurion who is leading the procession and who will have later to confirm the death and draw up the notification, seizes hold of a pilgrim, one Simon from Cyrene (in modern Libya), where many Jews lived. The Romans enjoy imposing humiliating tasks on Jewish pilgrims – and here was one such at hand![2] The centurion is impatient to escape from the crowd, with its unpredictable reactions, and get to Golgotha, a rocky hill on the outskirts of the city covered with gardens and tombs, which the Romans had made their place of execution.[3]

Crucifixion, the sentence that the priests had asked Pilate to impose on Jesus, was generally used by the Romans, but others, possibly the Persians, had invented it. The Empire reserved it as the penalty for failed rebels, unless they were Roman citizens, for whom it would have been too ignominious. In the previous century, six thousand slaves who had (with others) revolted under Sparticus and vanquished several Roman legions were crucified, forming a vast chain of pain and disgrace from Capua to Rome.

Death by crucifixion was an atrocious form of torture, 'the worst and the cruellest' according to Cicero.[4] A post was hammered into the ground, and when the victim arrived, carrying the other piece of wood, the *patibulum*, the two were fixed together, generally in the shape of a T. The condemned was usually attached to the cross with ropes, but nails were also used. The bones of a man crucified at the time of Jesus have been uncovered near Jerusalem; the feet, placed one on top of the other, were attached to the wood (of the post, since a support for the feet was not used before the third century) with a single nail.[5]

The victim who hung on a cross was continually close to suffocation; to gain breath, he pressed down on his feet – increasing his agony – or on a sort of a tilted ledge, the *sedula*, which cut into the buttocks but gave some support. The cause of death was not the haemorrhages caused by the nails hammered into the wrists and feet but suffocation and exhaustion. And if the victim survived too long, the Romans broke his legs, which ensured that he died of suffocation.

Pilate had a wooden notice proclaiming the reason for the condemnation fixed to the post on which Jesus was to be hung. This was the *titulus* and was obligatory. According to John, this one was written in Hebrew, Latin and Greek, and bore the derisive words 'Jesus the Nazarene, King of the Jews', or, in Latin, '*Iesus Nazarenus Rex Iudaeorum: INRI*'. Apparently the chief priests had not appreciated this and had tried one more manoeuvre, asking Pilate to write instead, 'This man said: "I am King of the Jews"'. But the procurator, impatient now and not displeased with the political implication of the inscription – a word to the wise is enough – or with the prospect of humiliating the Jews, merely replied, 'What I have written, I have written.' The Romans were fond of pithy sentences.

Jesus is dragged, pulled to Golgotha – 'brought', according to Mark,[6] as though Simon of Cyrene's aid was not enough. He is already near death. They offer him something to drink, wine mixed with myrrh.[7] This was customary, and was meant to numb the victim and relieve his suffering. Jesus simply wets his lips with it but refuses to drink. 'He wanted to depart life with perfect clarity of mind,'[8] wrote Renan.

The soldiers strip him. This was another Roman custom, the final humiliation of the condemned man. His clothes were then given to the executioners as a small bonus (*pannicularia*).[9]

They crucify him.

None of the four texts provides the tiniest detail here. They limit themselves to saying simply, 'They crucified him', as though the scandal of this terrible thing took away the writers' power of speech, froze their hands.

They crucify him. And others with him. Two 'robbers' according to Mark and Matthew, two 'criminals' in Luke, simply 'two others' in John. Many people today identify them as political rebels, possibly companions of Barabbas. One of them finds the strength to add his insults to the crowd's, but in Luke (alone) the other defends Jesus and recognises him for who he is. The episode is controversial, but full of a sense of hope. Indeed, Luke sees the whole Passion as a kind of combat in which Jesus scores points and from which he emerges, at the last, victorious.[10]

Crosses, contrary to popular belief, were quite low. These scarcely emerged above the disparate crowd, composed of the idly curious, bitter opponents, pilgrims arriving from the coast (they passed Golgotha on their route into the city) and a handful of the faithful. Only the women have apparently been brave enough to come. None of the texts has a single disciple present, apart from John, who says that the mysterious beloved disciple stood, with Mary, Jesus' mother, at the foot of the cross. Mary's absence in the other three gospels raises questions, especially if one thinks of what Luke and Matthew had written about her in the infancy narratives. The Acts of the Apostles,[11] however, most of which is believed to have been written by the author of Luke, speaks of Mary and Jesus' brothers being present with those who had assembled to pray after the announcement of the Resurrection....

People would have been shouting at the foot of the cross – insults, mostly, born of hatred in some cases, of disappointment in others. From what Jesus had said, they had believed he was going to establish an earthly kingdom and reign over a perfect world, yet now he was in agony, a human wreck, powerless, finished. And so the old challenge was issued – 'if you are so powerful, prove it by getting out of this', the old misunderstanding of Jesus' meaning.

The Roman legionaries had a little trick they liked to use: they drank *posca*, vinegar and water, an old soldier's recipe to combat great heat and racking thirst. They were required to carry some at all times. Taking pity on the dying man, one of them soaks a sponge in the mixture, puts it on a reed and holds it to his dried and bloody lips. The sun would be at its height.

Jesus, before or after having taken a few drops of this *posca*, cried, '*Eloi, Eloi, lama sabachtani?*', Aramaic for 'My God, my God, why have you deserted me?' A cry of distress? Christian commentators all point out that it is the first verse of Psalm 22, a text which indeed begins as a cry for help:

> Yet here I am now, more worm than man,
> scorn of mankind, jest of the people,
> all who see me jeer at me,
> they toss their heads and sneer,
> 'He relied on Yahweh, let Yahweh save him!
> If Yahweh is his friend, let Him rescue him!'[12]

But the psalm goes on to *praise* God, who has responded to this supplication:

> I shall proclaim Your name to my brothers,
> praise You in full assembly:
> you who fear Yahweh, praise Him!
> Entire race of Jacob, glorify Him!
> Entire race of Israel, revere Him!
> For He has not despised
> or disdained the poor man in his poverty,

has not hidden His face from him,
but has answered him when he called.[13]

The similarity between the mocking words that the Jews, according to the gospels, hurled at Jesus, and the words of derision in the psalm, is striking. The authors of the New Testament were evidently anxious to show that everything that had been prophesied by the Old had happened. It is difficult to view this cry of Jesus as historical fact, even though Mark and Matthew have included a detail that gives a 'realistic feel': hearing this 'Eloi, Eloi', the onlookers, most of whom probably did not understand Aramaic, presumed that he was calling on the prophet Elijah.

The afternoon wears on. Jesus will soon have been on the cross for six hours.[14] At the Temple, the ceremonies in preparation for the festival are beginning. Lambs are being slaughtered for the Passover meal.

At Golgotha, it is the end. 'It is accomplished,' cries Jesus. With the exception of Luke, always concerned to show the Passion as a victory, the evangelists do not have Jesus uttering a single word in praise of God, as though to show that he was human to the extent of dying in terror and torment.

Jesus dies.

Though the light has come into the world, men have shown they prefer darkness to the light.[15]

Jesus *died*. For the Jews best disposed to him, this was another proof – if such were needed – that he was *not* God. In the correspondence between Justin and Trypho that took place around the middle of the second century,[16] the rabbi writes: 'There is something incredible in wanting to show that God had allowed Himself to be begotten and to live as a man,' and 'You place all your hope in a crucified man.' The first Christians, all Jews, were ashamed of the crucifixion, which was the sign of a divine curse.

Jesus died, and the centurion who had been in charge of the

execution cried, according to one version, 'In truth this man was a son of God,' or, according to another, 'This was a great and good man.' This need not, it seems, be interpreted as the sign of a sudden conversion; in the centurion's language, influenced as it had been by Greek culture, 'son of God' was a common expression that designated a great man, a human hero.[17] But it is equally possible that the evangelist was the author of these words, added as a personal expression of faith.

Jesus died, and, according to Mark, the veil of the Temple was torn. Matthew adds that there was an earthquake, rocks split open and the bodies of many 'holy men', raised to life again, emerged from tombs and showed themselves to the inhabitants of Jerusalem. These are not, of course, historical facts. The veil of the Temple (which separated the holy place where priests regularly burnt incense from the Holy of Holies) was not torn – any more than the earth trembled, and so on. We are dealing once again with a *theologoumenon*. The tearing of the Temple veil signifies that from then on faith was no longer centred on the Temple, but on the Christ (it should also be remembered that the first Jewish Christians continued going to the Temple for some time ,and that Mark's text was written after this practice had ceased). All the events that Matthew describes also refer to Scriptures that announced the end of the world as we know it and the dawning of a new one.[18] This, for him, began with the resurrection.[19]

Jesus died and, according to John, the legionaries broke the legs of the two men who were crucified with him so as to hasten their death and get the affair over with; John adds that they refrained from doing this to Jesus, but pierced his side, from which 'blood and water' emerged. This piercing with a lance was not customary, and one cannot really see what point it had, since the soldiers had already seen that Jesus was dead. Doubtless it was a case of the evangelist wanting, once again, to prove that everything had happened according to Scripture: 'They will look on the one whom they have pierced.'[20] As for the fact that the soldiers did not break his legs, Jean-Paul Roux,[21] author of distinguished works on eastern religions, points out that many primitive legends featured men, even animals, who were resurrected on condition that their bones were intact. 'A huge portion of mankind,' he writes, 'believed that a lamb-god would die, his bones unbroken, and return to life.' John, who explains that the soldiers had not broken Jesus' legs for the simple reason that he was already dead, and who insists (although it is likely that this was a later addition to the text) that 'this is the evidence of one who saw it – trustworthy evidence and he knows he speaks the truth – and he gives it so that you may believe as well,'[22] immediately adds that 'all this happened to fulfil the words of Scripture: "Not one bone of his will be broken." '[23] Everything had been predicted.

Except for the cross.

An important man, a member of the Sanhedrin, now comes on the scene: Joseph, from Arimathea (north-west of Jerusalem), a supporter of Jesus' movement who is rich enough to possess a garden and, unusually, a tomb, at the gates of the city.[24] He asks Pilate if he can take the body so that it is not thrown into the common ditch for condemned men (Mark says that he 'went to' Pilate, which would have been a transgression of the Law forbidding Jews to defile themselves by entering a 'pagan' house). He must have acted very soon after the death, because the centurion, summoned by Pilate to confirm that the affair was over, has not yet had time to give his report. The procurator, magnanimous for once, grants the wealthy man's request, and Nicodemus goes to help him bury the body.

This is the moment of the dignitaries, the people with contacts who can get themselves listened to by the highest authority in the land. Jesus' usual companions, peasants, fishermen and tax collectors, have been reduced to silence ,and very likely to despair. The only disciples present at the tomb are several loyal and courageous women (although still no explicit mention is made of Mary, Jesus' mother).

Nicodemus brings 'about a hundred pounds' of myrrh and

aloes, according to John (the Roman pound was equivalent to about 11½ ounces, or about 325 grams). Myrrh, a resinous gum, was mixed with aloes[25] and used to embalm corpses, although the practice was usually reserved for the upper classes. Having embalmed the body, Nicodemus and Joseph wrap it in a winding sheet or a linen tunic: translations have differed.[26] If it were a linen tunic, the evangelists might have wanted to suggest that Jesus was the new High Priest, since that is what Annas had been wearing when last we saw him.

Later, according to Matthew, a new delegation of priests, now joined by the Pharisees, go to Pilate to ask him to place a watch on the tomb, for fear that Jesus' disciples would remove the body and claim that he had been resurrected, as he had prophesied. Pilate, no doubt thoroughly sick of all these visits, consents. However, the episode could not have happened when the evangelists say it did. A visit to Pilate 'the day after the Preparation, in other words on the sabbath day, was unthinkable', writes Gilles Becquet.[27] There are two possible interpretations. The delegation might have taken place at another time (though it is hard to see when, since the burial, of which the delegation, according to the text, was informed, could only have occurred just before the sabbath). Or else Matthew wants to deflect possible objections to the resurrection by showing that the well-guarded body could not have been stolen. The latter is by far the most likely explanation.

Matthew is in fact the most reticent about Jesus' appearances after his death. But he tells us that the guards who had been posted to watch the tomb, having seen that the stone closing the entrance had been rolled away (after an earthquake) and also 'an angel of the Lord' descending from heaven, go to tell the chief priests – a surprising thing for Roman legionaries to do. With the inducement of a bribe, the priests order them to say that Jesus' disciples have stolen the body. They also assure them that should Pilate come to hear about it, the chief priests would undertake to sweet-talk him so that the soldiers would not get into trouble. 'The soldiers took the money and carried out their instructions, and to this day that is the story among the Jews:' Matthew is clearly trying to scotch the rumours and to convince sceptics who cannot believe the unbelievable: the Resurrection.

Mary Magdalene had been unable to act on the sabbath. What this most faithful of the faithful had done during those long hours, what thoughts had passed through her mind, no one can say. No doubt the young woman from the village of Magdala, whom seven (*seven!*) evil spirits had persecuted before she met Jesus, had concluded that once again death had had the last word....

It is dawn. The sun is rising above the mountains in the east and just beginning to cast its rosy light onto the city, and Mary Magdalene can wait no longer. Alone – indeed, it might have seemed to her that she was the only living soul that morning – she hurries towards the tomb. She has no expectations of miracles or wonders. She is simply taking to the tomb perfumes and spices, which she has prepared with the other women who had followed every step of Jesus' journey towards death, perhaps because she thinks the body had been too hastily or inadequately prepared, or perhaps because it was customary to take spices to the dead on the third day.[28]

She is not hoping for anything. None of these loyal women are hoping for anything. But at the tomb they find the stone has been rolled away, and people dressed in white – like the young man in Gethsemane – tell them that Jesus' body is not there, for the very simple reason that he is alive. In John's version, the white messengers do not even have time to announce to Mary Magdalene that Jesus had been raised to life. It does not cross her mind that he might be living again: no sooner has she told them, 'They have taken my Lord away ... and I do not know where they have put him,' than she turns round and sees someone whom she takes for the gardener, someone who had perhaps had some hand in the stealing of the body.

But then she recognises him. It is him, Jesus. He entrusts her with telling the others, and she hurries away, delighted, overcome, released.[29] All good news sparks off a trail of joy, and we can picture from the gospel accounts one person telling others 'He is alive!', in a chain of life that mirrors the chain of death in which the men of power had passed Jesus from one to another.

'He is alive!' That declaration would alter the history of the world. Yet for many women and men, even those who admire Jesus and his message, it is unbelievable.

What does the historian have to say about it? Not one scholar would assert, point blank, that Jesus was resurrected. On the other hand, not one, at least among serious academics, can prove that he was not. By studying the texts and analysing their context, however, we can at least edge towards an answer and bring a little light to bear on the subject.

The first point that should be mentioned is that the Jews were quite familiar with the idea of resurrection. For them, the return to life of prophets like Elijah or Moses was in no way surprising.[30] As we have seen, Herod Antipas even believed for a while that John the Baptist had returned from the dead.[31] And when Mark, Matthew or Luke recount the resurrections of the daughter of Jairus or the son of the widow of Nain, they do not seem to think that these miracles are any more remarkable than the others. No more does John when he recounts the resurrection of Lazarus. At the same time, these resurrections involved only a survival, a prolongation of life, whereas far more was involved in Jesus' resurrection than resuscitation after the vital organs had ceased to function. He had taken on a new, other, life.[32] Luke prefers to say that Jesus was 'alive' rather than 'resurrected'.

Having underlined that, let us join the debate. In support of their declaration that Jesus was resurrected, the authors of the New Testament have a fact – the empty tomb – and witnesses.

The gospels relate the discovery of the empty tomb in various, and somewhat contradictory, ways. But for some scholars 'the very inconsistencies ... argue very persuasively that this actually happened':[33] people who had fabricated the whole story in order to strengthen the faith of the first Christian communities would surely have made sure that the versions matched. But one can also argue that the contradictions are awkward.

Two of these versions have received particular attention: John and Luke. As we will see in the Appendix, the gospels underwent several rewritings. Now, most critics believe the verses of John and Luke about the empty tomb[34] to have been written early, close to the time of the actual events,[35] while Mark's account is later.[36] But there are other early texts, such as those of Paul, which do not mention the empty tomb.

Another interesting clue is found in John. He has Peter and 'the disciple Jesus loved' running to the tomb, having been told the news by Mary Magdalene. It is a scene that has a 'realistic feel' to it, since several details are included that evidently have no particular purpose. Peter, for example, is outstripped by his companion who, arriving first at the tomb, hesitates to go in alone and waits for the older man. When he arrives, Peter enters the hole in the rock and sees 'the linen cloths on the ground, and also the cloth that had been over his head; this was not with the linen cloths but rolled up in a place by itself'.[37] If this is compared with the resurrection of Lazarus, it can be seen as a symbol. Lazarus had emerged from the tomb still wrapped in his burial cloths, whereas Jesus had truly entered a new life, free and unfettered. The episode also gives us a historical clue: if Jesus' followers, or others, had come in secret to remove his body, they would hardly have taken the time to leave behind the cloth in which he was wrapped.

Most modern scholars believe that the tomb really was empty. If it had not been, it is difficult to see how Peter and his companions could then have proclaimed the Resurrection to the town. The inhabitants would just have been able to retort: 'Oh, that's interesting – but impossible because his corpse is still in Joseph of Arimathea's tomb!' These scholars acknowledge that the empty tomb does not *prove* the resurrection, and Matthew's version clearly shows that there was a widespread story in the town that the disciples had removed the body. Another hypothesis is that Mary Magdalene, who would have witnessed the burial only from afar, might have mistaken the tomb. Or there could have been two burials: a temporary, hasty one before the festival began, and the permanent, proper one when the sabbath was over.

The empty tomb can therefore be considered only as an interesting element of the story. Although there have been people who have taken their belief in the resurrection to the very limit: even if Jesus' bones were found, they say, they would still believe in his rising from the dead because a body is much more than just flesh and blood. Human beings have a capacity to communicate with others and with the universe that cannot be described in purely physical or scientific terms – and there is also the 'spiritual body', of which St Paul speaks.[38] But here we leave the domain of the historian and enter that of the philosopher and the theologian.

Let us turn to the evidence for the Resurrection. Like the accounts of the discovery of the empty tomb by Mary Magdalene, it is contradictory. Matthew and Mark locates the Easter appearances in Galilee, Luke and John in Jerusalem. That is not enough to discount them, but it does raise questions if one is attempting to establish a chronology. Jesus' companions can obviously not have been simultaneously in two regions that were four days' walk apart.[39]

The accounts of Jesus' appearances after his Resurrection all have the same structure, three separate stages. First, there is the arrival. Jesus suddenly manifests (even through closed doors) where he is not expected, and is not immediately recognised. Second, the recognition. Jesus gives the women or his companions signs – almost passwords – that prove his identity and show that he is not a ghost (he asks doubting Thomas to touch him, or eats grilled fish with them). Third, he charges them with a mission, and promises them the help of the Holy Spirit.

It is therefore a literary genre. This again raises questions, but is not enough to rule out the historical truth of the appearances.

The writers of these texts are concerned to evoke a scene and its meaning rather than merely describe the facts of it in the manner of a modern historian or journalist. The Gospel of Luke illustrates this. He locates all the appearances in or near to Jerusalem on the same day, but the Acts of the Apostles, which he almost certainly also wrote, declares that 'for forty days [Jesus] had continued to appear to them and tell them about the Kingdom of God'.[40] The number forty is suspicious because of its symbolic meaning, but the discrepancy between one and forty also shows that these authors were not very worried about the accuracy of certain details. What is important to them is that Jesus had appeared to his companions. We should also note that, for once, they barely allude to the Scriptures to demonstrate that everything had been foreseen, precisely as though they had been overwhelmed by the unexpected.

There is another witness, who was not one of Jesus' companions: Paul. We can date his first letter to the Christians at Corinth with some accuracy, thanks to a Greek inscription discovered at Delphi, which reproduces a letter addressed to that town by the Emperor Claudius. Archaeologists have established that this letter was written in April or May 52, and it mentions the presence in Greece of the proconsul Gallio (brother of the philosopher Seneca), before whom Paul appeared.[41] Paul's first visit to Corinth would therefore have been at that time, and he would have met Gallio between July and October 51.[42] What does Paul say to the Corinthians? He reminds them that

> In the first place, I taught you what I had been taught myself, namely that Christ died for our sins, in accordance with the Scriptures; that he was buried; and that he was raised to life on the third day, in accordance with the Scriptures; that he appeared first to Cephas and secondly to the Twelve. Next he appeared to more than five hundred of the brothers at the same time, most of whom are still alive, though some have died; then he appeared to James, and then to all the apostles; and last of all he appeared to me too; it was as though I was born when no one expected it.[43]

We can leave aside what Paul had, as he said, been 'taught himself' about Christ dying for our sins, which has more to do with the beliefs of the early Christians than with what Christ actually said. The interest, in relation to the problem before us, lies elsewhere. Here is a man who is writing about events that had happened less than twenty years earlier and which had changed his life. His testimony is therefore important, although that does not of course mean that historians must accept it. And the possibility of a psychological explanation must not be ruled out.

The 'five hundred of the brothers' to whom Jesus had appeared 'at the same time' might cause such doubts: was this in fact some kind of collective ecstatic experience? The appearances to the apostles could also be explained, just about, as a sort of intense wish-fulfilment on their part – something is desired so strongly that it is actually conjured up in imagination, and the hallucinator becomes convinced of the reality of what he has 'seen'. But this was not the case with Paul who, when he set off for Damascus, was still 'breathing threats to slaughter the Lord's disciples'.[44]

The debate on the Resurrection has sparked off other explanations. It has been suggested, for example, that Jesus did not die on the cross, and that Joseph of Arimathea and Nicodemus put Jesus in the tomb, which was not hermetically sealed, so hastily because they wanted to keep him alive. They would simply have gone through the motions of a burial. In the eighteenth century, a theologian named Karl Friedrich Bahrdt even suggested that Joseph and Nicodemus had links with the Essenes, who were behind this scene: this would explain the appearance at the tomb of two men dressed in white, the usual garb of the members of that sect.[45] But if we suppose that Jesus were still living, we have also to suppose that no help could have been given him during the sabbath. The theory, which rests on no precise evidence, is difficult to accept.

An even stranger rumour, which circulated among the Jews, made Judas responsible for the removal of Jesus' body. Judas was a 'pious and wise man' who

had handed him over to his enemies on the Feast of Passover. Jesus
was stoned and hanged on a gibbet. But Judas removed the body of
his master and buried him in a garden, beneath a stream from which
he had diverted the water; he then restored the stream to its
natural course so that the body of Jesus the magician could not be
found.[46]

The most common Jewish explanation at first was of course
that Jesus' body had been removed by his disciples. But neither
the chief priests nor the Romans seem to have done anything
about trying to find it. And if the disciples had simply hidden the
body, would they have had such faith in Jesus that they would
willingly accept torture and martyrdom in his name?

Renan, who also believed that the tomb was empty but had no
theories about who took the body, concluded that 'we will never
know' where the faith in the Resurrection came from. He adds,
alluding to the 'seven demons' that had possessed Mary
Magdalene before she knew Jesus,

We can say however that the strong imagination of Mary
Magdalene would have played a critical role. The divine power of
love! In such sacred moments, the passion of a hallucinator gives
the world a resuscitated God! [47]

In arguing for this theory of hallucination – a theory that others would later hold – Renan highlights an important element in
this decisive episode: the role of women. It is to women that Jesus
first appears – Mary of Magdala and also, according to Luke, another Mary, the mother of James and John, and several others
who are not named. All of them go to tell the good news to the
apostles, 'but this story of theirs seemed pure nonsense and they
did not believe them'.[48] Naturally: in their eyes, these were old
wives' tales. Few ages or societies have given much credence to
women, and this one was no exception. Indeed, it was remarkable
that Jesus, unlike the other rabbis of his time, had always been
surrounded by women, that only the women of his group had

accompanied him to his death, and that women were the first witnesses of the disappearance of his body.

This last point is extremely important. For it scuppers the theory that has been repeated a thousand times over the centuries, that this was an operation mounted by Jesus' disciples, who had taken the body before announcing the Resurrection. If they had wanted to mount such an exercise in mass manipulation, as we would say today, they would have chosen messengers other than women. To have the Resurrection of Jesus announced by women, whoever they were, was the surest method of not being believed. St Paul, a misogynist typical of his time, but above all concerned to convince, was very wary about speaking of the appearances to the women when he announced that Jesus was living. The least worldly-wise of Jesus' companions would have realised that to get such a huge deception accepted it was preferable to use respectable intermediaries such as Nicodemus or Joseph of Arimathea, or another more or less secret member of Jesus' network in Jerusalem, or simply the first man to come along – who would have been more readily believed than a woman, even were she the wife of the steward Chuza.

Of course, this constitutes only an indication, a probability; it does not prove the Resurrection. From the perspective of historians, no such proof exists.

And so?

And so, two men were walking to Emmaus, a village a few miles from Jerusalem – no one knows exactly where. To Emmaus – in other words to emptiness and lost hope. They were tired, they had run out of dreams, of enthusiasm. It was all over. They had given themselves completely to Jesus' movement, certain that he was going to save the world from evil and Israel from the aristocracy of the Temple and the Romans. They had not had pride of place in his movement, belonging to those unknowns who had helped with the organisation and who were sometimes part of his audience, comforting those who had not been able to get near to him,

speak to him or touch his cloak. They had not asked for more.
They had been happy to sacrifice everything to help him. And this
is what it had come to. He had died without trying to defend himself, and all those whom they had seen pressing around him,
whom they had sometimes had to remove by force, had abandoned him. Even the leaders of the movement, the intimate companions whom he had chosen as his 'management', his confidants,
had hidden themselves away, frightened and defeated. It was said
that Peter himself, who had always been ready to push himself to
the fore and to speak for the others, had sworn on his life that he
did not know Jesus. They had thought they were taking part in a
unique adventure that would give their lives a radiant meaning
and purpose and that would lead them, lead everyone, to a world
of joy and fulfilment. All that was left them was a bundle of regrets, bitterness and remorse – it was all over.

Another man joined them, asking them to tell him their
troubles. He was that rarity, a man who knew how to listen. And
then he told them the history of the world, beginning with Moses
and the prophets. Their hearts, warming, began to open. Their
minds, slower on the uptake, would not recognise him until the
moment when, having shared bread with them, he disappeared.

Emerging from darkness and despair, they set off again, back
to Jerusalem. The people they found there were in the same
despair as they had been, a few poor specimens, a handful of
peasants and fishermen, who had proved cowards and turncoats.
They had some contacts with the important people, on whom they
thought they could count, but most of them had suddenly disappeared into thin air. They could not stay in that hostile city much
longer and would have to leave, at night, their heads bowed and
their hearts dead.

Now, those bent men straightened themselves and began con-
fronting every danger, risking their very lives, to declare that
Jesus was alive and that they had the best proof of it: they had
seen him; they had even eaten with him. But it was not what they
said that was the best proof. It was they themselves, those poor,

semi-literate nobodies who resuscitated Jesus' movement, repeating everywhere his words of love and liberation – words that few people would actually put into practice, but which nevertheless would leave an indelible mark on humankind.

Something happened, then, during that time, some explosion of faith that changed those people. They said that that 'something' was their meeting with the living, resurrected Jesus, and they said it even when to say it cost them their lives. No one can prove beyond doubt that that was what really happened. Everyone has the right to doubt it. The God that Jesus proclaimed respects our freedom to the extent of allowing us to doubt Him or reject Him.

And so history cannot say whether Jesus is alive or whether he died forever on 7 April AD 30. What it can say, however, is that something happened during that time which turned those men and women around, and that their transformation would transform the world.

Appendix

Sources

I do indeed think that we can now know almost nothing concerning the life and personality of Jesus, since the early Christian sources show no interest in either, and are moreover fragmentary and often legendary; and other sources about Jesus do not exist.[1]

This pronouncement by the German Lutheran Rudolf Bultmann in 1926 caused something of a stir. Bultmann and other German authors believed that the four gospels were written relatively late, long after the events they described and the words they reported, and that they should be considered as no more than compilations of various stories and traditions – a mixture of moral tales, anecdotes, true and fictional words of Jesus – that had gradually been transformed by the first Christian communities in the laudable aim of witnessing to their faith. These people had altered and obscured the image of their Lord to suit their purpose.

Was it therefore impossible to write a life of Jesus? Some people were too quick to draw that conclusion from Bultmann's findings; he liked to express himself bluntly, and this passage taken out of context gives an over-simplified picture of his views. For he also believed that it was possible to form a coherent impression of what Jesus had preached, and maintained that certain of the events described by the gospels were true. But his words rang out like a challenge, which scholars took up, striving – as this book has often shown – to distinguish between what was 'from Jesus' and what was not, to tease out the evangelists' stylistic additions, their objectives in writing, the cultural influences to

248

which they had been subjected, and the sources they had used. They have also been concerned to establish what elements of the gospels could have been, as these scholars put it, 'productions of the Christian community'. Stories, in other words, that had evolved out of these people's new-found fervour and that were fairly distant from the actual history of Jesus.[2]

Today, no scholar would dare make such a bald statement as Bultmann's – and, paradoxically, this is partly due to the challenge that he himself issued and the methods of research that he initiated. As Eugen Drewermann, hardly a conformist himself, writes:

> The exegesis of the last two decades, following Bultmann, is no longer based on that radical scepticism.... Here and there, certain hypotheses about the historic Jesus are held to be plausible and acceptable and ... the earliest Church is no longer seen as the omnipresent and overwhelming influence on the story of Jesus that it once was.[3]

And a disciple of Bultmann's, Günther Bornkamm (frequently mentioned in this book), commented:

> Quite clearly what the gospels report concerning the message, the deeds and the history of Jesus is still distinguished by an authenticity, a freshness, and a distinctiveness not in any way effaced by the Church's Easter faith. These features point us directly to the earthly figure of Jesus.... Although the gospels do not speak of the history of Jesus in the way of reproducing the course of his career in all its happenings and stages, in its inner and outer development, nevertheless, they do speak of history as occurrence and event. The gospels give abundant evidence of such history. This opinion may be boldly stated, despite the fact that on historical grounds so many of the stories and sayings could be contested in detail.[4]

Thanks to such scholarship, to archaeological discoveries and to research into Judaism at the time of Jesus, we continually know more about Jesus and above all about what he said; scholars disagree, sometimes significantly, about the events of his life but are far more united about his words. This book has attempted to gather together that body of knowledge. We need now to look at some important details about the sources.

References to Jesus himself in non-Christian sources are rare, but they do exist. Most important of these is the Jewish historian Flavius Josephus; born in AD 37 to a priestly family in Jerusalem, he fought against the Romans, was taken prisoner, and subsequently lived in Rome, where he wrote the history of his people – in which he mentioned Jesus. Over the succeeding centuries Christian copyists fraudulently added phrases that were extremely unlikely to have emerged from the pen of a Jew, since they were favourable to Jesus: 'He was the Christ,' for example, and 'On the third day he appeared to them restored to life.' The deception discovered, people tended to reject the whole of the text on Jesus. However, an Israeli scholar, Professor Shlomo Pines, discovered a version of Josephus among some Syrian writings that seems authentic. It is short:

> At this time, lived Jesus, a wise man who performed good deeds; his virtue was recognised. Many Jews and people of other nationalities became his disciples. And Pilate sentenced him to death on the cross. But those who had become his disciples continued to preach his doctrine. They reported that he had appeared to them three days after his crucifixion and that he was alive; accordingly he was perhaps the Messiah [another translation reads 'he was considered as the Messiah'], concerning whom the prophets have recounted wonders.[5]

This sympathetic but slightly sceptical testimony seems to report what the first Christian communities were saying about Jesus. A little later, the same author speaks of the stoning, at the instigation of a chief priest, of 'James, brother of Jesus who is called Christ'.[6]

Jesus is also mentioned in ancient Jewish texts. These references are generally fairly hostile, and seem not to have been written before the fifth or sixth century. Writing about the events after the burning of Rome, for which responsibility was pinned on the Christians, the Roman author Tacitus says in his *Annals* that Nero inflicted

> the utmost refinements of torture on those, despised for their abominable crimes, whom the people called Christians. This name was derived from Christus, who, under the reign of Tiberius, had been put to death by Pontius Pilate. Suppressed for a brief time, this despicable superstition arose again, not only throughout Judaea where the evil had originated, but even in Rome.[7]

This text was probably written around AD 115–16.

Finally, the existence of a sect that had abandoned temples and the sacrifice of animals and that worshipped a certain Christus (or Chrestus), whom they considered a god, was mentioned in a letter from Pliny the Younger, a governor in Asia Minor, to the Emperor Trajan.[8] Suetonius said in *The Twelve Caesars*, written around 120, that Claudius had expelled Jews from Rome in AD 49 because they 'caused continual disturbances at the instigation of Christus'.[9]

As Günther Bornkamm wrote,

> These pagan and Jewish sources are of importance only in so far as they confirm the fact which was otherwise well known, that in the early days it never occurred even to the fiercest adversary of Christianity to doubt the historical existence of Jesus at all. This was reserved for an unrestrained, tendentious criticism of modern times.[10]

Today, no serious historian questions Jesus' existence. But since the above is the sum total of non-Christian sources, the only means we have of knowing anything more about him are the Christian texts. We should ask two main questions about these: how reliable are they, and how were they compiled?

The first point to be made is that we do not have any originals of ancient works, only copies of copies, and that includes the gospels. However, the copies of the gospels are older than those of other works. The oldest manuscripts of other texts date from the eighth century, whereas the oldest manuscripts of the gospels date from the fourth century. The actual writing of the gospels and the earliest complete copies that we have of them are therefore separated by only three centuries. In other words, these texts have come down to us in a better state than many other literary, religious or philosophical works from the ancient world.[11] Four centuries separate Virgil from the oldest manuscripts of his work, thirteen centuries in the case of Plato, and sixteen in that of Euripides. Obviously, the more a text is copied and recopied, the greater the risk that alterations will be made to it, and the copies of the gospels are therefore more free from such adulteration. Scholars have been able to reconstitute the texts as they would have been around AD250, and the discovery in Egypt of papyri containing fragments of the gospels, such as the Bodmer papyri dating from the early third century or, better still, the Rylands (so called because it is kept in the John Rylands library in Manchester), which dates from before AD 150 and contains several verses from John, confirm the validity of the texts in our possession. So do the quotations from the gospels found in various documents written between the end of the first century and the end of the second. It is important to note that, with the exception of John, and contrary to what is often said, the gospels were written shortly after the events, when witnesses to them were still alive.

The story of the gospels merits a very large volume in itself – and there are indeed many such books, so voluminous is the research on the subject and so extensive the debate. One of these debates polarises those who uphold the 'oral tradition' against those who favour the 'written tradition'. This argument can be roughly summarised as follows. According to the oral-tradition camp, the first Christian communities sent out missionaries to take their message in person to the Mediterranean world, since this was almost the only way of transmitting a message on a large scale in an age in which few people knew how to read and write. People had developed techniques that allowed them to remember the texts transmitted by word of mouth more easily, particularly the Jews, the disciples of rabbis, who had been taught to repeat faithfully the teachings of their master. That said, 'memory can play tricks; many a slip is possible between the hearing of a thing and its repetition to another person'.[12]

'Objection!' cry other scholars. Palestine was not a country with a strong oral tradition, for the simple reason that it was situated at the heart of the Near East, where writing probably originated. At the time of Jesus, alphabetic writing had already been in existence for more than a thousand years. It was a nation of scribes (not all of whom were Jesus' opponents). Some of the apostles were undoubtedly illiterate: Peter ends his first Epistle 'I write these few words to you through Silvanus.'[13] On the other hand, to take only one example, Matthew the tax collector must necessarily have been able to keep written accounts. It is also likely that there were people among Jesus' lesser-known disciples who could read and write. These people would have taken notes, so important did they feel the Master's words to be.

Adherents of both camps are agreed on one thing: anthologies of Jesus' sayings (*logia*), designed to help the missionaries, began to appear quite soon after his life. These *logia* would have been used in the writing of the gospels. In what language were they written? In Aramaic, the language of the people? Hebrew, the language of rabbis and scholars? Or even Greek, widely used in some towns?

Claude Tresmontant, who teaches the philosophy of science at the Sorbonne, and who has translated the gospels, has vigorously defended the theory that the logia were first written in Hebrew.

> When one reads the Gospel of Matthew carefully, in its current version, that is in the Greek, and then the Gospels of Mark and of Luke, one is struck by the realisation that typical Hebrew expressions have constantly been simply reproduced in Greek.[14]

Tresmontant adds that these translations are more faithful to the original; the translators were not concerned about writing litera-ture but simply strove to follow the Hebrew texts that they had before them as closely as possible.

'*Traduttòre: tradditòre*' ('translator equals betrayer'), say the Italians. Thought is expressed and framed in language, and is necessarily influenced by it. By attempting to return to Hebrew sources of the gospels, of which we possess only Greek texts, Tresmontant and others have shed interesting light on the debate. But their theory is strongly contested by the great majority of scholars, who detect underneath the Greek of the gospels not Hebrew but purely Aramaic ways of speaking or writing. Some even believe that Aramaic *logia* existed at the time of Jesus.

The debate demonstrates what knotty problems face those who study the gospels.[15] By comparing the texts, these scholars soon discovered that many passages were the same (apart from the Gospel of John, which is almost completely original). The gospels, like most sacred books, are divided into small paragraphs called verses. Now, around 600 of the 1,068 verses in Matthew's gospel, and 350 of the 1,149 verses in Luke's gospel, are similar to ones in Mark. In addition, Matthew and Luke have another 235 verses in common. From which the question naturally arose: had they all copied one another? Or had Mark been copied by the two others? Or were the similarities explained by the fact that they had re-ferred to a common source, the famous *logia*?

The debate on this would, again, easily fill a library. Most scholars believe in the existence of two main sources, Mark and 'Q' (from the German *Quelle*, meaning 'source'). But there is no unanimity. Others think that the writers had access to a wider range of documents. A good summary of the various complex positions is found in Philippe Rolland, who argues, in his recent and scholarly book, that Mark, Matthew and Luke, called the Synoptic Gospels, were partly inspired by a version of Matthew written in Hebrew.[16]

Mark. The gospel of Mark, or at least the Greek text that we have, seems to have been written first. According to Irenaeus, the Bishop of Lyon who played a large part in the story of the gospels, 'Mark, disciple and interpreter of Peter, also wrote down for us what Peter preached.'[17] Moreover, in an epistle, Peter calls Mark by the friendly 'my son'.[18] Most scholars locate Mark's text between the fire of Rome in AD 64 and the destruction of the Temple in 70. It was therefore written very close to the events it describes. As well as the testimony of Peter, Mark drew on the various traditions and beliefs of the earliest Christian communities.[19] Some scholars have even detected similarities to Paul in his text, suggesting an influence. Mark writes in a simple, lively style, apparently for non-Jews: he explains Jewish customs, gives geographical details, is rarely concerned to explain that everything was carried out according to the Scriptures, and insists on the universal import of Jesus' message. His gospel is the shortest. It is focused on the trial, the Passion, the death and the Resurrection.

Matthew. The gospel of Matthew would have been written second, again at least in its Greek version: for some scholars, there was a Hebrew or Aramaic Matthew before Mark and from which Mark may even have drawn some of his material. Pretty well all the research dates Matthew's text at around AD 80. Some commentators think he was contemporary with Mark, or even earlier, and this was also the belief of the early religious writers whom we call the Church Fathers. Matthew did not intend to write a clinically objective text; his aim was to convince (and also, at times, to moralise). He wrote for the Jews, constantly referring to the Old Testament,[20] to demonstrate that Jesus had fulfilled its promises. Matthew was completely immersed in Hebraic culture – as shown, for example, by his frequent use of the symbolic numbers three and seven.

Luke. According to several second-century writers, the gospel of Luke was written by a Syrian, originally from Antioch, a doctor who had accompanied Paul on his travels – although many scholars have contested this last point. As we have said, almost all attribute the Acts of the Apostles and the Gospel of Luke to the same person, because of the similarity in style and structure and because both texts are dedicated to a certain Theophilus. It is also possible that Luke met Peter in Rome between AD 61 and 63.

The date of the writing of this gospel has given rise to a battle of the experts which does not seem to be anywhere near to a resolution: between AD 60 and 80, according to the various opinions. In his preface, Luke declares that he has decided to write his gospel 'after carefully going over the whole story from the beginning'.[21] Some have concluded that Luke knew Mary personally, but this hardly seems possible, since she would have been born around 25 BC, and it is a theory that is not in any case backed up by any evidence. Luke is more cautious about dates and numbers than Mark and Matthew (he often uses the word 'about'), but certain passages indicate that he did not know Palestine personally.[22]

Luke, a polished and literary writer, seeks above all to show that the biblical story, from the birth of Israel to the emergence of the Church under the inspiration of the Holy Spirit, and focusing on the central event of the coming of Jesus, is the unfolding of a single divine plan. He is mainly addressing pagans, who have been influenced by the Greeks. Given Luke's obvious aim, his text cannot be viewed as scientifically accurate, but he had met many witnesses, and probably seen other texts that have today disappeared. As he writes in his preface: 'Many others have undertaken to draw up accounts of the events that have taken place among us, exactly as these were handed down to us by those who from the outset were eyewitnesses.'[23]

John. The gospel of John is very different from the three others. First, it was written later. Almost all scholars date it around the year AD 100, perhaps a little earlier. As several Church Fathers asserted, it seems to have been preceded by another 'edition', if not two or three, the first of which was written by the apostle John,[24] but this theory cannot be definitively verified.

John loved symbols, as we have seen in regard to the wedding at Cana, for example. But his historical import, independent of the three others, is nonetheless considerable, particularly in regard to

Jesus' visits to Jerusalem. On the other hand, the words that John attributes to Jesus are often 'composed' by a writer who is above all concerned to demonstrate his subject's divinity.

Other sources. Other Christian sources exist: primarily the Epistles and the Acts of the Apostles, but the information they give about the historical Jesus is limited. Paul's letters, for example, say much about Jesus and his teaching, but in the way of biographical detail tell us only that Jesus, a Jewish descendant of David, had instituted the Eucharist during a meal with his disciples before undergoing various ordeals, dying under Pontius Pilate and then being resurrected. Finally, in the Acts of the Apostles, Paul attributes a saying to Jesus unknown in the gospels: 'There is more happiness in giving than in receiving.'[25]

This leaves the gospels that are called 'apocryphal' (which did not originally mean 'false' but 'hidden'). It seems that fairly quickly, in the first and second centuries, numerous texts grew up recounting Jesus' words or episodes from his life. Many have disappeared, and their existence is known only because they are mentioned — usually with disdain — by Church Fathers such as Origen, Irenaeus, Jerome, Eusebius of Caesarea or Epiphanius of Salamis. Some of these apocrypha were popularly considered to be 'inspired'. Some gave rise to traditions such as the Presentation of Mary at the Temple or the Feast of St Anne, supposed to be the mother of Mary, and they also contributed much to medieval art, although Renan considered them 'flat and puerile additions, usually based on the canonical gospels and adding nothing of worth.'[26] Many are devoted to Jesus' childhood, which they furnish with marvellous happenings: in the pseudo-gospel of Matthew, for example, lions and leopards come to worship the baby Jesus during the flight into Egypt, and the infant makes palm trees bend down so that he can give their fruit to his mother.[27] Many of these texts, all written after the lifetimes of people who had actually known Christ, seem to have been influenced by other eastern religions.

Between the second and the fourth centuries, the Church came

257

gradually to distinguish between the 'canonical' and the 'apo-cryphal' gospels. One man in particular seems to have played a decisive role in this: Irenaeus, a native of Smyrna, where he was a disciple of Polycarp, who had in turn been a disciple of John. These apocryphal gospels may not generally be of much use to the historian, but a special place must be given to one called the Gospel of Thomas, an anthology of words attributed to Jesus – exactly 114 *logia* – which came to light in Upper Egypt, near Nag Hammadi, at the end of the Second World War, when a jar containing a dozen papyrus manuscripts written in Coptic and dating from the third or fourth centuries was uncovered in the cave-dotted mountainside. Although they were very much later than Jesus' lifetime,[28] the original text was certainly written earlier.

One can imagine the excitement that scholars felt at this discovery. Over half of these *logia* already featured in the four gospels, and others seemed to have been influenced by the eastern religions that were very much in vogue in the third and fourth centuries. Perhaps a dozen might have been authentic. One, for example, that other Christian writers had cited: 'He who is near me is near the fire. He who is far from me is far from the Kingdom.' But in any event, the text casts barely any new light on the life of Jesus. The four so-called canonical gospels, enriched by all our knowledge about them, therefore remain our principal sources.

As we have seen throughout this book, the gospels contradict one another on many details, and sometimes on important facts (such as the number of journeys to Jerusalem). We have also seen that not everything they say can be considered historically accurate, although at that time every Jew, immersed as he had been in knowledge of the Scriptures, believed that the meaning of an event was more important and truthful than the facts surrounding it. Throughout the Mediterranean basin, those who undertook to write histories were not very concerned about writing what was absolutely accurate and literally true.

The gospels have been scrutinised and examined more than any other texts of that time, although some of these seem *a priori* more debatable.[29] Questions are still being asked about the texts and translations of Matthew, Mark, Luke and John, but such inquiry is positive, because it means that scholars continue to be inspired to further research and debate. 'Criteria of authenticity' have been developed that allow us to verify the historical accuracy of a saying or an event.[30]

The most recent discoveries seem to confirm certain of the gospel accounts. For example, the famous parable of the Pharisee and the publican,[31] where Jesus has the Pharisee self-righteously declaring, 'I thank you, God, that I am not ... like the rest of mankind.' The phrase 'I thank you, God, that ...' is found only once in the Old Testament, at the beginning of a poem in Isaiah,[32] and is unknown in any contemporaneous Jewish texts. Scholars wondered where Jesus could have taken such a phrase from – until the discovery of manuscripts at Qumran: it is used fourteen (out of eighteen) times at the beginning of Essene hymns. This confirms Luke's text, but also seems to suggest that Jesus was having a little fun at the Pharisees' expense, because Pharisees and Essenes were hardly bosom pals likely to borrow one another's language.

Or, for example, the meal taken at the publican Levi's house, recounted by Mark.[33] Jesus found Levi 'sitting by the customs house', which indicates that there was a frontier there, between Capernaum and Bethsaida. For a time, it was thought that the story was an invention of the first Christian communities to sanction meals between Jewish and non-Jewish Christians: if Jesus had eaten with publicans and fishermen, they could do as much. Today, however, we know that such a frontier did indeed exist, but had been abolished between AD 39 and 46, in the reign of Agrippa I, under whom the eastern and western parts of the Jordan were united.

Another example concerns Pilate, whose role – and even existence – has sometimes been questioned. Gerd Theissen of Heidelberg University comments ironically that if there had been in first-century Palestine a 'Committee for Misleading Later

Historians',[34] dedicated to creating a false picture of contemporary events, they would have had their work cut out, since they would have had to give false information about Pilate to Josephus, Tacitus and Philo of Alexandria, plant brass coins inscribed with Pilate throughout Palestine, and write an inscription on a step of the theatre at Caesarea to the effect that Pilate had rendered homage to his emperor. Theissen writes:

> The chance distribution of remains and sources about Pilate, convince us that Pilate lived. What the gospels write about him does not contradict the other sources, but cannot be derived from them. In the case of Pilate there is no doubt that the gospels have an 'historical background'. One could argue in a similar way for Herod Antipas.

The evangelists relate words and episodes that run counter to the objectives of the early Church. Thus, whereas the Church was anxious to convert Gentiles, Matthew attributes the following to Jesus: 'Do not turn your steps to pagan territory, and do not enter any Samaritan town; go rather to the lost sheep of the House of Israel.'[35] The fact that the evangelists reproduce such sentiments – somewhat mysterious and contradictory to many others – demonstrates a certain integrity on their part. Similarly, the early Church had hesitated to include the famous episode of the adulterous woman,[36] for fear, if St Augustine is to be believed, that it would be interpreted as condoning her behaviour.

Even more serious for the Church is the fact that the gospels do not mention the concept. The famous phrase attributed to Jesus: 'You are Peter [rock] and on this rock I will build my Church'[37] is of uncertain authenticity. The absence of other and firmer allusions in the gospels means that the question of whether Jesus had truly wanted to found a church is still debated.

Finally, as Xavier Léon-Dufour writes:

> Why do the gospels not eliminate certain sayings of Jesus which raise immense difficulties about his divinity: e.g. his statement that

'the father is greater than I' (John 14:28), his prayer in Gethsemane, his cry on the cross 'My God, my God, why hast though forsaken me?' If the evangelists were really writing naked apologetic, they made a poor success of it, stressing as they do the sufferings, the weakness, and the disappointments of Jesus.[38]

Fr Léon-Dufour also points out that certain later copyists of the text tried to modify Jesus' anguished cry as he was dying by changing it to: 'My strength, my strength, it is forsaking me,' and that the gospels show that Jesus does not know the day or time of the coming of the Kingdom.

We could go on with the list. And the conclusion of all this is inevitable: the gospels, our best – indeed almost our only – source of knowledge about Jesus, are at once complex and simple, obscure and enlightening, products of their age and applicable to all ages. We cannot reasonably deny that they are honest testimonies, and we must hope that the work of scholars will continue to shed light on them.

Notes

Chapter 1

1. The age at which boys became adults, from a religious perspective, was set at thirteen, but exceptions were occasionally made in the case of gifted boys. Several authors consider that the episode of the boy Jesus and the scribes in the Gospel of Luke was in fact his bar mitzvah. But that ceremony, which is now in common usage throughout the world for Jewish boys, seems not to have existed at the time of Jesus. According to the *Dictionnaire encyclopédique du judaisme*, Cerf, 1993, p. 31, no trace of the bar mitzvah can be found before 1400.

2. Psalm 122:1–2.

3. Flavius Josephus, *The Wars of the Jews*, III, 1–3.

4. Psalm 137:5.

5. Herod began the construction in 20 or 21 BC.

6. Erected on the foundations whose stones today form the Wailing Wall.

7. His good behaviour is confirmed by the Gospels of Matthew and Luke, the only ones to deal with Jesus' childhood, although not his independence of spirit. However, from the great independence that he later demonstrated, we can legitimately presume that it also existed in childhood.

8. A subject that would provoke much debate.

9. The Greek word used in the gospel, *teknon*, means, 'my little one', and literally, 'you to whom I gave birth', which, as France Quéré comments (*Jésus enfant*, Desclée de Brouwer, 1992), neatly combines emotion with reproach.

Chapter 2

1. Pierre Teilhard de Chardin, *The Phenomenon of Man*, trans. from French by Bernard Wall, Collins, 1965.

2. 1 Corinthians 15:2.

3. Luke 3:23.

4. John 8:57.

5. In his principal work *Adversus Haereses* or *Against Heresies*.

6. Charles Perrot, *Jésus et l'Histoire*, Desclée de Brouwer, 1979, p. 86. See also Oscar Cullman's *La Nativité et l'arbre de Noël*, Cerf, 1993.

7. The monk Dionysius based his calculations on Luke, according to whom Jesus had begun his 'public life' at the age of thirty, in the 'fifteenth year of Tiberius Caesar's reign, when Pontius Pilate was governor of Judaea, Herod tetrarch of Galilee', etc. Now, the fifteenth year of Tiberius's reign occurred in the year 782 of the Roman calendar. 782 − 30 = 752. Simple. The only problem is that Herod died in 750, and Matthew and Luke assert that Jesus was born during his time. Historians have pointed out that before reigning alone Tiberius had shared power with his predecessor Augustus; Luke's 'fifteenth year of Tiberius Caesar's reign' would therefore be in 779 according to the Roman calendar, and Jesus would have been born in 3 BC.

There remains the reference to Quirinius as governor of Syria at the time of the census. A theory has been advanced that he began his period of office only at the end of a census that had begun much earlier. This is possible: a census in Gaul had met with such opposition from the inhabitants that it took forty years to complete − and the Jews were no less opposed to Roman rule than the Gauls. A census begun in Herod's lifetime might therefore not have been completed until the time of Quirinius, ten years later.

Some people have based a theory that Jesus was born in 6 or 7 BC on the conjunction of Saturn and Jupiter that occurred at that time, which would have given the appearance of a very brilliant star such as the one Matthew has guiding the Magi. But this reference can obviously not be upheld by serious historians.

8. According to France Quéré, 'these errors in dating are based on the deliberate negligence of the evangelists who did not take the trouble to adjust or check their facts'. In their eyes, this period was not important and deserved no better than a vague outline since 'the age of the emperors was not favoured by God' (France Quéré, *Jésus enfant, op. cit.*, pp. 55 and 61).

9. Gabriel specialised in very important announcements in the Bible, particularly those concerning 'the end of time' (cf. Charles Perrot, 'Les récits de l'enfance de Jésus' in *Cahiers Evangile*, no. 18, p. 43), and was an 'assistant at the throne of God', one of His very close collaborators (cf. F. Neyrinck, 'L'Evangile de Noël', in *Etudes religieuses*, no. 749, p.25).

10. Zechariah is punished because as a priest he would know the case of Isaac,

born when his father Abraham was 100 and his mother Sarah 90 years old, and should therefore have accepted the news without a murmur. As for Mary, she is 'confronted with a situation that is radically new: the Bible has no other incidents of conception without sexual union' (Hugues Cousin, *Evangile de Luc*, Centurion, 1993, p. 29).

11. 1 Samuel 2:4.

12. Luke 1:52.

13. Luke 1:53.

14. Justin, *The Dialogue with Trypho*, LXXXVIII, 8.

15. Cf. Christian-Bernard Amphoux, *La Parole qui devint Evangile*, Seuil, 1993, p. 15; Hermann Strack and Paul Billerbeck, *Das Leben Jesu nach Jüdischen Quellen*, Munich; and particularly Celsus, a pagan who lived in Rome, author of *Of the True Doctrine*, written in AD 178 (see also *Against Celsus* by Origen, I, 28).

16. Matthew 1:24.

17. Luke 3:38.

18. Matthew 1:16. It must be noted that Matthew has Joseph descending from Jeconiah, of whom the prophet Jeremiah said: 'none of his descendants will have the fortune to sit on the throne of David' (Jeremiah 22:28–30). Bishop Irenaeus saw this as an additional proof of Jesus' virgin birth (*Against Heresies*, III, 21, 9). This confirms the obvious contradiction between the virgin birth and the descent from David.... The whole of this complex debate is well summarised in Raymond E. Brown's *The Birth of the Messiah*, Doubleday, pp. 505ff.

19. Romans 1:3.

20. Galatians 4:4.

21. Luke 2:49.

22. Charles de Guignes, *Histoire des Huns*, Paris, 1756.

23. XIX, 8. Cf. M. Philolenko, *Les Interpolations chrétiennes des testaments des douze patriarches et les manuscrits de Qumràn*, Paris 1960. The 'Essenism' of these testimonies has however been disputed.

24. Josy Eisenberg, *La Femme au temps de la Bible*, Stock, 1993, p. 369.

25. Justin, *The Dialogue with Trypho*, written in AD 155.

26. Matthew 1:22–3.

27. John 1:45.

28. C. H. Dodd, *The Interpretation of the Fourth Gospel*, Cambridge University Press, 1953, p. 260, note 1. Ignace de la Potterie gives a different, although not entirely convincing, interpretation in his 'La conception virginale de Jésus selon saint Jean', in *Marie, dans le mystère de l'Alliance*, Desclée de Brouwer, 1988, pp. 99–172.

29. In this regard, Eugen Drewermann writes (*La Parole qui guérit* [*Wort des Heils, Wort der Heilung*], Cerf, 1991): 'If one says that Mary's virginity is only symbolic, most people think that that means it must then have been imaginary and subjective, and therefore unreal. *We must re-learn that symbols communicate a reality that cannot be translated into any other language, that there are truths that cannot be expressed in any other form but through myths, sagas and tales*' [author's italics].

Chapter 3

1. 2 Samuel 24:2–24.

2. Luke says that there was no room for them at the inn. But no one at that time would have dreamed of taking to an inn a young woman about to give birth, to a caravanserai where people ate and slept cheek by jowl. What is more, men were never present at births – they did not get involved until the circumcision. There are many midwives in the Bible, and not one obstetrician. Luke's claim is therefore surprising. Unless he never spoke about an inn. For the Greek text uses the word *katalyma* which does not mean 'inn' anywhere else in the gospels or other literature. France Quéré comments (*Jésus enfant, op. cit.*): '*Katalyma* is a room, whose etymology leads us to suppose that it was a place where one deposited one's belongings: a kind of left luggage.' And she suggests that Joseph, looking for a secluded and sheltered place where his wife could be free from the stares of the curious, had thought of a luggage room but had found it was littered 'with all the paraphernalia that this forced tourism necessitated' and in which they were perhaps disturbed by all the comings and goings of people taking or leaving belongings. In desperation, they removed to a nearby stable.

3. Joachim Jeremias, *Jerusalem at the Time of Jesus*, trans. from German by F. H. and C. H. Cave, SCM Press, 1969 (reissued SCM, 1985), p. 66.

4. Mark 3:13–19.

5. Ruth 4:17. On this subject, cf. Josy Eisenberg, *La Femme au temps de la Bible, op. cit.*, p. 38.

6. Luke 1:60.

7. Luke 2:22.

8. Luke 2:23.

9. Luke 2:34–35.

10. Micah 5:2. According to André Paul ('L'Evangile de l'enfance selon Matthieu', *Lectures bibliques*, 1984, pp. 133–7), Micah's text had been 'reworked, transformed and amplified' by the evangelist in order to emphasise that Jesus, born in Bethlehem as a son of David and fulfilling the divine promises transmitted through the prophets, was indeed the Messiah. Many scholars also underline the similarities between the account of Jesus' birth and the *midrash* of Moses (the *midrash* were texts consisting of updated Scriptures for use in the synagogues, almost as though we were today to describe Jesus' life with the help of slang). It seems that the earliest Christians had thus 'slipped' certain accounts about Jesus' birth into the biblical accounts of his childhood (cf. Charles Perrot, 'Les récits de l'enfance de Jésus', *art. cit.*, pp. 11–16).

11. 1 Samuel 16:1.

12. John 7:42–3.

13. Matthew 2:11.

14. *La Bible du peuple de Dieu*, Ecole Biblique, Jerusalem, vol. 4, Cerf-Centurion, 1973.

15. The tradition that they were kings developed later, and even gave them names: Gaspar, Melchior and Balthasar, one of whom was black.

16. 'Let them come forward now and save you, these who analyse the heavens, who study the stars and announce month by month what will happen to you next. Oh, they will be like wisps of straw and the fire will burn them. They will not save their lives from the power of the flame' (Isaiah 47:13).
    And in Leviticus, that guide to laws and regulations: 'Do not have recourse to the spirits of the dead or to magicians; they will defile you. I am Yahweh, your God' (19:13).

17. Matthew 2:13.

18. Matthew 2:15. The 'oracle' quoted is Hosea (11:1).

19. Exodus 11:4–5.

20. Exodus 12:11–23.

21. Charles Perrot, *Jésus et l'Histoire, op. cit.*, p. 76. See also the same author in 'Les récits de l'enfance de Jésus', special edition of the journal already quoted, which begins with Etienne Charpentier's observation: 'The childhood narratives have too often in the past been read as folk tales whereas they are, above all, theology.' Not history.

22. Cf. *Jésus aujourd'hui. Historiens et exégètes à Radio-Canada*, vol. 2: *Vie, message et personnalité*, Bellarmin-Fleurus, 1980.

23. C. H. Dodd, *The Founder of Christianity*, Collins, 1971 (reissued Shoreline, 1993).

24. Used of Samuel (1 Samuel 2:26).

Chapter 4

1. Deuteronomy 22:8.

2. Genesis 9:4–5.

3. Acts 10:11–14. On the other hand, there are the words given to Jesus by Mark (7:18–19): 'Do you not understand either? Can you not see that whatever goes into a man from outside cannot make him unclean, because it does not go into his heart but through his stomach and passes out into the sewer? (Thus he pronounced all foods clean.)' However, some people consider that these words, and particularly the parenthesis, originate from Paul.

4. Deuteronomy 11:8–9.

5. Ernest Renan, *Vie de Jésus*, Arlea, 1992, p. 82.

6. *Ibid.*, p. 71.

7. The discovery in 1961 of an inscription at Caesarea referring to Pilate as 'prefect' suggests that the title was also used for the governor of the province of Judaea.

8. Josephus, *Antiquities* XVIII, 11–25.

9. Cf. Jean Giblet, 'Un mouvement de resistance armée au temps de Jésus' in *Revue théologique de Louvain*, no. 5, 1974, pp. 410–26, who, without denying the importance of the opposition to the Romans, concludes: 'At the time of Jesus, signs of revolutionary preparation were hardly apparent and, above all, there are few indications of operations undertaken by armed revolutionary groups.'

10. According to Joachim Jeremias, *Jerusalem at the Time of Jesus, op. cit.*

11. Matthew 20:1–16.

12. Cf. *Dictionnaire encyclopédique du judaïsme, op. cit.*, p. 55.

13. John 7:49.

14. H. Daniel-Rops, *Jesus in his Time*, trans. from French by R. W. Millar, Eyre & Spottiswoode, 1950, p. 134.

15. *Vie de Jésus, op. cit.*, p. 21.

16. Luke 4:16–20.

17. John 8:3–5.

18. Numbers 15:37–9.

19. On waking, he praised 'He who stretches the earth over the waters, for His grace is eternal'. While tying the laces of his sandals, he thanked God for having 'seen to all his needs'. While fastening his belt, he invoked the Eternal 'who encircles Israel with His power'. And when he went to the corner that served as lavatory, he blessed God for having 'fashioned man wisely and created in him entrances and exits'.

20. Mark 6:3.

21. Matthew 13:55–6.

22. Mark 3:32.

23. John 7:5.

24. Acts 1:14.

25. Galatians 1:18–19.

26. 1 Corinthians 9:5.

27. *Antiquities* XX, 200.

28. John 19:25.

29. Fr Xavier Léon-Dufour, in vol. 2 of his *Lecture de l'Evangile selon Jean*, published with the imprimatur, Seuil, 1990, writes in a discreet note (p. 212): 'Who are these "brothers" of Jesus'? Criticism has tended to conclude that they are, according to the meaning of the Greek word *adelphos*, brothers in the sense of blood. *For reasons of a theological nature*, Catholics usually return to the Hebrew term *ah* which can have a very wide meaning: people of the same family.' [Author's italics at *'for reasons of a theological nature'*.]

    Claude Tresmontant, a lay commentator who argues, in essence, that the gospels were first written in the very midst of the events they described and in Hebrew – a theory rejected by most other scholars – writes (in *Le Christ hébreu: la langue et l'âge des Evangiles*, Œil, 1984, p.91): 'This expression [brother of the Lord] *should not upset anyone*. One has only to consult ancient Hebrew literature to see how and in what sense the ancient Hebrews used the Hebrew term *ah*, which has been translated into Greek as *adelphos*.'

    In support of his argument, Tresmontant cites several passages from Genesis, for example the one in which Jacob's uncle, Laban, calls him his 'brother' (Genesis 29:15). He adds, quoting Deuteronomy, 'To designate what we, in twentieth century French, call brothers, Hebrew used a particular expression: brother, the son of your father,... sister, the daughter of her father,... my brothers, sons of my mother.'

All these examples are taken from the Old Testament. [The author underlines 'should not upset anyone' because such a reassurance seems to him significant.]

30. Colossians 4:10.

31. Luke 2:25.

32. Matthew 1:25.

33. *Jésus enfant, op. cit.*, p. 113, note 25.

34. He reminds 'readers of the Catholic faith that the *Magisterium* to which they are submitted and the role that they are called to accord to Tradition should *also* play a part in their reading and understanding of Scripture. This last is therefore not the *sole* standard of faith for them. This is particularly pertinent in relation to Marian doctrine' (*Jésus enfant, op. cit.*, p. 6).

According to *Larousse*, the *Magisterium* is 'the whole of that which, taking its authority in the name of Christ, is charged with the interpretation of revealed doctrine (pope, ecumenical councils, bishops)', and 'tradition' is 'the doctrines of faith not directly contained in written Revelation but based on the continuing teaching and institutions of a religion'.

In other words, these are undoubtedly both authorised and respectable interpretations, but not history.

35. André Chouraqui, *La Vie quotidienne des hommes de la Bible*, Hachette, 1978, p. 156.

36. Genesis 30:2.

37. Psalm 128:3.

38. 1 Corinthians 7:25–8.

39. 1 Corinthians 7:5.

40. This refers to a gospel attributed to James and one attributed to Peter. According to the James text, Mary's parents had decided to consecrate her to the Lord when she was twelve years old, and the High Priest of Jerusalem picked out an elderly widower as her guardian. This was Joseph. However, having to go away for four years, he was astonished on his return to find the girl pregnant and unable to say how she had become so since she had not had relations with a man. Both were arrested by the

High Priest, but their integrity was eventually recognised. Joseph had been entrusted with Mary's care when he was ninety years old, no less, when he already had six children, four boys and two girls.

41. In which case there are perhaps distant descendants of Joseph and Mary living today.

Chapter 5

1. Luke 1:15–16.

2. Matthew 3:4.

3. 2 Kings 1:8.

4. Cf. Jean-Paul Roux, *Jésus*, Fayard, 1989, p.68.

5. In his *Odes*, Horace applies the phrase *praesens divus*, 'propitious divinity', to Augustus.

6. Isaiah 59:4 and 9–11.

7. Matthew 3:7 and Luke 3:7.

8. Matthew 3:9 and Luke 3:8.

9. Matthew 3:10 and Luke 3:9.

10. Mark 2:19.

11. *Antiquities* XVIII, 116–19.

12. The whole of this very vivid scene is in Luke 3:10–14.

13. John 1:19–23.

14. Stagnant, or 'dead', water was held to be totally impure. The Temple's need for fresh water was such that a system of channels via the terraces and a huge underground network had to be built. During excavations of the Herodian quarter of Jerusalem, where the priests and their families lived, archaeologists discovered numerous purification basins (cf. Jacqueline Génot-Bismuth, *Jérusalem ressuscitée*, Œil–Albin Michel, 1993).

15. On this point, cf. Charles Perrot *Jésus et l'Histoire, op. cit.*, pp. 98–9. But others believe that almost all the Jewish groups that practised water rites appeared in the last decades of the century (cf. Simon Legasse, *Naissance du baptême*, Cerf, 1993, pp. 51-4).

16. *Wars of the Jews*, II, 8.

17. Luke 1:80.

18. *Wars of the Jews*, II, 2.

19. John Drane, *Jesus and the Four Gospels*, Lion Publishing, 1979, p. 42.

20. Matthew 3:12 and Luke 3:17.

21. John 1:29.

22. 'Jesus is not here the new religious victim, he is the one through whom God intervenes in the world by offering humanity a perfect reconciliation with Himself' (*Lecture de l'Evangile selon Jean, op. cit.*, vol. 1, p. 174).

23. Matthew 3:13–14.

24. Quoted by St Jerome, a Church Father who lived in the fourth century and who contributed much to exegetical commentary.

25. Luke 3:21.

26. *Lecture de l'Evangile selon Jean, op. cit.*, p. 178.

27. Jacques Guillet, *Jesus Christ, Yesterday and Today*, trans. from French by John Duggan, SJ, Geoffrey Chapman, 1965, p. 46.

28. David Flusser, *Jesus*, trans. from German by Ronald Walls, Herder & Herder, 1969, p. 29.

29. Isaiah 42:1.

30. This is a variant: the *Jerusalem* gives, 'You are my Son, the Beloved; my favour rests on you.'

31. Psalm 2:7.

32. Matthew 15:24.

33. Oscar Cullman, *La Nativité et l'arbre de Noël, op. cit.*, pp. 31ff.

34. Which is confirmed by the Judaeans' reply to Jesus (John 2:20): 'It has taken forty-six years to build this sanctuary.' According to Josephus, the works began in 19 BC, which would take us to AD 27.

Chapter 6

1. Exodus 16:13.

2. Joel 1:10.

3. Numbers 20:5.

4. Deuteronomy 8:3.

5. Psalm 91:11–12

6. Deuteronomy 6:16.

7. Deuteronomy 6:13.

8. At Matthew 12:22–4, Jesus heals a blind and dumb demoniac, as a result of which the crowd are on the point of acclaiming him as the 'Son of David', but the Pharisees object that 'the man casts out devils only through Beelzebub, the prince of demons'. To which Jesus replies, with impeccable logic, that that would be absurd, for Satan would not banish Satan.

9. 1 Corinthians 1:22.

10. He very often specifies 'the next day' or 'on the last day of the festival' or, 'It was the time when the feast of Dedication was being celebrated in Jerusalem. It was winter …'

11. According to some interpretations, Jesus himself recruited Philip.

12. For example, during the miracle of the loaves.

13. Cf. Xavier Léon-Dufour, *Lecture de l'Evangile selon Jean, op. cit.,* vol. 1, pp. 195–6.

14. The whole of this episode is recounted in John 1:35–51.

15. Matthew 8:23–7.

16. Pliny, *Natural History*, V, 15.

17. Luke 16:3.

18. Mark 8:27.

19. Mark 7:24.

20. Cf. Gerd Theissen, *Le Christianisme de Jésus*, Desclée de Brouwer, 1979, pp. 95 and 121–2.

21. Matthew 6:25.

22. For example, Matthew 10:9–14, Mark 6:8–11, Luke 10:5–12.

23. Matthew 8:14.

24. Luke 10:38.

25. Luke 7:37.

26. Luke 8:2.

27. Mark 1:17.

28. Matthew 10:24.

29. Matthew 23:8.

30. John 8:31–2.

31. Mark 9:40.

32. Matthew 8:22.

33. Luke 9:59–62.

34. Luke 14:26.

35. Luke 12:52.

36. Matthew 10:22.

37. Mark 3:21.

38. Luke 10:1.

39. Numbers 11:24–30.

40. Genesis 10:1–32.

41. Mark 3:14–15.

42. Cf. the contribution of Jean Delorme, professor at the Catholic University of Lyon, in *Jésus aujourd'hui. Historiens et exégètes à Radio-Canada, op. cit.*, vol. 3: *Heritage, image et rayonnement*, pp. 22ff.

43. Mark 6:30.

Chapter 7

1. John, the only evangelist to recount the wedding at Cana and the miracle that Jesus performs there, specifies that it took place 'on the third day' (which is rendered in the *Jerusalem Bible* as 'three days later'). This has much intrigued translators and exegetes: on the third day after what? Not finding a solid answer, some have even suggested that it is a reference to the Resurrection three days after the crucifixion. Most now believe that John had simply meant to refer to a Tuesday, the Jewish week beginning on Sunday and ending on the seventh day, the sabbath – the only day to have a name, the others simply being numbered. Among the Jews, Wednesday was the traditional day for the marriage of virgins, but Galilean peasants frequently diverged from this rule.

2. Cf. Leon Marcel, *Regard sur Jésus à la lumière de saint Jean*, Saint-Paul, 1993, pp. 34–5.

3. John 2:11.

4. John 20:30.

5. Georges Chantraine, 'Les signes de l'amour' in *Les Miracles*, special edition of the review *Communio*, September 1989.

6. John 6:11.

7. Xavier Léon-Dufour, *Lecture de l'Evangile selon Jean, op. cit.*, vol. 1, p. 215.

8. Matthew 11:18–19 and Luke 7:18–30.

9. The whole scene in Matthew 11:1–15 and Luke 7:18–30.

10. The whole scene in John 3:22–30.

11. Matthew 14:4.

12. Matthew 14:9–12.

13. John 1:8.

14. Deuteronomy 21:20.

15. Jean-Paul Roux, *Jésus, op. cit.*, p. 166.

16. Ecclesiastes 10:19.

17. Psalm 104:15.

18. Ecclesiasticus 31:28.

19. Amos 9:13.

20. Isaiah 25:6.

21. St Thomas Aquinas, *Super Evangelium*, 5, 'Joannis lectura', II, 7, 358. Quoted by Xavier Léon-Dufour, *Lecture de l'Evangile selon Jean, op. cit.*, vol. 2, p. 237.

22. John 1:17–18.

23. Ernest Renan, *Vie de Jésus, op. cit.*, p. 133.

Chapter 8

1. John 20:30.

2. Acts 2:22.

3. Quoted by John Drane, *Jesus and the Four Gospels, op. cit.*, p. 116.

4. 'The deaf, that day, will hear the words of a book and, after shadow and darkness, the eyes of the blind will see' (Isaiah 29:18–19) and 'Your dead will come to life, their corpses will rise' (Isaiah 26:19).

5. Mark 7:32–6.

6. Mark 8:26.

7. Mark 1:44.

8. Mark 8:12.

9. Matthew 16:2–4.

10. René Girard, *Quand ces choses commenceront ...*, Arlea, 1994, p. 177.

11. Paul Valéry, *Suite*, Gallimard (cf. *Le Dournon des citations français*, Belfond, 1992).

12. Victor Hugo, *Les Travailleurs de la Mer*, I, 17.

13. Ernest Renan, preface of the 13th edition of *Vie de Jésus*, *op. cit.*, p. 10.

14. Jean Rostand, *Ce que je crois*, Grasset, 1965, p.75.

15. 'We cannot use electric lights and radios and, in the event of illness, avail ourselves of modern medical and clinical means and at the same time believe in the spirit and wonder world of the New Testament. And if we suppose that we can do so ourselves, we must be clear that we can represent this as the attitude of Christian faith only by making the Christian proclamation unintelligible and impossible for our contemporaries.' Bultmann, who had a great influence on modern theological commentary, believed that the knowledge of the power and laws of nature had brought to an end 'faith in spirits and demons.... Likewise, illnesses and their cures have natural causes and do not depend on the work of demons and on exorcising them. Thus, the wonders of the New Testament are also finished as wonders....' (Rudolf Bultmann, *New Testament and Mythology, and other basic writings*, trans. from German by Schubert M. Ogden, SCM, 1984, pp. 4–5).

16. Günther Bornkamm, *Jesus of Nazareth*, trans. from German by James Robinson, Hodder & Stoughton, 1960, p. 131 (reissued in a translation by Irene and Fraser McLuskey with James Robinson, Hodder & Stoughton, 1973).

17. This pool has caused doubt to be shed on John's account: who could imagine the existence of a five-sided pool at that time? However, excavations of that site in 1960 uncovered the remains of two rectangular basins surrounded by colonnades between which a narrow channel formed the fifth portico.

18. John 5:3–9.

19. Cf. John Romer, *Testament: the Bible and history*, O'Mara, 1988.

20. Acts 2:22.

21. Mark 13:22.

22. Matthew 8:1–35.

23. Etienne Trocmé, 'Le christianisme jusqu'à 325', *Histoire des religions*, Gallimard, in the collection 'Encyclopédie de la Pléiade', vol. 2, p. 194.

24. Mark 5:41.

25. Charles Perrot, *Jésus et l'Histoire, op. cit.*, pp. 177–99.

26. Mark 9:38.

27. John 9:1–7.

28. Mark 8:22–6.

29. Mark 6:5.

30. Matthew 17:27.

31. John 4:46–54, Matthew 8:5–13, Luke 7:1–10.

32. *Talmud B. Berakhot*, quoted by Xavier Léon-Dufour, *Les Miracles de Jesus*, p. 137.

33. Mark 11:12–21.

34. *La Bible du peuple de Dieu, op. cit.*, p.187.

35. Mark 5:1–13.

36. Georges Chantraine, 'Les signes de l'amour', *art. cit.*

37. *Ibid.*

38. Psalm 65:8.

39. Job 9:8.

40. 1 Kings 17:17–24 and 2 Kings 4:8–37.

41. 2 Kings 4:1–6 and 4:42–4.

42. Mark 6:4. In this famous episode appear what the evangelist calls Jesus' brothers: James, Joseph, Judas and Simon. But the last part of the passage, rarely mentioned by commentators, in which Jesus declares that a prophet 'is only despised in his own country, among his own relations and in his own house', raises questions. There is a progression in the phrase, like a camera that gradually 'zooms' onto the detail of a scene: his country, his relatives, his house. And 'his own house' means 'his intimate family'. Mary was in his house, but she barely figures in the scene. Does she understand this 'prophet' who was her son? What does she do? And say?

43. Mark 6:5.

44. Mark 3:7–12, 4:1, Matthew 13:34 and 8:1, and Luke 6:19.

45. Mark 2:13–19.

46. Mark 6:7–13.

47. Luke 9:6, Mark 6:13.

48. At the beginning of his gospel (3:6), Mark states that 'the Pharisees went out and at once began to plot with the Herodians against him, discussing how to destroy him'. But most scholars believe that this was an 'anticipation' of events, added by the author or authors of the text who wrote without being overly concerned with chronology. Shortly after the miracle of the loaves, Mark (8:15) has Jesus saying to his disciples: 'Be on your guard against the yeast of the Pharisees and the yeast of Herod,' meaning, at least, that he classed them together. Later, Luke has the Pharisees coming to warn Jesus: 'Leave this place, because Herod means to kill you' (Luke 13:31).

49. Mark 6:31.

50. Matthew 14:13.

51. Luke 9:10.

52. John 6:1. On this subject, see Xavier Léon-Dufour, *Lecture de l'Evangile selon John, op. cit.*, vol. 2, p. 101.

53. According to some writers, the mention of Passover is not chronologically accurate, but should be linked to the institution of the Eucharist at the Last Supper. In other words, the implication is that the Jewish Passover would soon be replaced by the Christian Easter. On this subject, see the Jesuit Ignace de La Potterie in the edition (already cited) of the international Catholic review *Communio* devoted to miracles.

54. Matthew 14:21.

55. John 6:10.

56. Mark 6:35–6. Mark has a tendency to put the disciples in the role of villains of the piece.

57. John 6:7.

58. Mark 6:37.

59. John 6:11. In the other gospels, Jesus 'raised his eyes to heaven' as though asking his Father to perform the miracle. Similarly, John has Jesus distributing the bread by himself – which is unlikely. In the other texts, the task is given to the disciples, whom, if one sees the episode as a prefiguring of the Eucharist, Jesus would later also teach the sharing of the Eucharistic bread.

60. John 6:14.

61. Ruth 2:14.

62. Psalm 23:1–2.

63. Mark 6:34.

64. Fr Léon Marcel, *Regard sur Jésus à la lumière de saint Jean, op. cit.*, p. 102.

65. Mark 6:41–2.

66. Mark 14:22.

67. In *L'Homme qui devint Dieu*, particularly in the second volume, *Les Sources* (Livre de Poche, 1993, p.292), Gérald Messadié takes up what had already been a longstanding theory among exegetes of the so-called 'liberal' school, basing his argument on a clue that he calls 'convincing': the reference to the twelve baskets of leftovers. Where did these baskets come from, he asks, 'if they had not brought them'? He is not sufficiently cautious about this symbolic number of twelve, which demonstrated above all the generosity of God. In any case, the presence of baskets proves nothing: they could just as well have originally been empty as filled with provisions.

68. Luke 8:3.

69. Gerd Theissen, *The Shadow of the Galilean, the quest of the historical Jesus in narrative form*, trans. from German by John Bowden, SCM Press, 1987 p. 120.

70. A. G. Herbert, 'History in the feeding of the Five Thousand', in *Studia Evangelica*, II, Akademie-Verlag, Berlin, 1982, p. 68.

71. H. Clavier, 'La multiplication des pains dans le ministère de Jésus', *Studia Evangelica*, I, p. 447.

72. Cf. on this point Xavier Léon-Dufour, *Lecture de l'Evangile selon Jean, op. cit.*, vol. 2, pp. 117ff.

73. John 6:26–7.

74. John 6:34. In the English *Jerusalem*, this is rendered as 'Sir'.

75. John 6:35–40.

76. *Lecture de l'Evangile selon Jean, op. cit.*, p. 138.

77. John 6:51.

78. John 6:55.

79. John 6:66.

80. John 6:68–9.

81. Matthew 14:22 and Mark 6:45.

82. Mark 6:52.

83. Mark 8:1–10.

84. Mark 8:17–18.

85. Jeremiah 5:21 and Ezekiel 12:2.

86. John 4:14.

87. John 4:15.

88. Albert Camus, *The Plague* [*La Peste*], trans. from French by Stuart Gilbert, Hamish Hamilton, 1948 (repub. Penguin).

89. Anne Reboux-Caubel, *Peut-on ressusciter?*, Centurion, 1989, p. 34.

90. John 10:33.

91. John 10:38.

92. John 11:1–44.

93. Psalm 42:6–12. On this point see Xavier Léon-Dufour, *Lecture de l'Evangile selon Jean, op. cit.*, vol. 2, pp. 423 and 424.

94. Mark 11:11.

95. Luke 10:38–42.

96. *L'Homme qui devint Dieu, op. cit.*, pp. 280 and 281: 'First described by Ambroise Paré,' writes Gérald Messadié, 'catalepsy has been described far more scientifically in the twentieth century by the Frenchman Henri Baruk. In this state, the body becomes soft and plastic, 'like plasticine' (Norbert Sillamy, *Dictionnaire de psychologie*). A cataleptic coma can last for days, months and even years. It was probably such a coma that gave rise to the story of Sleeping Beauty.'

97. Ernest Renan, *Vie de Jésus, op. cit.*, p.203.

98. *Ibid.*, p.202.

99. Xavier Léon-Dufour, *Lecture de l'Evangile selon Jean, op. cit.*, vol. 2, p. 408.

100. Luke 16:19–31.

101. Cf. J. Kremer, *Mélanges J. Dupont*, Cerf, pp. 571–4. Fr Léon-Dufour (*Lecture de l'Evangile selon Jean, op. cit.*, vol. 2, p. 409) believes the second hypothesis is 'more likely'.

102. *Ibid.*

103. Irenaeus, *Against Heresies*, V, 13.

Chapter 9

1. Matthew 6:2.

2. John 3:13.

3. John 4:17–18.

4. Mark 1:22.

5. The figure is approximate because some are so brief – one or two sentences – that their categorisation as parables is problematic.

6. For example, the parable of the fig tree that bore no fruit (Luke 13:6-9). The owner of the vineyard wants to cut it down, but his servant pleads for its reprieve: 'leave it one more year and give me time to dig round it and manure it; it may bear fruit next year....' This story is reminiscent of another found, according to Gerd Theissen (*The Shadow of the Galilean*, *op. cit.*), in the so-called Ahikar romance, of which 'many versions were already widespread in pre-Christian times'; in this story, the tree is about to be felled and begs, 'Transplant me, and if I do not bring forth fruit even then, cut me down.' But it is important to remember that plants and animals never speak in Jesus' parables; these are not the tales of La Fontaine or Aesop. Other examples can be found in D. La Maisonneuve, 'Paraboles rabbiniques', in *Cahiers Evangiles*, 50.

7. Luke 16:1–9.

8. Luke 16:13.

9. Mark 4:3–9.

10. Mark 4:13–20.

11. Mark 4:10–13.

12. Mark 4:33.

13. Isaiah 6:9–10: the prophet has for audience a corrupt and avaricious people who 'add house to house and join field to field' and who refuse to listen to him. So the Lord says to him:

> Go and say to this people,
> 'Hear and hear again, but do not understand;
> see and see again, but do not perceive.'
> Make the heart of this people gross,
> its ears dull;
> shut its eyes,
> so that it will not see with its eyes,
> hear with its ears,
> understand with its heart,
> and be converted and healed.'

Cf. on this subject 'Les Paroles scandaleuses de Jesus' in Fêtes et saisons, no. 465, May 1992, pp. 23-4.

14. Zechariah 9:9–10. According to scholars, the texts attributed to Zechariah are of diverse origin. This one perhaps dates from the fourth century.

15. Psalm 72:11–14.

16. Mark 1:15.

17. Cf. C. H. Dodd, *The Founder of Christianity*, *op. cit.*, and D. Marguerat, *L'Homme qui vient de Dieu*, Ed. du Moulin, pp. 20ff.

18. Luke 17:20–21.

19. Mark 10:15.

20. Matthew 11:12. Matthew uses the expression 'the Kingdom of Heaven' not to describe an extraterrestrial domain but because, unlike Mark and Luke, he was writing for the Jews. The Jews did not like pronouncing the name of God, for fear of inadvertently breaking the commandment: 'You shall not utter the name of Yahweh your God to misuse it' (Exodus 20:7).

21. Matthew 13:33.

22. Luke 13:18–19.

23. Matthew 6:7–14 and Luke 11:1–4. Luke's version is shorter and omits, principally, the third request: 'Your will be done, on earth as in heaven.'

24. Luke 17:10.

25. Sigmund Freud, *Civilisation and its Discontents*, trans. from German by Joan Riviere, International Psycho-Analytical Library, no. 17, 1930, p. 90.

26. Luke 6:27–8.

27. Deuteronomy 6:5.

28. Leviticus 19:18.

29. David Flusser, *Jesus*, *op. cit.*, p. 70.

30. *Ibid.*, p. 74. The rabbi Hillel, to whom Flusser refers, lived between 70 BC and AD 10. As President of the Sanhedrin, he was the highest Jewish authority on matters of religion and legislation. He had formulated the golden rule: 'What is distasteful to you, do not do to your neighbour; that is the whole law, the rest is but commentary.' He enjoined people to turn away from worship of power and state and to embrace the ideal of a Jewish community based on the love of God and one another.

31. Matthew 23:23–4.

32. Mark 2:27.

33. Mark 10:17–27.

34. Ernest Renan, *Vie de Jésus, op. cit.*, p. 129.

35. Psalm 69:33.

36. Mark 10:35–45. In judging the incongruity of this behaviour on the part of the sons of Zebedee, one must remember that Mark never misses an opportunity of emphasising the disciples' foolishness.

37. Luke 22:25–7.

38. John 13:4–7.

39. Mark 12:13–17.

40. Luke 15:11–32.

41. Matthew 22:2.

42. Luke 22:30.

43. Luke 15:6.

44. Matthew 13:44.

45. Matthew 16:21–4.

46. Matthew 11:30.

47. Jean-Paul Roux, *Jésus, op. cit.*, p. 283.

48. Luke 22:19.

49. On this point, cf. Jean Vassal, *Les Eglises, diaspora d'Israël?*, Albin Michel, 1993, p. 101.

50. Cf. on this question of original sin, Pierre Gibert, *Bible, mythes et récits de commencements*, Seuil, 1986. He shows that the dogma of original sin does not have its origin in the story of Adam and Eve but in St Paul (Romans 5). For Paul the salvation that Christ brought concerned the universal and undying evil in man. But he did not, any more than Christ, develop the idea that Creation had been spoilt by original sin and that a sacrifice, in the person of Jesus, was necessary to restore a partnership with God. It was St Augustine who established this sequential explanation, which was soon developed into an absolute truth.

Chapter 10

1. Luke 11:37–54.

2. Luke 13:31.

3. Matthew 5:17.

4. Matthew 5:21–48.

5. Luke 7:36–50.

6. John 7:16.

7. John 5:18.

8. Gérard Israël, 'Y-a-t-il une pensée juive du christianisme?', in *Les Nouveaux Cahiers*, review published under the auspices of the Alliance israélite universelle, no. 113.

9. Eduard Schweizer, *Jesus*, trans. from German by David E. Green, SCM, 1971. p. 36.

10. Cf. on this point Pierre Grelot, 'L'Arrière-plan araméen du Pater', in *Revue biblique*, 1984, p. 531.

11. As François Refoulé commented ('Le Notre Père, point de vue exégétique', in *Unité des chrétiens*, no. 39, July 1980), 'It is important to note that the 'Our Father' contains no Christological elements: it does not mention Jesus, or his role in the coming of the Kingdom, or his power to forgive sins.' A Jew could unhesitatingly recite the 'Our Father' and it sometimes – if rarely – happens that Jews and Christians recite it together.

12. *Art. cit.*

13. Mark 14:36.

14. Joachim Jeremias, *Abba. Jésus et son père*, Seuil, 1972, p. 89. On this thesis, see the study of Jacques Schlosser in *Le Dieu de Jésus*, Cerf, pp. 179–209. In addition, Prof. J. M. Van Cangh believes that in calling God *Abba* ('Daddy'), 'Jesus was unique' and without precedent; no other prophet or founder of a religion had gone so far ('Bible et verité', in *Le Supplement*, no. 188, January 1994).

15. For a more complete study of the 'Our Father' and particularly its translation, see, apart from the texts cited above, Max-Alain Chevallier, 'Relire le Notre Père', special edition, *Réforme*, n.d.

16. Mark 10:13–16.

17. Proverbs 10:1.

18. Proverbs 29:15.

19. 'Whoever refuses honour to the Son refuses honour to the Father who sent him' (John 5:23).

20. Rudolf Augstein, *Jésus, Fils de l'homme*, Gallimard, 1975, p. 46 [*Jesus: Menschensohn*, C. Bertelsmann Verlag, 1972].

21. 'In Christianity, the individual became so important that he could no

longer be sacrificed,' Nietzsche wrote towards the end of his life, 'all "souls" being equal before God – thus threatening the survival and the good of the species. Christian altruism is a life-threatening concept.... All great movements, wars, etc., lead people to sacrifice themselves, and the ranks of the strong are continually depleted. The weak, in contrast, have a terrible instinct to retreat, to survive, to support their own. This so-called mutual welfare is supposed to be virtue and philanthropy ...' (*Nachgelassene Fragmente* [Posthumous Fragments] 1888–1889, Walter de Gruyter, 1972). Nazism, which sought scapegoats and sacrificial victims 'for the good of the species' took the inspiration for its fundamentally anti-Christian schema from Nietzsche.

22. The Church Father Epiphanius quotes this gospel (Havis XXX, 16–14). On this text, see the article 'Apocryphes', p. 79 in *Dictionnaire des religions* (PUF, 1984), edited by Paul Popard.

23. Hosea 6:6.

24. However, when Jesus is asked to pay the Temple tax (in the episode of the golden *stater* in Matthew 17:24–7), he declares that the Jews are free to pay it or not, but that he will do so, so as not to 'offend' them. Some scholars believe that the passage does not report Jesus' actual words but was inserted in order to resolve a problem that confronted the first Christian communities: these Judaeo-Christians were obviously unsure of what to do in regard to the Temple tax.

25. Ecclesiasticus 12:1–7.

26. *Antiquities* XVIII, 15.

27. Cf. Jackie Feldmann, 'Le second Temple, comme institution economique, sociale et politique', in *La Société juive à travers l'histoire*, vol. 2: *Les Liens de l'Alliance*, edited by Shmuel Trigano, Fayard, 1993, p. 170.

28. Claude Tresmontant, *Le Christ hébreu: la langue et l'âge des Evangiles, op. cit.*, p. 180.

29. Matthew 23:27–8.

30. *Dead Sea Scrolls*, IV, 7–8.

31. Luke 7:36–50.

32. John 3:2.

33. John 9:1–34.

34. John 9:40–41.

35. Charles Guignebert, *Modernisme et tradition catholique*, Paris, 1908, p. 78. 'The avenging stones', as Guignebert puts it, would kill Stephen, a

contemporary of Jesus who, having announced that he had seen Jesus 'standing at God's right hand' was dragged outside Jerusalem and stoned (Acts of the Apostles 7:8–58).

Chapter 11

1. Cf. Gerd Theissen, *Le Christianisme de Jésus, op. cit.*, p. 69.

2. Luke 13:34 and Matthew 23:37.

3. John 7:1–36.

4. He signed it with the insignia of a palm tree, this being the emblem of royalty. Cf. H. Daniel-Rops, *Jesus in His Time, op. cit.*, p. 176.

5. Luke 7:5.

6. John 6:51.

7. John 6:68-69.

8. The agent of God could not, in Jewish eyes, have been a boy who had once played in a village street. His origin must be marvellous and mysterious. In addition, two traditions and beliefs about the Messiah already existed. For some, as we have seen, he would be the descendant of David (the theme taken up by the childhood narratives in Matthew and Luke). For others, his presence on earth would be hidden until the moment when he would suddenly present himself (or be presented) to his people. The rabbi Trypho, in his dialogue with Justin in the second century, says: 'Even if the Messiah has been born and is living somewhere today, he is unknown' (Dialogue VIII, 4). An episode in the gospels has incited long discussions on the question of this 'hidden Messiah'. Jesus asks his disciples what is being said about him. Then he asks, 'Who do you say I am?' to which Peter replies, 'You are the Christ'. Mark concludes the passage by saying that 'he gave them strict orders not to tell anyone about him' (Mark 8:27–30). There are very similar passages in Matthew and Luke, but no such allusion in John. Several explanations of this have been suggested: Jesus wanted to quell any false hopes that his contemporaries might have had of his being an earthly king; he wanted to assign all that he did to God; he did not want to use his power and his real identity to impose the reign of God on men; he was prepared even to denigrate himself, allowing himself to be ridiculed and hounded, such was his respect for men's freedom.

9. John 10:22-42.

10. Psalm 82.

11. Cf. Jackie Feldmann, 'Le second Temple, comme institution economique,

sociale et politique', in *La Société juive à travers l'histoire, op. cit.*, vol. 2, p. 168. The account of this meeting is in John 11:47–54, who also alludes to it during Jesus' trial (18:14).

12. John 4:21–3. 'The day he uttered these words,' wrote Renan, 'Jesus really became the son of God. For the first time, he made the declaration on which the edifice of eternal religion would be built. He founded a pure religion, outside time and nationality, which all elevated souls would practise until the end of time' (*Vie de Jésus, op. cit.*, p. 151). However, in this same dialogue John has Jesus saying something that contradicts this: 'You worship what you do not know; we worship what we do know; for salvation comes from the Jews' (verse 22). Renan argues in a note that this phrase 'seems to be the clumsy addition of the evangelist, terrified by the audacity of the words he was reporting'. Later, others such as Rudolf Bultmann emphasised that when John used the word 'Jews', it was to designate the chief priests, the Pharisees, the Sadducees – in other words, Jesus' enemies. When he wants to speak of the people who had been faithful to the Covenant, he uses the word 'Israel'. He would obviously not have said that salvation would come from Jesus' enemies, and the phrase must therefore have been an addition. But exegetes such as Xavier Léon-Dufour (*Lecture de l'Evangile selon Jean, op. cit.*, vol. 1, p. 370) see no contradiction between verse 22 and the others: the passage, they say, highlights both the import of the meeting between the Samaritans and Jesus and *also* the fact that the one God had chosen the Jewish people to be His witness to the nations and had forged with them the first Covenant, to which the whole of humanity was called. The Jewish Jesus was therefore acknowledging the origin of his message *while also* giving it a universal meaning.

13. Matthew 17:17, Mark 11:1–10 and Luke 19:28–40.

14. Some versions have 'colt', rather than 'young donkey'.

15. Cf. Jean-Paul Roux, *Jésus, op. cit.*, pp. 335 and 336.

16. Judges 5:9–10.

17. Matthew 21:5, referring to Zechariah 9:9 – obviously not the husband of Elizabeth, but the author (perhaps authors) of a text written between the seventh and the sixth centuries BC and mainly devoted to the coming of the Messiah.

18. John 12:12–19.

19. Cf. Xavier Léon-Dufour, *Lecture de l'Evangile selon Jean, op. cit.*, vol. 2, p. 452, note 27.

20. 1 Maccabees 12:41–51. The books of Maccabees are not part of the Jewish

canon, and Protestants (as well as St Jerome) consider them apocryphal. But Josephus gave the first book enough credit to paraphrase much of it in his *Antiquities* (XII–XIII).

21. Psalm 118:26.

22. Jean-François Six, *Jésus*, Somogy, 1972 (reissued by Seuil, 1974), p. 124).

23. John 12:15.

24. John 12:19.

Chapter 12

1. John 2:13–16 and Matthew 21:10–17, Mark 11:15–19, Luke 19:45–8.

2. Cf. Xavier Léon-Dufour, *Lecture de l'Evangile selon Jean, op. cit.*, vol. 1, p. 248.

3. John 2:21–2.

4. S. G. F. Brandon, *Jesus and the Zealots: a study of the political factor in primitive Christianity*, Manchester University Press, 1967, p. 333.

5. Mark 15:7.

6. Luke 23:18–19.

7. S. G. F. Brandon, *Jesus and the Zealots, op. cit.*, p. 341.

8. *Ibid.*, p. 334.

9. Cf. Francis Schmidt, *La Pensée du Temple. De Jérusalem à Qumràn*, Seuil, 1994, pp. 250ff.

10. E.P. Sanders, *Jesus and Judaism*, SCM Press, 1985.

11. David Flusser, *Jesus, op. cit.*, p. 108.

12. Mark 13:1, but also John 2:18–22, Mark 14:57–8 and 15:29.

13. For the debate on this, see Francis Schmidt (*La Pensée du Temple. De Jérusalem à Qumràn, op. cit.*, pp. 250ff) who concludes that Jesus' action 'to all intents and purposes signified a break with the Temple and with its thinking'. On a similar, though more forcefully expressed, theme, see Paula Fredriksen, *From Jesus to Christ: The Origins of the New Testament Images of Jesus*, Yale University Press, 1988, pp. 111ff.

14. Mark 14:41.

15. Matthew 21:32.

16. Psalm 118:22–3.

17. Matthew 21:33–46, Mark 12:1–2, Luke 20:9–19.

18. Isaiah 5:1–7.

19. Matthew 22:1–14, Luke 14:16–24.

20. Matthew 22:41–6, Mark 12:35–7, Luke 20:41–4.

21. John 12:23.

22. For the debate on this subject, cf. notably: Charles Perrot, *Jésus et l'Histoire, op. cit.*, pp. 207ff; Günther Bornkamm, *Jesus of Nazareth, op. cit.*, chap. 'The Messianic Question'; Eugen Drewermann, *L'evangile de Marc: images de la rédemption*, Cerf, 1993, p. 44, note 30; and finally, amongst many others, David Flusser, *Jesus, op. cit.*, p. 103, for whom Jesus had initially spoken of the 'Son of Man' in the third person because he was expecting this to be someone else, but then 'in the end, the conviction gained strength that he himself was the coming Son of Man'. Nothing, however, corroborates such a theory, especially since Jesus spoke in his own name from the beginning of his ministry: 'I tell you solemnly …'

23. Ezekiel 2:1 and Daniel 8:17.

24. Daniel 7:13–14.

25. Günther Bornkamm, *Jesus of Nazareth, op. cit.*, pp. 177–8.

26. Matthew 26:6-13, Luke 7:37-38, Mark 14:3-9, John 12:1–8.

27. Paul even suggests to the Corinthians who wanted, perhaps in the name of Christianity, to cease wearing the veil, that they should have their hair cut off or shaved.

28. John 6:70.

29. John 13:27.

30. John 11:57.

31. Zechariah 11:4–13.

32. These two hypotheses are advanced principally by Jean-Claude Barreau, *Biographie de Jésus*, Plon, 1993, pp. 205 and 206.

33. John 6:71 and 13:26.

34. Ernest Renan, *Vie de Jésus, op. cit.*, p. 210.

35. H. Daniel-Rops, *Jesus in his Time, op. cit.*, pp. 363–4.

36. Xavier Léon-Dufour, *Lecture de l'Evangile selon Jean, op. cit.*, vol. 3, p. 64.

37. Matthew 26:24.

Chapter 13

1. On this subject, cf. Gilles Bernheim, 'L'Eucharistie, le corps, le sang', in *Les Nouveaux Cahiers*, no. 113, pp. 6ff.

2. Cf. Robert Aron, *Jesus of Nazareth: The Hidden Years*, trans. from French by Frances Frenaye, Hamish Hamilton, 1962 pp. 66–74.

3. According to the various translations, this could have been a high room inside the house, a terrace or a fairly large reception room provided with benches. Cf. J. Decroix, 'Le Cénacle', in *Bible et Terre sainte*, no. 98, p. 9.

4. Luke 22:13, Mark 14:12–16, Matthew 26:17–19.

5. *Jesus of Nazareth: the hidden years, op. cit.*, p. 74.

6. Jacqueline Genot-Bismuth, *Jerusalem ressuscitée, op. cit.*, p. 117.

7. John 13:6–17.

8. The second meaning is the more likely. In fact, the same phrase appears in Matthew (10:16–24): Jesus tells his disciples that they will be persecuted and that he is sending them out 'like sheep among wolves'. And after emphasising that 'the disciple is not superior to his teacher,' he concludes: 'If they have called the master of the house Beelzebub, what will they not say of his household?' John puts this phrase at the moment of Jesus' washing of his disciples' feet, but it could well have been said earlier.

9. Matthew 26:20–25, Mark 14:17–21, Luke 22:14–23, John 13:21–30.

10. John 12:27.

11. He would never name him, as though he wished to cast him as the idealised, perfect disciple. But at the end of his gospel he states that he was his source: 'This disciple is the one who vouches for these things and has written them down, and we know that his testimony is true' (John 21:24). On the origin of John's gospel, see appendix.

12. John 1:5.

13. Cf. Xavier Léon-Dufour, *Lecture de l'Evangile selon Jean, op. cit.*, vol. 3. p. 57. Renan, having pointed out that John had recounted the meal 'at inordinate length', sees his silence on this point as 'proof that the sect (the Judaeo-Christian community out of which the gospel had arisen) whose tradition he represented did not regard the institution of the Eucharist as peculiar to the Last Supper.'

14. John 6:51–7.

15. Matthew 26:26–9, Luke 22:18–20, Mark 14:22–5.

16. 1 Corinthians 11:23–6.

17. Gilles Bernheim, *art. cit.*, p. 62.

18. Acts 2:42.

19. Cf. Joseph Bonsirven, '*Hoc est corpus meum*. Récherches sur l'original araméen', *Biblica* 29 (Rome, 1948), pp. 205–19.

20. Jeremiah 31:31–2. 'See, the days are coming – it is Yahweh who speaks – when I will make a new covenant with the House of Israel ... but not a covenant like the one I made with their ancestors on the day I took them by the hand to bring them out of the land of Egypt.'

21. This is the theory of Annie Jaubert, *La Date de la Cène*, Gabalda J., 1957.

22. *Babylonian Talmud*, tractate *Sanhedrin*, V, 2, 43a: 'On the eve of Passover, Jesus the Nazarene was hanged ... he practised sorcery and led Israel astray by seduction.' The text apparently dates from the second century.

23. Mark 15:42 and John 19:31.

24. John 13:33–8.

25. John 14:1–31.

Chapter 14

1. Luke 22:35–8.

2. Marie-Emile Boismard, 'Synopse des quatre Evangiles en français', vol. 2: *Commentaire*, Cerf, p. 388.

3. *Jesus and the Zealots*, *op. cit.*, p. 341.

4. Luke 22:51.

5. There is another possible name, derived from the oldest text (the Chester Beatty papyrus): *Gessamanei*, meaning either 'valley of fats or oils' or 'abundant valley'. Cf. Amédée Brunot, 'Gethsemani' in *Bible et Terre sainte*, no. 99, March 1968.

6. Matthew 26:36–46, Mark 14:32–42, Luke 22:40–46, John 18:1.

7. Cf. Jean-Paul Roux, *Jésus*, *op. cit.*, p. 364.

8. Genesis 32:23–3.

9. 1 Kings 19:1–21.

10. Psalm 42:10–11.

11. John 18:36.

12. Matthew 26:64.

13. Luke 22:70.

14. Jacques Guillet, *Jesus Christ, Yesterday and Today*, op. cit., chap. 7.

15. Charles Guignebert, *Jésus*, Albin Michel, 1969, pp. 211-12.

16. The medical *Larousse* (1981 edition) states: 'Hematidrosis is an extremely rare disorder, occurring through apparently intact skin. It is possibly connected to the manifestations observed in certain stigmatics.' It was undoubtedly this phenomenon that gave rise to the French expression 'to sweat blood and water'.

17. Certain translations of Mark give the impression that the Jewish authorities had called on a group of thugs, 'an armed rabble', but this seems improbable, since they already had a Temple police force at their disposal.

18. Acts 21:27–36.

19. Mark 15:7.

20. Mark 14:51–2.

21. Gérald Messadié, *L'Homme qui devint Dieu*, op. cit., pp 35–6.

22. Mark 16:3.

23. Luke 24:4, Matthew 28:3, John 20:12.

24. Cf. on this point Menahem Stern, 'La société juive à l'époque du second Temple: prêtrises et autres classes', in *La Société juive à travers l'histoire, op. cit.*, vol. 1, pp. 379ff.

25. John 18:12–24.

26. Mark 14:65, Matthew 26:67–8, Luke 22:63–5.

27. This is notably the thesis of Jacqueline Genot-Bismuth, professor of Ancient and Medieval Judaism at the Sorbonne, in *Jérusalem ressuscitée, op. cit.*, p. 218.

28. Josephus, *Antiquities* XX, 199–203.

29. In *Jésus aujourd'hui. Historiens et exégètes à Radio-Canada, op. cit.*, vol. 2, p. 134. On this question, cf. in this same collection the whole of chap. 12, pp. 129ff and also David Flusser, *Jésus, op. cit.*, chap. entitled 'The Son'.

30. 'A man may be put to death only on the word of two witnesses or three; and no man may be put to death on the word of one witness alone' (Deuteronomy 17:6).

31. On all these points, see Simon Legasse, *Le Procès de Jésus*, Cerf, 1994, and also the analysis of this book in *Esprit et Vie*, June 1994, p. 364.

32. 'The rabbis knew the position in their country better than anyone and if they said (thereby lowering their own status) that they did not have the right to try criminal cases, that must be right,' quoted by Jean Becq, 'Ponce Pilate et la mort de Jésus', in *Bible et Terre sainte*, no. 57, June 1963.

33. Letter quoted in the *Legatio ad Gaium* (302), and by David Flusser (*Jesus, op. cit.*, note 220), to which Flusser however adds: 'it may be no accident that the list of crimes adds up to seven'.

34. The prefect had military and policing powers while the procurator was responsible for administrative affairs.

35. Robert Aron, *Jesus of Nazareth: The Hidden Years, op. cit.*, pp. 141–2.

36. Tacitus, *Histories*, V, 5.

37. Cf. Joseph Meleze Mordzejwski, 'Les Juifs dans le monde gréco-romain', in *Les Nouveaux Cahiers*, no. 113.

38. In fact, the provision of water formed part of the High Priest's obligations, and *should* have been financed by the Temple. Pilate's offence was that of arrogating the High Priest's role to himself.

39. Luke 13:1.

40. Matthew 27:11–14, Mark 15:2–5, Luke 23:2–5.

41. John 18:29–38.

42. The existence of this custom has been contested. According to David Flusser, *Jesus, op. cit.*, p. 126, it is confirmed by rabbinic sources. But Raymond E. Brown, in a detailed study, *The Death of the Messiah: A Commentary on the Infancy Narratives in Matthew and Luke*, Geoffrey Chapman, 1994, is very sceptical about it (pp. 814–15). See also Simon Legasse, *Le Procès de Jésus, op. cit.*, p. 108.

43. Mark 15:6–8.

44. Philo of Alexandria, *In Flaccum*, 36–9.

45. The Jews meted out only forty strokes, with whips made of leather; a third of the strokes were inflicted on the chest, the rest on the shoulders. The apostle Paul underwent this punishment five times, a formidable experience – but less degrading, painful and potentially fatal than the kind of flagellation reserved by the Romans for foreigners.

46. This is what Jesus' words in Matthew (23:34–6), for example, would seem to indicate: 'I am sending you prophets and wise men and scribes: some you will slaughter and crucify, some you will scourge in your synagogues and hunt from town to town; and so you will draw on yourselves the blood of every holy man that has been shed on earth, from the blood of

Abel the Holy to the blood of Zechariah son of Barachiah whom you murdered between the sanctuary and the altar.'

47. Acts of the Apostles 3:17.

48. Xavier Léon-Dufour, *The Gospels and the Jesus of History*, trans. from French by John McHugh, Collins, 1968, p. 212. On this subject see also *ibid*, pp. 266-7, and also, notably, Ignace de La Potterie, 'Deux livres récents sur le procès de Jésus', in *Biblica* 43, Rome, 1962; Weddig Friche, *Chronique du procès Jésus*, Liana Lévi, p. 207 and Eugen Drewermann, *L'Evangile de Marc: images de la rédemption, op. cit.*, pp. 54 and 55.

Chapter 15

1. 'The people stayed there watching him' (Luke 23:35).

2. Cf. David Flusser, *Jesus, op. cit.*, p. 131.

3. *Golgotha*, Aramaic word meaning 'skull'. The Latin *calvarius* (from which the French 'calvaire' and English 'calvary' derive) means 'a hillock bare like a bald skull'.

4. Cicero, *Contra Verres*, II, 5–14.

5. Nicu Haas, 'Anthropological observations on the skeleton from Giv'at ha-Mitvar' in *Israel Exploration Journal*, Jerusalem, vol. XX, no. 12, 1970. Historians and commentators had long contested the notion that Jesus has been nailed to the wood – which is indicated only in John (the appearance to Thomas, John 20:27) – until this discovery in 1968.

6. Mark 15:22.

7. According to Mark 15:23. Matthew (27:34) speaks about 'gall', but this was undoubtedly an error based on the desire to demonstrate that everything had happened in accordance with the Scriptures. Psalm 69:21 says: 'They gave me poison to eat instead, when I was thirsty they gave me vinegar to drink.' This version was widely accepted because it seemed to show the readiness of the brutes who killed Jesus to add to his sufferings. Cf Jean-Paul Roux, *Jésus, op. cit.*, p. 396.

8. Ernest Renan, *Vie de Jésus, op. cit.*, p. 225.

9. Some people have questioned this episode, which is recounted by all four gospels, seeing in it simply the desire to evoke the Scriptures. This time, Psalm 22:18: 'They divide my garments among them and cast lots for my clothes.' But it was a Roman custom to give the victim's clothes to the soldiers, who would share them out in one way or another.

10. Cf. Xavier Léon-Dufour, *The Gospels and the Jesus of History, op. cit.*, p. 265.

11. Acts 1:13.

12. Psalm 22:7–9.

13. Psalm 22:22–5.

14. On the problem of the timings on the Friday, cf. notably Eduard Schweizer, *Jesus, op. cit.*, pp. 9–10 and Jean Carmignac, 'Qumràn et le courant essénien au temps de Jésus' in *Jésus aujourd'hui. Historiens et exégètes a Radio-Canada, op. cit.*, vol. 1: *Sources, méthodes et milieu*, pp. 106 and 107.

15. John 3:19.

16. Numerous translations have been published. See also Adalbert Hamman, 'La philosophie passe au christianisme', in *Lettres chrétiennes*, 3, Paris 1954. The passages quoted here are from LXVIII, 1 and X, 3.

17. Cf. John Drane, *Jesus and the Four Gospels, op. cit.*, p. 50.

18. For example, the book of Daniel (12:2): 'Of those who lie sleeping in the dust of the earth many will awake, some to everlasting life, some to shame and everlasting disgrace.'

19. Cf. Pierre Grelot, 'L'interpretation des sources de la vie de Jésus' in *Jésus aujourd'hui. Historiens et exégètes à Radio-Canada, op. cit.*, vol. 1, pp. 6off.

20. Zechariah 12:10.

21. Jean-Paul Roux, *Jésus, op. cit.*, p. 401.

22. John 19:35.

23. This is a quotation from Psalm 33:31.

24. A 'disciple' according to John (19:38), but 'a secret one because he was afraid of the Jews', which confirms the existence of some sort of clandestine network.

25. This was probably not medicinal aloes, a foul-smelling plant, but a perfume derived from aloes-wood, a sweetly scented Indian wood. Cf. H. Daniel-Rops, *Jesus in his Time, op. cit.*

26. A very technical debate. Cf. Claude Tresmontant, *Le Christ hébreu d'Evangiles: Année A, op. cit.*, pp. 298-9.

27. Gilles Becquet, Robert Beauvery, Roger Varro, *Lectures d'Evangiles: Année A*, Seuil, 1974, p. 305.

28. Of the many debates, arguments and studies on this passage, one concerns the 'third day'. Certain translations imply that the Resurrection took place after three days, that is, after seventy-two hours had elapsed. In the

language of the Jews, Jesus was raised from the dead on the third day, that is two days after his death and burial.

29. John 20:11–18.

30. David Flusser, *Jesus, op. cit.*, p. 122.

31. Mark 6:4.

32. Cf. on the concept of resurrection among the Jews and in Greek thinking, predominant in the Mediterranean at that time and familiar to us today, Jean-François Six, *Jésus, op. cit.*, pp. 184ff.

33. Eduard Schweizer, *Jesus, op. cit.*, p. 48.

34. John 20:1–2 and Luke 24:12.

35. Cf. Arthur Nisin, *Histoire de Jésus*, Seuil, 1961, pp. 33–8.

36. Mark 16:1–8; the words attributed to the angel correspond to the beliefs of the Christian communities.

37. John 20:1–8.

38. Cf. on this subject Xavier Léon-Dufour, 'La mort et la résurrection de Jésus', in *Jésus aujourd'hui. Historiens et exégètes à Radio-Canada, op. cit.*, vol. 2, p. 141.

39. Cf. id., *Les Evangiles et l'histoire de Jésus, op. cit.*, pp. 448 and 449.

40. Acts 1:3.

41. Acts 28:12–17.

42. Cf. Stanislas Lyonnet, 'Les témoignages chrétiens du premier siècle' in *Jésus aujourd'hui. Historiens et exégètes à Radio-Canada, op. cit.*, vol. 1, p. 54, but also Jerome Murphy-O'Connor, *St Paul's Corinth*, Veritas Publications and Michael Glazier Books, 1983.

43. 1 Corinthians 15:3–8.

44. Acts 9:1.

45. Cf. Johannes Lehmann, *Dossier Jésus*, Albin Michel, 1972, p. 49.

46. Passage from the *Toldoth Jeshu*, a collection of ancient Jewish texts quoted in Fouard, *Vie de Jésus Christ*, Paris, 1882, vol. 2, p. 453.

47. Ernest Renan, *Vie de Jésus, op. cit.*, p. 231.

48. Luke 24:10.

The Sources

1. Rudolf Bultmann, *Jesus and the Word*, trans. from German by Louise Pettibone Smith and Erminie Huntress Lantero, Charles Scribner Sons, 1934, reproduced in *Rudolf Bultmann: Interpreting Faith for the Modern Era*, ed. Roger Johnson, Collins, 1987, pp. 94–5.

2. On this point, see among others, François Refoulé, 'Jésus dans la culture contemporaine', in *Les Quatres Fleuves*, Seuil, no. 4, 1975, and id., 'Comment connaissons-nous Jésus?' in the collection *Jésus*, Hachette-Réalités, pp. 75ff, Charles Perrot, *Jésus et l'Histoire*, op. cit., pp. 35ff, Mgr de Solages, *Critique des Evangiles et méthode historique*, Privat, 1972, pp. 79ff.

3. Eugen Drewermann, *L'Evangile de Marc: images de la rédemption*, op. cit., p. 87.

4. Günther Bornkamm, *Jesus of Nazareth*, op. cit., pp. 24–5.

5. Cf. on this subject, André Pelletier, 'L'originalité du témoignage de Flavius Josèphe sur Jésus', in *Recherches de science religeuse*, no. 52, 1964, pp. 177–203.

6. *Antiquities* XX, 1.

7. Tacitus, *Annals* XV, 44.

8. Pliny the Younger, *Letters* X, 96.

9. Suetonius, *Life of Claudius* XXV, 4.

10. Günther Bornkamm, *Jesus of Nazareth*, op. cit., p. 28.

11. Mgr de Solages, *Critique des Evangiles et méthode historique*, op. cit., pp. 37ff.

12. C.H. Dodd, *The Founder of Christianity*, op. cit., p. 20.

13. 1 Peter 5:12.

14. Claude Tresmontant, *Le Christ hébreu: la langue et l'âge des Evangiles*, op. cit., p. 24. His argument has been opposed, notably by Pierre Grelot (*Evangile et tradition apostolique: réflexion sur un certain Christ hébreu*, Cerf, 1984), a recognised authority on Aramaic.

15. Charles Perrot (*Jésus et l'Histoire*, op. cit., pp. 27 and 28) gives a concise summary.

16. Philippe Rolland, *L'Origine et la date des Evangiles*, Saint-Paul, 1994, pp. 17-19.

17. Irenaeus, *Against Heresies*, III, 1.

18. 1 Peter 5:13. Mark is cited eight times in the Acts of the Apostles or the Letters, sometimes accompanied by Peter or Paul.

19. Xavier Léon-Dufour, *The Gospels and the Jesus of History*, op. cit., pp. 128–9.

20. Cf. *Matyah: Evangile selon Matthieu*, ed. André Chouraqui, Jean-Claude Lattès, pp. 50–51.

21. Luke 1:3.

22. Xavier Léon-Dufour, *The Gospels and the Jesus of History*, op. cit., p. 147.

23. Luke 1:1–2.

24. Cf. Marie-Emile Boismard and Arnaud Lamouille, *Un Evangile préjohannique*, Gabalda J., 1993.

25. Acts 20:35.

26. Ernest Renan, *Vie de Jésus*, op. cit., p. 45.

27. *Les Evangiles de l'ombre*, Lieu Commun, 1983, pp. 46–7.

28. *The Gospel of Thomas*. Cf. also Henri-Charles Puech, *En quête de la gnose*, vol. 2: *Sur l'Evangile selon Thomas*, Gallimard, 1978.

29. For example, historians consider that Apollonius of Tyana, a contemporary of Jesus whose life was recorded by Philostratus in the third century, long after the events, is authentic, at least in regard to the essential details.

30. There are several criteria:
    - Linguistic: Jesus spoke Aramaic and the phrases in the gospels containing Aramaic words are probably authentic, as are the passages that can be easily translated into Aramaic.
    - Originality, or in the language of scholars, dissimilitude: this criterion has been widely used since Bultmann and is based on a simple notion; sayings of Jesus that are mirrored in the Judaism of the time or that resemble the beliefs of the early Church are suspect, for these sources may have introduced them into the text of the gospels. On the other hand, when Jesus says something unique and original, it is probably authentic: when he calls God *Abba*, for example. That said, this criterion must be used with care because our knowledge of Judaism at the time of Jesus and of the beliefs of the early Church is not complete. Moreover, Jesus might have said things that had a parallel in Judaism, or that, more probably, influenced the beliefs of the primitive Church; he did not break away completely from the former and was the originator of the latter.
    - Convergence: if texts that do not have the same source recount the same saying or episode, these are likely to be authentic.

298

- Consistency: if a saying is consistent with the whole of Jesus' teaching, it merits consideration.

None of these criteria is indicative in itself of authenticity. If they are all present, however, we can begin to formulate probabilities and occasionally certainties. A careful study of literary forms can also allow us to detect differences in style between two episodes, or two verses of the same episode, and thus possible additions (cf. on this point Charles Perrot, *Jésus et l'Histoire, op. cit.,* p. 41).

An example of the depth of research necessary to establish authenticity may be given in relation to three announcements made by Jesus about his death and resurrection (Mark 8:31, 9:31, 10:33–4, also recounted in Luke and Matthew). Did Jesus really utter these words or did his disciples attribute them to him after the events? To answer that, the following elements must be analysed: structure of the text; literary style and vocabulary; comparison with the accounts of the Passion of Jesus and with the way in which the resurrection was proclaimed by the early Church; ease of translation into Aramaic; comparison of this translated text with Jesus' usual manner of expression. And, despite the enormous research undertaken, scholars have not arrived at a common position on these passages. Almost all, however, believe that at least certain details would have been added after Jesus' death and Resurrection.

31. Luke 18:9–14.

32. Isaiah 12:1.

33. Mark 2:13–17.

34. Gerd Theissen, *The Shadow of the Galilean, op. cit.,* p. 66.

35. Matthew 10:5–6. Words repeated in a different form in Matthew 15:24: 'I was sent only to the lost sheep of the House of Israel.'

36. John 8:1–11.

37. Matthew 16:18.

38. Xavier Léon-Dufour, *The Gospels and the Jesus of History, op. cit.,* p. 154.

Index